STAY OFF THE SKYLINE

Related Titles from Potomac Books

The Outpost War: The U.S. Marine Corps in Korea, Vol. 1: 1952
By Lee Ballenger

The Final Crucible: The U.S. Marines in Korea, Vol. 2: 1953
By Lee Ballenger

Marine Rifleman: Forty-three Years in the Corps
By Wesley L. Fox

STAY OFF THE SKYLINE

THE SIXTH MARINE DIVISION ON OKINAWA—AN ORAL HISTORY

LAURA HOMAN LACEY

POTOMAC BOOKS, INC.
WASHINGTON, D.C.

First Paperback Edition 2007
Copyright © 2005 by Potomac Books, Inc.

Library of Congress Cataloging-in-Publication Data

Lacey, Laura Homan, 1962–
     Stay off the skyline : the Sixth Marine Division on Okinawa : an oral history /
     Laura Homan Lacey.—1st ed.
         p. cm.
     Includes bibliographical references and index.
     ISBN 978-1-59797-050-1 (alk. paper)
     1. World War, 1939–1945—Campaigns—Japan—Okinawa Island.   2. United States.
Marine Corps. Division, 6th.   3. World War, 1939–1945—Personal narratives, American.
4. Marines—United States—Biography.   5. Oral history.   6. Okinawa Island—History,
Military.   I. Title.
     D767.99.O45L33 2005
     940.54'25229—dc22
               2005018399

Potomac Books, Inc.
22841 Quicksilver Drive
Dulles, Virginia 20166

First Edition

10 9 8 7 6 5 4 3 2 1

CONTENTS

Acknowledgments		vii
Preface		ix
Chapter I	The Word	1
Chapter II	Memory	15
Chapter III	Their War Begins	21
Chapter IV	Love Day	43
Chapter V	War Becomes Real	57
Chapter VI	The Attractions of War	139
Chapter VII	The Bomb	167
Chapter VIII	Homecoming	185
Chapter IX	War's Wisdom	195
Chapter X	Sea Stories	203
Notes		219
Selected Bibliography		231
Index		239
About the Author		243

ACKNOWLEDGMENTS

There are many people to acknowledge when accomplishing something of this magnitude. Thanks to my family: Keith, Sean, Morgan, and Ryan who have patiently listened to stories for years now. They have tiptoed out of rooms as I transcribed, and watched as I thrashed at night, overcome by others' memories. They have loved me in spite of it all, and I am grateful.

To Dave Davenport and George Feifer, who first taught me the story of the Battle of Okinawa—I am forever in your debt. To the Marine Corps: I am honored that they had faith enough in this project to name me the Gridley Fellow for 2002. In addition, I am grateful to Mike Miller of the Marine Corps University Archives for the use of the facility and for being a valued friend.

I must thank my mentor and friend Dr. Joyce Goldberg, who has spent hours slashing away with her purple pen, aspiring for me to be better, and inspiring me to find my best without adjectives. Dr. Gerald Saxon validated my belief in stories and taught me to be a gatherer of tales. Monica Drake provided continued support and wonderful ideas and editing.

This tale of fighting men is dedicated to the Sixth Marine Division. It is a glimpse into the past of a generation quickly fading. They taught me well how war affects men. They taught me to listen, to laugh, and to cry for men long gone. They have taught me to be grateful to all those who serve.

This work is dedicated to the men and boys of World War II: Gerald Dibert, General Day, Dick Bush, Bill Sams, Bill Pierce, Dick, George, Pete, Claud, Norris, Bob, Harry, Paulie, Charlie, Ken, John, Tom, Jim, Ray, De Joralemon, and most of all, to James Chaisson, my personal hero.

Above all it is dedicated to Marines—past, present, and future—my father, my husband, and my sons.

PREFACE

THE BEGINNING OF THE END

The Battle of Okinawa was fought on a small Japanese island in the spring of 1945. It was the biggest battle in the Pacific and the last battle of World War II. More than 200,000 people perished in the eighty-two-day campaign. Many veterans attribute President Harry Truman's decision to use an atomic bomb against Hiroshima, at least in part, to the outcome of this bloody battle, yet America's collective memory does not include it in its remembrances of pivotal battles of World War II. Few people, except those directly affected, remember it at all. One group of men who does remember is the Sixth Marine Division, which was formed to fight the Japanese on Okinawa and then mainland Japan. The Sixth was not a novice unit, but one made up of some of the toughest units in the Marine Corps and augmented with fresh, eager troops from the United States. Their memories of the Battle of Okinawa are the focus of this work.

An outsider can sit at a gathering of the Sixth Marine Division Association and hear wonderful sea stories (that is, accounts that may or may not be embellished). The men will laugh often but cry only after they are comfortable in your presence. One veteran tells the story of exploring a cave on Okinawa. He turns at all of the bends in his mind; he points out all of the rooms and recalls what they contained; he unconsciously grips an imaginary rifle as he snakes his way through; he smells the death in the place. Today it is just as he remembers it, although he has not been there in more than fifty years. Most interesting of all is that one can move to the next table and hear another member of the same unit repeat the same incident with uncanny similarity. Is this an example of collective memory? Perhaps, but could it also be that those memories, created almost sixty years ago, were imprinted on the men's brains because they were so intense? As the scientific community begins to understand the workings of the mind, it is adding professional support to the idea that memories are far more valid to historians than previously thought.

Capturing the memories of this unique unit, whose collective history as a fighting unit is shorter than its history as a veterans' association, is historically significant. Once these men are gone their war memories will also disappear, and few people will have the privilege of hearing the tales they have to tell. Thus, to capture their voice, to remember and record that moment in history in which they participated, is imperative. It is, perhaps, the last chance to hear their version of what happened and to see the war from their perspective. By exploring this last great battle of World War II, we can learn much about what war does to young men, about how people of that generation felt, about how they thought, and about how they interacted with one another. We can explore the realities of combat, and we can gain insight into the way men remember war.

Each of the forty men interviewed here, and each of the manuscripts, letters, or memoirs cited, contains a unique perspective that paints a picture of the men who fought and lived through the Battle of Okinawa. There are some voices that will remain missing—those who never came home or those who came home too damaged to contribute to these recollections of war. The men who did survive feel an obligation to those who never made it back. In fact, it is often their most important reason for getting the story right. They fear their story being misrepresented more than they ever feared the Japanese. For many veterans, the need to tell their story has come late in life, in part because they began to hear inaccurate accounts of the war as they remembered it. They argue that analyses of the battle are seldom created by the men who fought the war. Instead, the authors of these critiques are people either who were not on the front lines or who have all the advantage of hindsight. For others, the controversy over the exhibition of the Enola Gay, so close to their own fiftieth anniversary, was a catalyst to get the story straight. Collectively, these veterans of the Battle of Okinawa realized their story must be told.

Any fighting man of World War II understands the phrase "stay off the skyline" and its myriad of meanings. He understands that it once meant doing a job—but not volunteering—while still persevering to live and fight another day. When uttered on departure, it meant to take care and be cautious. The men still use this phrase with each other today. Perhaps it is done as a reminder of life's capriciousness, or perhaps as a validation that they were there, walked that skyline, and survived. This is not only the story of the Sixth Marine Division but also a story of the Marines' war in the Pacific in general—what it felt like, smelled like, and sounded like. It is probably as close as the reader will ever get to the best and worst life experiences of these men. These are the memories of a generation that understood the importance of getting a job done; a generation that volunteered or was drafted; a generation that left loved ones behind and went off on an adventure as men have done from the beginning of time; and a generation that shaped much of the twentieth century for good and for ill. This is the story of eighty-two days on an island in the Pacific Ocean that would forever shape these men and their memories.

THE WORD

AN UNFAMILIAR AND HISTORICAL STAGE

Sixty years ago on an island in the Pacific, American and Japanese troops fought and killed each other as never before. Caught in the crossfire of these warring powers were the native inhabitants of Okinawa. The loss of life on Okinawa and the many historical firsts that occurred during the battle there should, at the very least, give Okinawa notoriety equal to Normandy. Yet, although there is a wealth of scholarship regarding the Battle of Okinawa, neither historians nor the general public has given it recognition equal to that paid to D-Day in the European Theater of World War II. This omission from history is a great disappointment, not least to those who survived the battle.

The political strategy of "Europe First" relegated war in the Pacific to secondary status. The places of battle in the Pacific were remote and unfamiliar-sounding to Americans, and at that time, few Americans had cultural ties to the Pacific. There were no familiar reminders of American society in the jungles of Asia as there were in the countries of Europe.[1] Europe was familiar. The Pacific was not.

The Battle of Okinawa is distinguished among battles, yet it is often unrecognized in discussions of the great battles of World War II. More than 250,000 people, including both military personnel and civilians, lost their lives. Approximately 150,000 Okinawans, about one-third of the population, perished.[2] At the battle's end, somewhere between one-third and half of all surviving civilians were wounded.[3] No battle during World War II, except Stalingrad, had as massive a civilian casualty count. The Japanese were determined to fight to the last man, and they almost achieved their objective; in defeat, 100,000 Japanese combatants died rather than surrender.[4] In the end, fewer than 10,000 members of General Mitsuri Ushijima's Thirty-second Army were taken prisoner.[5]

The number of U.S. casualties was staggering as well. The U.S. Navy sustained the largest number of casualties ever in a single battle with almost 5,000 killed and an equal number wounded.[6] The Navy also sustained the largest loss of ships in its history with thirty-six lost and 368 damaged.[7] At Okinawa, the U.S. Tenth Army incurred its greatest losses in any campaign in history.[8] The Tenth Army, which was initially made up of 183,000 Army, Navy, and Marine personnel, lost 7,613 troops, and more than 30,000 wounded troops were evacuated from the front lines for a minimum of a week.[9] Moreover, the largest number of U.S. combat fatigue cases ever recorded occurred on Okinawa.[10]

The Battle of Okinawa saw many history book firsts, beyond being the first time U.S. troops fought on Japanese soil. The battle occurred during a time of unprecedented historical significance. The two highest-ranking officers to die during World War II were the commanders on Okinawa: Gen. Mitsuri Ushijima and Gen. Simon B. Buckner.[11] Furthermore, when Gen. Roy Geiger, a Marine aviator, assumed temporary command until Gen. Joseph W. Stillwell arrived, it was the first time that a Marine commanded a fighting force as large as a field army.[12]

DEFENDING THE HOME GROUND

In the spring of 1945 a new motivation existed for Japanese resistance in the bloody fighting in the Pacific. The stakes were raised when, for the first time, Japan's military machine began defending home territory by conscripting civilians, holding back airplanes, and training suicide squadrons. Although the Japanese may not have viewed the Okinawans as their equals, or even as Japanese, the island was a Japanese colonial possession. The Satsuma clan, a feudal shoganate, conquered the island during the seventeenth century and, over the centuries, subsequently impoverished the once wealthy kingdom.[13] Both U.S. and Japanese forces realized that Okinawa's location, some 350 miles from Kyushu on the southern tip of mainland Japan, could be the U.S. stepping-stone onto mainland Japan.[14] Okinawa was positioned as a virtual "springboard to victory" for the Allies.[15] From Okinawa, the Allies could launch an attack on the mainland by air or sea.

OPERATION ICEBERG

The plan for taking Okinawa was called Operation Iceberg, and it began on Easter Sunday, April 1, 1945. The landing was referred to as "L-Day" or "Love Day" (for "Landing Day"), and perhaps befitting of April Fool's Day, it encountered virtually no opposition. This lack of opposition was unexpected and unprecedented.

The commanders for Operation Iceberg were Adm. Raymond Spruance and Vice Adm. Marc Mitscher of Task Force Fifty-eight; Vice Adm. Richmond Kelly Turner of Task Force Fifty-one; and Lt. Gen. Simon Bolivar Buckner of the Tenth Army. Maj. Gen. Roy S. Geiger led the Third Amphibious Corps with three Marine Divisions: the First, Second, and Sixth; and the Army's Twenty-fourth Corps, made up of the Seventh, Twenty-seventh, Seventy-seventh, and Ninety-sixth Infantry Divisions.[16] The total number of assault troops for the initial landing was estimated at 182,821.[17]

Many other aspects of L-Day were unprecedented. The Tenth Army itself was unique. The combination of Adm. Chester Nimitz's and Gen. Douglas MacArthur's forces created a joint task force—not just a U.S. joint task force but one that also included Great Britain. The British Task Force, commanded by Vice Adm. Sir Bernard Rawlings, turned over operational control to Admiral Spruance, U.S. Navy, Commander, Fifth Fleet.[18] This combination of Marines, soldiers, and naval personnel created the largest group of Americans and Allies to land in the Pacific—548,000 before war's end.

The U.S. Navy assembled a theretofore-unprecedented armada in April 1945, with 1,300 ships lying in wait off the coast of Okinawa.[19] In fact, the effort in the spring offensive of 1945 in the Pacific was far greater than the previous spring's offensive in Europe. During the Normandy invasion, the Allies employed 150,000 troops, 284 ships, and 570,000 tons of supplies, all of which required a very short supply line. In the invasion of Okinawa, there were 183,000 troops, 327 ships, and 750,000 tons of supplies.[20] On Okinawa, in Japan's backyard, maintaining the supply line seemed an incomprehensible feat.

World events overshadowed the life and death struggle on Okinawa during the spring of 1945, and these developments shaped contemporary attitudes regarding Okinawa.

In February 1945, the Battle of Iwo Jima raged. The loss of life and the willingness of the Japanese to fight to the last soldier were beyond the comprehension of most Americans. On Iwo Jima, by noon of March 2, 1945, Americans had counted 7,127 enemy dead and had taken only thirty-two prisoners.[21] On March 9–10, 1945, the massive bombardment of American incendiary bombs destroyed much of Tokyo.[22] Five days after L-Day the Soviet Union entered the war and joined the Allies on the Pacific front.[23] Twelve days after L-Day, April 12, 1945, Franklin D. Roosevelt died. Many of the young troops fighting could remember no other president, nor did many of them know anything about their new commander in chief, Harry S Truman. The famous war correspondent, Ernie Pyle, who captured the imaginations of the home front and the hearts of troops in the foxholes, was killed early in the battle, and his frontline stories no longer made their way back to the states.[24] On May 8, 1945, while the Marines of the Sixth prepared to move out and relieve the army on the southern end of Okinawa, the Germans surrendered.[25] On July 2, 1945, while the Sixth Marine Division rested, trained, and prepared for the expected invasion of mainland Japan, the first atomic bomb was detonated in New Mexico. For the first time an alternative to invasion seemed possible.[26] On the morning of August 6, 1945, an atomic bomb exploded over Hiroshima.[27] Three days later, on August 9, 1945, Nagasaki suffered a similar fate.[28] Japan finally bowed under the weight of this new technology; in Tokyo Bay, on September 2, 1945, aboard the USS *Missouri*, World War II ended.[29]

Ironically, because Okinawa was the final battle of World War II, the war's end obscured the battlefield accomplishments. In 1945, journalist Sid Moody of the Associated Press summarized it best: "Before Hiroshima there was Okinawa. Because of Okinawa, in considerable part there was Hiroshima."[30]

As with the rest of the world, the troops who fought on Okinawa were stunned by, and then celebrated, Japan's capitulation. However, their relief quickly diminished with the discovery that, unlike most of the combat-hardened troops in Europe, they would not be heading home. Instead, they became the occupation forces in Japan and the liberation forces in China. Some of these soldiers and Marines returned more than a year later and found an America that had gotten on with life and proved uninterested in hearing about some little island in the Pacific. In a country where 16 million citizens had served in an unprecedented national effort, the people were war weary.[31] Average American citizens either had their own wartime experiences or could not comprehend what these men had lived through; neither did it seem to matter much by then. The Battle of Okinawa lost its place in history because the history being made in 1945 was itself so monumental.

HISTORY OF THE SIXTH MARINE DIVISION

The Sixth Marine Division has a special place in military history and especially in Marine Corps history. Its place has been underrecognized in part because, unlike most other divisions, the Sixth never reactivated after World War II. The Sixth was formed on Guadalcanal in September 1944. It was commanded by Maj. Gen. Lemuel Shepard, a veteran of World War I, who had been commanding the First Marine Brigade on Guam.[32] The core of the division was made up of battle-hardened Marines, some of whom were veterans of Eniwetok, while others had fought on Saipan. These seasoned veterans of the Central and Western Pacific were augmented with newly trained replacement troops who arrived from the United States, and with special troops such as Corpsmen, reconnaissance, tanks, engineers, and other auxiliary units.[33]

Many of the new Marines had previously held stateside billets. They were freed up after 1943 when the Women's Reserve began taking over clerical and other noncombat positions stateside. The Reserve's numbers grew to 18,000, and this substantial expansion freed able-bodied men to go overseas. The Commandant of the Marine Corps from 1944 to 1947, Gen. Alexander A. Vandegrift, said the addition of women to the Marine Corps accounted for the ability to put "the Sixth Marine Division in the field."[34] The division was composed of four regiments: the Fifteenth Marines, which was the artillery regiment and consisted of artillery units previously attached to other units; the former Raider Battalions, which became the Fourth Marine Regiment; the Twenty-ninth Marine Regiment, which was brought up from battalion to regimental strength; and the Twenty-second Marine Regiment, which was the first Marine regiment organized for independent duty after the United States entered the war. Although it was a new division, the Sixth entered the Battle of Okinawa with more combat experience than any of the other Marine divisions in initial assaults.[35]

The Sixth Marine Division did not fight alone on Okinawa. Many other military units fought bravely as well. The Tenth Army consisted of five army divisions: the Seventy-seventh, the Ninety-sixth, the Twenty-seventh, the Eighty-first, and the Seventh. The Second and the First Marine Divisions fought on Okinawa as well. These divisions were all supported by naval, amphibious, and tactical air forces. Jack Jackson of Weapons Company, Seventh Marines, First Marine Division, remembered that "while the Sixth was a great division, in some ways they were lucky to have the First on their left flank who knew how to do things the Marine way."[36] Regardless, the Sixth Division would be a new, untested element for General Ushijima's Thirty-second Japanese Army. As the Okinawan-termed "Typhoon of Steel" rained on Naha, Okinawa's capital, the local Japanese newspaper ended its final issue, warning, "This Sixth Marine Division is a fresh unit. Among the badly mauled enemy it is a tiger cub and their morale is high." The newspaper concluded that defeating the Sixth would be the key to Japan's victory.[37]

THE "TYPICAL" MARINE

The average Marine during World War II was a nineteen-year-old who entered the Marine Corps between 1941 and 1945. He was Caucasian, five feet nine inches tall, and weighed about 140 pounds. He most often came from the rural south or the urban north, had two to four siblings, and a father—who was also the primary breadwinner—and mother at home. Marines were almost equally Protestant and Catholics. They did not drink, smoke, or display tattoos. Most of them had spent very little time away from home.[38] Of course, the Corps included both seasoned veterans and newly recruited Marines. Sixteen-year-olds who lied about their age shared the rank of Private First Class (PFC) with thirty-four-year-old men. Sixth veterans remember that many of the older troops served before the war in the Civilian Conservation Corps (CCC). Some had even been given the choice of going to prison or joining the Marine Corps. These troops came from both respectable families, and from families perceived as less savory.

The Marines of the Sixth were children of the Great Depression. When Germany began its assault on Europe in 1939, there were still between 8 and 9 million unemployed in the United States. Not until 1943, two years after Pearl Harbor, did unemployment end for most Americans.[39] Hard times were nothing new. A Sixth veteran explained that many of the men he knew had never had indoor plumbing before boot camp. The seasoning of this generation came long before the first invasion of a Pacific island or before boot camp, whether boot camp took place at Parris Island, South Carolina, or San Diego, California. The prospect of a job—any job—shaped this generation. Historian Gerald F. Linderman writes that they "brought with them into the service the values they attached to work."[40] The very ideals of democracy were tested during the 1930s in a country founded on the ethic that hard work brings success. The Dust Bowl swirled, unemployment skyrocketed, communism continued its emergence around the world, and every aspect of society felt the strain.[41] Still, because of the National Origins Act of 1924, a sharp decline in immigration had occurred, and it resulted in a far more homogeneous citizenry than had existed before in the United States. Without the influx of peoples from different lands, there was a burgeoning sense of national identity and shared historical experience.[42] Despite hard times, the generation that grew up during the thirties also witnessed a resurgence of patriotism.[43]

In April 1945, Ernie Pyle became acquainted with the Pacific Marines and tried to describe "who they were." He wrote that their battles in the Pacific had been so fierce that his imagination turned them into men from Mars, and he was almost afraid of them. Instead, he found them "confident but neither cocky or smart-aleckey. They had fears, and qualms and hatred for the war the same as anybody else. They want to go home as badly as any soldier I've ever met."[44] Pyle tried to understand the minds of the Marines he had chosen to follow. He found them to be young, sentimental, and compassionate. They bowed to Okinawan civilians on the road and adopted all sorts of animals as pets. He concluded, "Marines do not thirst for battles. I've read and heard enough about them to have no doubts whatever about the things they can do when they have to. They are o.k. for my money, in battle and out."[45]

THE MEDIA INFLUENCE

Not everyone who lived through the thirties struggled continuously. Although times were difficult, movies became an inexpensive diversion for this generation. In fact, many veterans mentioned choosing the Marines because of movies they had seen. These films helped foster patriotism and a preference for the Marine Corps. From the early days of filmmaking, the Marine Corps recognized Hollywood's ability to reach potential recruits and used motion pictures as a part of their "public relations operations."[46] Although other branches also used Hollywood to highlight their image, the Marine Corps mastered it. Movies such as *The Star Spangled Banner* (1911) and *The Unbeliever* (1918) helped create the image of the Marine Corps as an elite unit.[47] *What Price Glory* (1926) was one early movie that made an impression on the public. After it appeared in theaters, the Marines reported more recruits than any time since World War I.[48] The director, Raoul Walsh, explained that years later a general told him he had joined the Marines after seeing *What Price Glory*.[49] Other movies such as *Tell It to the Marines* (1926), *Devil Dogs of the Air* (1935), and *The Singing Marine* (1937) helped entice many Marines into the Corps before the attack on Pearl Harbor.[50] These prewar movies "showed the boys having fun and meeting broads."[51]

The Marines on Okinawa, many of whom had been too young to enlist before Pearl Harbor or even during the early war years, continued to be conditioned by movies such as *To the Shores of Tripoli* (1942), *Wake Island* (1942), *Guadalcanal Diary* (1943), *Gung Ho!* (1943), and *Marine Raiders* (1944).[52] Hollywood discovered quickly that even in wartime the motion picture industry could combine propaganda and patriotism with exciting entertainment.[53] Many of the Marines who enlisted after seeing these films were looking for the same excitement.

PREPARING FOR INVASION

The Japanese on Okinawa were prepared for an invasion. As early as 1943 the Ryukyus—the islands comprising Okinawa—had been part of the "Absolute National Defense Zone" for Japan.[54] Japan's Thirty-second Army came into being on March 22, 1944, with a mission to defend the Ryukyus, build airfields, and help hold the Tojo Line in the Central Pacific.[55] As the situation deteriorated for them, so did the infrastructure of the Japanese military machine. Arguments over how to use assets created a situation in which General Ushijima's loss was unavoidable.[56]

The Japanese knew they could not win on Okinawa; therefore their mission, or *jikyusen*, became a battle of attrition.[57] For every Japanese soldier killed, the army must kill ten Americans. For every Japanese plane destroyed, an American boat must also be destroyed. The objective was to destroy or, at the least, delay the U.S. Pacific Fleet. This would give the Japanese time to prepare the homeland. The southern end of Okinawa seemed ideal for Ushijima's battle. It was honeycombed with caves that had been reinforced (often by conscripted labor) to create interlocking defenses, making it easy to defend. Ridges, rocky embankments, trees, and foliage made it a good place to fight a battle of attrition. The Japanese employed delaying tactics and sent groups to slow the Allies, but Ushijima's plan was always for a southern standoff below the Shuri-Yonaburu Line.[58] Meanwhile, the U.S. fleet supplied the troops on land, leaving the fleet exposed to Japanese air and naval attacks. This, argued Tokyo's leaders, would further slow the Allies' attack on the mainland.[59]

At the beginning of the campaign, Ushijima commanded approximately 110,000 troops. Twenty thousand came from the Okinawan

Home Guard and made up the Twenty-fourth Division; the Sixty-second Division; the Forty-fourth Independent Mixed Brigade; and the First, Second, Third, Twenty-sixth, Twenty-seventh, Twenty-eighth, and Twenty-ninth Independent Brigades. Before the invasion, a U.S. Special Operations report predicted, "It can safely be assumed that most of the troops entrusted with the defenses of Okinawa will be Manchurian trained." The Japanese Thirty-second Army consisted of tough combat veterans,[60] and Ushijima's artillery was the heaviest concentration encountered up to that point by the Allies in the Pacific.[61] Furthermore, the Thirty-second Army had naval, amphibious, and air assets at its disposal.[62]

BATTLE PLANS

The Battle of Okinawa became an important part of the overall U.S. Pacific military strategy. Known as the "industrial heart of Japan," southern Honshu between Shimonoseki and the Tokyo plain was a central goal for the Pacific campaign to reach.[63] This strategy entailed taking successive steps toward mainland Japan, commonly known as "island hopping." One plan, code-named Operation Causeway, considered Formosa as the next target island of the Pacific island-hopping plan in the spring of 1945. Allied occupation of Formosa (now, Taiwan) would enable them to provide support to China as well as establish air bases from which to bomb mainland Japan. An alternate plan, Operation Iceberg, called for the invasion of the Ryukyus. The Ryukyus were within medium bomber range of mainland Japan and would provide airfields for both bombers and fighters. In theory, Okinawa would provide good anchorage, and the islands would help establish support positions for the invasion of Kyushu and eventually industrial Honshu.[64]

The Formosa plan was rejected because military planners believed the island could be neutralized without an invasion. On October 5, 1944, Admiral Nimitz advised his command that the plan for Formosa had been deferred and that General MacArthur would invade Luzon in December 1944. The Pacific forces then seized Iwo Jima on January 20, 1945, and subsequent positions in the Ryukyus by March 1, 1945.[65]

FROM LOVE DAY TO MEZADO RIDGE

Although few Marines in the Sixth, besides Major General Shepherd, knew of their ultimate destination, the division had been planning and training for a landing months before its departure from Guadalcanal in March 1945. After a rest and rendezvous stop at the Ulithi Atoll in the Carolines, the division's briefings and preparation began in earnest.

The fleet began moving into place around the Ryukyus chain in March 1945. The first kamikaze assault of the Okinawan campaign occurred on March 18, 1945. The Navy began softening up the island on March 21, which made the landing easier for the assault troops when they came ashore. The naval bombardments removed walls, foliage, and other barriers while also killing Japanese troops. The Okinawans referred to the attack as the "Typhoon of Steel." Members of the Tenth Army occupied the Kerama Islands off the coast of Okinawa from March 25 through March 28, which gave the Allies a place for fuel replenishment and pre-invasion bases.[66]

L-Day began early on April 1, 1945. The first waves of troops went in at 8:30 a.m. The landings took place on the west coast of Okinawa on the Hagushi beaches, known to the troops as Green Beach and Red Beach. The plan called for U.S. forces to spread out and sever the island in two. The Marines of the First and Sixth Divisions were to move from west to east and then go north. After landing, the Tenth Army headed south. On L-Day the Second Marines conducted a diversionary operation on the southern end of Okinawa, but the expected bloody landing never materialized. Instead, the Tenth Army virtually strolled onto the island with little opposition.

It was the Sixth's responsibility to take care of the Tenth Army's left flank. The Fourth, Twenty-second, and Fifteenth Regiments, the lead contingents for the Sixth, achieved their first day's objective by 10:30 a.m. The Tenth Army controlled the Yontan and Kadena airfields. By that evening the Twenty-ninth Regiment, which was held in reserve and did not anticipate an Easter landing, was on land. Equipment and 60,000 troops were on shore by the end of the first day, which was more than the scheduled L-2 (i.e., two days past L-Day) objective. By L-7, the Marines had secured Nago, Okinawa's second largest city, and were headed farther north. The division ran into resistance on the Motobu Peninsula in mid-April, especially on the well-fortified positions around Mount Yae-Dake. Organized resistance on the northern two-thirds of the island ended on April 20, and the division thought its job was finished.

However, word began to filter back that events were not going smoothly in the south. The Army was mired down. The Twenty-seventh Army already had a reputation for performing poorly in previous island fighting; now the Marines were being ordered to bail them out. In April, Marine Corps Commandant Gen. Alexander Vandergrift visited the island and discussed an amphibious assault on the southern end of the island in contrast to Buckner's plan of continued frontal assault. This later became a major point of debate in the battle's history. Specifically, the debate revolves around the contention that a southern assault would have been less costly in terms of time and lives lost. Buckner prevailed, and at the end of April the Marines began replacing the Army on the front lines. They were about to run headlong into the Shuri-Yonaburu Line.

The Japanese military was unsure of where the Allies might land next and removed troops from Okinawa to Formosa. This decision condemned the Japanese Thirty-second Army to fight a defensive battle. Rather than meeting the Tenth Army at the beachhead, the Thirty-second Army moved to the Shuri-Yonaburu Line, which geographically cut the island in half north of Naha in the eastern quadrant. At the center of the Shuri-Yonaburu Line was Shuri Castle—the pride of the Okinawans. The Thirty-second Army's goal was to inflict as much damage as possible from that spot. From the walls of Shuri Castle, Ushijima and his staff watched the Americans land, positioned their guns while Japanese soldiers dug interconnecting tunnels, and waited.

One problem for the Tenth Army was the rain, which by May 9 had begun in earnest. Everything became muddy. Moving supplies and equipment proved almost impossible and often had to be accomplished hand-over-hand. Asa Kawa River seemed to be the biggest obstacle between the Sixth Marine Division and Naha. The river was breeched by the Twenty-second Regiment one yard at a time; after that, all that stood between the division and Naha were three seemingly insignificant hills: Half Moon, Horseshoe, and Sugar Loaf.

From May 12 to May 18 some of the most savage fighting in Marine Corps history took place. Composed of mutually supported defensive positions consisting of mortar, artillery, machine guns, and tunnel complexes, the Shuri-Yonaburu Line cut Okinawa in half from east to west. The tunnels, an estimated 60 miles of interconnected passages, made movement and flanking maneuvers easy for the Japanese. In addition, the Marines ran into what they referred to as "spider holes," hideaways flush with the ground and covered with brush or dirt, in which the Japanese hid, maneuvered behind the lines of U.S. troops, and then emerged to shoot Marines in the back. The troops had to be constantly vigilant about what might be behind them. The Marines had found the flank of Ushijima's line of defense and the Japanese were unwilling to give it up without a tremendous payment. Finally, under the cover of darkness the remnants of the Thirty-second Army headed farther south. At the Battle of Sugar Loaf, the Marines assaulted the hill eleven times before the Japanese left it and prepared for a final stand on the southern tip of Okinawa. The Marines of the Sixth suffered more than 2,000 casualties.[67]

Once again the Marine command staff attempted to convince Buckner to make an amphibious landing, and he finally concurred. The Marines staged their amphibious assault on the Oroku Peninsula after less than 36 hours of planning. The Japanese naval forces had made the Oroku Peninsula their base of operation and, under Admiral Ota, they chose to stay in the elaborate cave system on Oroku and fight to the last soldier. After two days the Naha airfield fell to American hands, and the Sixth secured the peninsula within ten more days.

The land flattened as the troops moved south. There were many barriers to the progression of the Marines: cane fields, terrified civilians, and desperate Japanese troops to name but a few. Small hills, usually fortified, made the fighting treacherous and chaotic. The last battle for the Sixth on Okinawa, Mezado Ridge, was fought on June 17. On June 21, 1945, George Company, Twenty-second Regiment, the same outfit that raised the flag on the northern end of Okinawa, did the honors on the southern end. The battle for Okinawa was over.

MEMORY

Since before Thomas Jefferson chided John Adams in their twilight years about Adams's failing memory (an argument about the way Adams had described events during the founding of the United States), the debate regarding the value of memory has been ongoing. Even at the beginning of the nineteenth century Adams was concerned about how the Founding Fathers' actions would be remembered.[1] Perhaps in the twilight of the World War II veterans' lives a similar concern about how they will be remembered exists. Men who, for years, went on with the business of living, raising families, making money, and participating in a society whose preeminence in the world they helped ensure, seldom took time to speak of the bloody, muddy days of war. Now, as they confront their own mortality, some want to make sure that their story is correctly recorded. However, to the historian, the question of the value of memory remains.

It is understandable why war memories are so persistent to combat veterans. For most young troops, war is their first contact with "the world of great doings"—as well as an exile from their real lives.[2] Everything in war is strange. This dislocation from the familiar, which often happens in war, is preserved in a part of the mind separate from everyday occurrences.[3] To understand the changes war instills in combatants requires distance and perspective. As author Samuel Hynes states, the "memory dawdles and delays."[4]

War stories are written in retrospect, and even in narrative form they always struggle for a place in history. As John Hersey wrote in the foreword to *Into the Valley*, "There are as many truths about a given battle after it as there were participants."[5]

War stories often seem out of place in comparison to other historical analyses. They are autobiographical and they do not normally address grand strategies of battle. Because they seldom explain tactics, war stories appear as merely small-scale experiences that differ from person to person.[6] Lt. Col. S. L. A. Marshall pointed out after the November 1943 battle on Makin that no one knew exactly what had transpired, but every man remembered what he had done and seen.[7] Combatants see very little of the battle in which they participate, and they rarely remember the battle exactly as do the troops around them; however, that has never been the purpose of war narratives. War narratives are read when one wants to understand what troops do in battle and what battle does to them.[8] They give war a degree of humanity—taste, smell, and emotions—which is its own kind of history.

Until the 1940s, the use of oral history had been considered too unscientific for most academics. Oral history, currently in recovery, battles for legitimacy; the oldest type of history, it has to fight years of marginalization.[9] A national mythology helps support these experiences.

By the early 1940s, it was discovered that oral history could be especially useful for documenting events in combat, and it has always been valuable in telling the story of World War II and central to the creation of the culture surrounding the "greatest generation."[10] Dr. James Burns, one of the early combat historians for the army, concluded in 1947, "The type of history desired could not be written from records alone."[11] The records that were produced by the military amounted to "truths in uniform." These documents left untold large segments of the story's action.[12] By themselves, the records were overwhelming and did not always supply the accurate information required by historians.[13]

New truths about combat history, combined with technological advances, allow for the processes within combat to be evaluated. With the invention of the radio, tape recorder, television, and the creation of specialized television programming such as the History Channel, the combatants' story of World War II became an oral record as the stories of no war before was technologically capable of becoming.

However, critics believe that the war stories veterans tell are just that—stories. They doubt the value of oral history, which they see as mere embellishment of the past. Others question the reliability of war stories, arguing that deadly struggles of combat are so horrific and the experiences so surreal that no human can accurately remember what happened. Following this logic, historian Gerald F. Linderman wrote in relation to Civil War veterans that combat produces an almost narcotic effect, blurring and blunting emotions.[14] Furthermore, as Ralph Waldo Emerson so aptly wrote, "Time dissipates to shining ether the solid angularity of facts."[15] Some critics have concluded that former soldiers in their seventies or eighties cannot possibly remember a brief sojourn on a Pacific island fifty-seven years ago with any degree of accuracy.

For each of these arguments, there is an equal number of affirmations regarding the value of oral history. As a form of documenting the past it has gained increasing credibility. History, writes oral historian Paul Thompson, "is not just about events, or structures, or patterns of behavior, but also about how these are experienced and remembered."[16] Information that a historian might not even think to look for often reveals itself in an oral interview.[17] Moreover, an interviewer may ask the same question of different sources multiple times and from just one source recover an insight that adds clarity to an historical question. Additionally, in an oral interview subsequent questions for clarification can ferret out information that might never be culled from a piece of paper.[18] Interviews can shed light on the "unwritten rules of relating to others that characterize any group and explore experiences and gives meaning to them that public documents might clearly be lacking."[19]

In truth, different criteria must be applied to the history that memory provides. How individuals perceive an event gives insight not only into the event in question, but it can also describe an individual's environment at a particular moment. The study of collective memory has become increasingly popular in recent years, even as a "general category of knowledge."[20] By definition, collective memories are "shared remembrances that identify a group giving a sense of its past."[21] For insight into a period of time and the people who lived it, a study of memories of a specific group can add invaluable clarity. Memories will always be subjective, but at last historians are beginning to see that they are not something to be ignored.

Some critics of oral histories charge veterans with assimilating considerable information about combat after it occurs The argument proceeds that veterans' memories are not their own, but a collected memory formed from what they learned after the fact. It is indeed accurate to say that during World War II the average infantryman or artilleryman knew little about the battles in which they participated. However, any additional knowledge should be viewed as an enhancement of memories—allowing the veteran to understand his own part in an event more clearly—rather than an obstacle to them.

Refuting the argument that as humans age their retention of past events is diminished is a difficult task, but current scientific inquiry concerning the study of memory is making it easier. Current data suggests that the effects of aging are less significant than previously suggested. Examples of individuals, especially the elderly, who are incapable of remembering what they had for breakfast but who can remember minute details from fifty years ago, help to refute critics of memory. Long-term memory comes back to us as we age. Current studies demonstrate that while important memories are imprinted right away, superfluous information is lost with equal speed.

An event that occurred two minutes ago, although it seems immediate, is actually already just a memory stored in the brain.[22] Researchers indicate that the most significant memory loss occurs within the first twenty-four hours. This period of rapid loss is more significant than at any other period.[23] Over the next few days, the "curve of forgetfulness" evens out and retained memories remain notably consistent, barring illness or injury.[24] Researchers also believe certain events or periods in an individual's life are more significant than others. Significant events include a first date, a medical trauma, marriage, the birth of children and, unarguably, war.[25]

Another point of debate regarding the value of memory and oral history specific to combatants is the frequent inability or unwillingness of men to retain the horrific experiences of battle. Remembering these experiences is far too painful, and men often repress them for mental self-preservation. Veterans often become, to varying degrees, hardened to the horrors of combat, but to believe that combat-seasoned men simply forget their wartime experiences is far too simple an assumption. Many veterans of World War II still complain about sleepless nights due to war memories, or of easily becoming tearful over a buddy lost half a century ago. Scientists are now beginning to study the possible link between fear and memory. Far from adding doubts about memory, the results substantiate the accuracy and value of war stories.

Dr. James McGaugh of the University of California Irvine studies the mind, memory, and fear, and he has found evidence to support the credibility of war stories. He states, "Everything that we do as humans depends on our memory. Your notion of your own past is nothing but a memory in your brain, something changed in your brain."[26] The documented processes of fight-or-flight that humans and other animals experience when they are threatened are triggered by a surge of the hormone adrenaline. McGaugh explains that humans not only instinctively react to danger, but they also learn from the process—thus decreasing the chance of repeating that potentially life-threatening situation.[27] This same instinctive process of fight-or-flight, McGaugh has discovered, creates a reaction in the brain that helps store memories.

McGaugh's experiments have concentrated on the relationship between fear, the adrenal gland, and memory. McGaugh believes that an almond-shaped portion of the brain called the amygdale seems to hold the key to memory. When stimulated by adrenaline, the amygdale sends messages to the rest of the brain instructing it to remember the event in question. According to McGaugh, "Life goes by, trivial things happen to us, important things happen to us . . . a brain probably has some limited capacity of some kind. Wouldn't it be nice to have a brain that stored to a more intense extent those things that are more important and to a lesser extent those things that are trivial. We have a brain that does that."[28] The linkage between how humans remember an event and what *actually* happened is emotion.

THEIR WAR BEGINS

Exit Civilian, Enter Boot

—Gilbert Bailey, *Boot*

Most of the Marines who fought with the Sixth on Okinawa were too young to enlist at the time of Pearl Harbor, yet most veterans cite Pearl Harbor as one of the reasons they wanted to fight the Japanese. They felt a need to avenge the sneak attack of December 7, 1941. As with most life-altering events, the veterans remember what they were doing when they heard about the attack. Most of the men heard the news on the radio and subsequently sat with their families listening to the early reports. Interestingly, most of the men who were interviewed had no idea in 1941 where Pearl Harbor was. This insular worldview soon changed.

NEW RECRUITS

Immediately after Pearl Harbor, many young men who were already enrolled in colleges and universities wanted to volunteer for military service. Often discouraged by recruiters or professors who told them to finish their education, they either left school to join the fight or finished out their education in the V-12 program. The V-12 program, or Navy College Training Program, began in 1943 and was designed and implemented to meet both the short-term and long-term needs of the Navy. The program commissioned officers by keeping young men in school and preparing them for the military in the interim.[1] Because of the intense patriotic fervor after Pearl Harbor, many of the early officer candidates had to wait for extended periods to be called up after enlisting.

Members of the Sixth who were veterans of other campaigns also enlisted; however, after 1942, Selective Service took over the process of enlistment and young men were filtered through that agency. Because of their commitment to a volunteer force, the Marines found ways around Selective Service. Marine recruiters culled young men from the induction line, that is, the line to join. Often they were young men who had previously expressed an interest in the Marine Corps. They then began a journey that would ultimately make them Marines.

The education of Marines began long before they came off the train in Yemassee, South Carolina; San Diego, California; or, for officers, in Quantico, Virginia. They knew the Corps was the outfit to which they wanted to belong. Movies and Marine public relations had been effective in creating an image of the Marines that generated a special allure. Being in the military became the norm for that generation, but being a Marine was special.

The veterans of the Sixth had seen older brothers or neighbors head off to war or come home on leave in uniform. As Paul Fussell writes in *Wartime*, World War II was "uniquely a publicity war."[2] Young men joined the Corps for a variety of reasons: patriotism or vengeance over Pearl Harbor, societal pressure, or simply because they were drafted. Many wanted to join the Marine Corps because of its reputation. The Marines would be where the fight happened; Marines volunteered; Marines were tough. Perhaps for these same reasons, many of the veterans remember their parents' trepidation regarding their choice to become Marines.

SURVIVING BOOT CAMP

Much has been written about the process of breaking enlistees down and making them Marines. As Gilbert P. Bailey wrote in *Boot,* "No one ever likes boot camp; yet somehow, grimly, you do like it, in spite of hell. And there is plenty of that."[3] More than fifty years after that assessment the words still ring true. Anyone who has undertaken the challenge is still as proud of becoming a Marine as any other accomplishments in their lives. Whether they were officers or enlisted, everyone began as a "boot." Surviving boot camp is something they all had in common, and that bond was and is still extremely strong.

Almost every Marine can recall the name of his drill instructor (DI), and usually the names of the entire team of instructors who helped in the Marine metamorphosis. A study of basic training in 1976 concluded that "91 percent of trainees had a positive view of their drill sergeant, and no less than a quarter of them took him as their role model."[4] Many have gone to great lengths to find their DI later in life. In one poignant case, a former Marine sat beside the bed of his DI as the man lay dying, some thirty years after their first contact. The DI was often a Marine's first example of leadership, and the standard set by this authority figure in this formative period was what young recruits based their judgment of other Marines on in the future. Almost every veteran who was interviewed, when asked what would be most helpful for a new recruit on April 1, 1945, had fundamentally the same answer—the lessons taught by their DI. The DI did his best to eliminate weaknesses because the business of war must be taken seriously. Most remember that the breaking down ended after about the third week of boot camp; then enlistees began learning their new profession. They followed orders in unison without thinking about them. They were no longer a group of individuals, but a solid unit. In fact, this loss of self was essential in the months ahead.[5] Upon completion of boot camp, most went home on leave to show their families that they were changed—they were now U.S. Marines.

After boot camp the Marines went on to specific forms of advanced training. Most headed to Camp Lejeune for advanced infantry school. Some went to artillery, machine-gunner, or war dog school. New Marine officers had a different experience. Officer candidates, who in the morning had been PFCs, left Platoon Leaders Class at Quantico, Virginia, and traded barracks in the afternoon to become Reserve Officer Candidates in advanced training as second lieutenants. At one point the officers being trained overwhelmed the system, and at least one class of officers was sent to Camp Lejeune to train. As Henry Kemp commented, "The need for second lieutenants to be used as 'cannon fodder,' was so great they couldn't get them trained fast enough."[6] From there, the East Coast Marines boarded trains and went to Camp Pendleton for a short time. Then they were sent on to San Diego where they boarded ships for the Pacific. The time had come to prove themselves in combat.

For many young Marines the last few days in the United States were a fun time. They had pictures taken to send home, often using the photographer's dress blue uniforms because they did not own their own. The pictures from those days show these Marines with their hats perched at a jaunty angle, which was considered "salty." Some mentioned calling home before leaving or making a tape to send back to their loved ones. Others went to the many United Service Organization (USO) shows for their last taste of stateside normalcy.

The trip to the Pacific began aboard ship, which was often a Marine's first experience on the sea. Space was at a premium on the ships, there was no air conditioning, and many of them became seasick. Charlie Rittenbury of the Fifteenth Marine Regiment, who went overseas on the USS *Sea Bass*, commented in an interview that "no fish deserved to have its name used on a boat like that."[7] Still, there were diversions: long chow lines, boxing matches, ship newspapers, contests, and the legendary rite of passage from pollywog to shellback when new Marines crossed the equator. This brutal but expected hazing was a highlight of the trip through the equatorial Pacific. Marines who have saved very little else from those days still have the certificate acknowledging that they crossed the equator.

Troops filtered into Guadalcanal either as veterans from other Pacific islands or as novices from the States. Over a five-month period, the Sixth Marine Division was formed and trained. Other troops who joined the Sixth and fought at Okinawa also arrived on the shores straight from training, unseasoned even by the standards of the recruits who had trained on Guadalcanal.

STATESIDE MEMORIES

Whitaker: F/2/29*

[Richard "Dick" Whitaker turned nineteen en route to Okinawa. It was his first landing. He was from Saugerties, New York.]

Every town in America, I'm sure, had something called an honor roll. It usually started out to be a little white painted sign with guys' names on it as they went into the service. And because it was a work in progress these weren't cast in stone or bronze. They were just painted signs and they kept getting bigger. The one in Saugerties was located on the main street, right opposite the high school, and it kept getting bigger and bigger, and they had wings on it. It just got to be enormous! Every time someone went in the service, their name went up. Then, if they got killed a star went up. The sign in the window . . . and you know about this. . . . Every house in Saugerties that had a husband or a brother or a son in the service had a star in the window. Then, every once in a while, you'd see the gold star in the window, meaning that somebody got killed, and that was very sobering in a small town. That is also what fed the desire of younger men to go and be part of the war. Because the pool of young men in a town like that kept growing smaller.

Rittenbury: H&S/3/15

[Charlie Rittenbury was from rural North Carolina. Okinawa was his first landing. He had a girl back home, and the thought of getting back to her is what kept him going.]

---

*In keeping with the terminology used by the participants, I have used the accepted shorthand for unit designations. F/2/29, for example, refers to company, Second Battalion, Twenty-ninth Marines or Marine Regiment. HQ refers to the Headquarters Battalion.

Pearl Harbor . . . I was sixteen years old and a junior in high school. Three of my friends and myself were sitting in the local drugstore that Sunday morning. At about 11:00 a.m. on December 7, 1941, they interrupted a music program for a special bulletin and, of course, they announced that our fleet had been bombed at Pearl Harbor. There had been many casualties and many dead. I had never heard of Pearl Harbor. It had never been taught in school. We had a globe and I never had found it on the globe, and neither had anyone else that I was with ever heard of Pearl Harbor.

We were so infuriated over this sneak attack of the Japanese that we all immediately went to Raleigh and joined the military. Of course, the four of us were split up. Two went to the Army, one went to the Seabees [a military engineer group], and I was the only Marine in my graduating class.

We had to wait. Well, I actually lied about my age, but I took the papers home, the documents. Mother and Dad said, "No way are we going to sign for you to get killed; you're just a boy." Well, part of that was certainly true. That's all I was, a boy, when I went to Parris Island. I had to wait until 1943, and I joined the Navy and was accepted. There were 250 of us on our way to Camp Parry, Virginia boot camp. They announced that they needed five volunteers for the Marine Corps out of those 250. I stepped out first and four of my buddies from Wilmington, North Carolina, joined me, and we stayed together throughout the rest of the war at Okinawa.

Back in 1938, in the little town of Middlesex, a career Marine came home on leave. I thought he was the most handsomely dressed military man I had ever seen. He was in his dress blues. He was a Master Gunnery Sergeant, with all of those stripes up and down him. He called me over to his house. He was sitting on the front porch and he said, "Aren't you about old enough to become a Marine?" I think he'd had a few beers, by the way, and I said, "Yes, I'd like to go." He said, "Well, why don't you become a Marine? I think you'd make a good one." He was the first encouragement, and because of his gentle appearance and demeanor, I think that's what led me to select the Marine Corps.

Manell

[Alan Manell taught himself photography, and when he was picked to be a combat photographer he was the only amateur who was retained. He was already combat-hardened by the time he reached Okinawa.]

A clerk came out with a switch list and he said, "The Japs just bombed Pearl Harbor." I said, "Yeah, so what." He said, "Well, I guess it belongs to us." I said, "No kidding, where is it?" He said, "I don't know, but I think it's out in the Pacific from the way they're talking."[8]

Niland: L/2/22

[George Niland was from Boston; his father was a fireman. Operation Iceberg was his first landing.]

I was fifteen. I was walking up the street with two of my friends. Both, incidentally, who happened to join the Marine Corps. They were both older than I. We heard that Pearl Harbor had been bombed by the Japs. I didn't even know where Pearl Harbor was. None of us did, but it was America. Those little . . . rascals attacked Pearl Harbor. They killed Americans. I don't know if I can explain how I felt. I was infuriated. I was just a kid. I was infuriated. I had always considered the Japs as people who copied our products and, ya know, they didn't have a very good reputation in this country anyway. For them to have done that, to have attacked us with no provocation. . . . There probably was political provocation, but I didn't know about it and the average American didn't know about it. The kids who were killed in Pearl Harbor were just average American kids, and it infuriated me. I wished I was seventeen then so I could go . . . I wanted to avenge that. The reason I joined the Marine Corps . . . I thought it was the best organization in the world. I was so proud to be a Marine. I wanted to win a Congressional Medal of Honor at seventeen. Can you imagine how stupid I was? That was my feeling.

Joralemon: H&S/3/15

[DeWitt Joralemon came from the Bronx. He had graduated from high school early and had spent some time in college. He had already served in the Merchant Marines by the time he enlisted.]

> That was just a common feeling and, believe it or not, to hear the Marine Corps hymn just sent shivers through me. I wasn't alone. The Marine Corps held a mystique, probably a great deal of which came from World War I and so forth. That they are the superior elite fighting force. . . . That was a common thing. So you want to be a hero, you want to fight Japs, or whatever you want to do, you become a Marine.

Miller: I/3/29

[Charles Miller was convinced that the only outfit to be in was the Marine Corps. He enlisted after Pearl Harbor.]

> I was kind of dumb and foolhardy, and I always liked their uniforms. They looked so spiffy, and I wanted to be the finest and the toughest. . . . I joined the Marine Corps for one reason, and one reason only, and that was to be a hero.

Taylor: Sixth Recon. Sniper Scout

[Charles Taylor was born in Topeka, Kansas. He had almost completely finished officer training when he decided to enlist. He was seventeen when he volunteered for a reconnaissance unit.]

> I was at the University of Wichita during Pearl Harbor. I had entered that fall. Both of my parents were dead. The following spring we were out for track. There was a Marine out there recruiting. Four of us went up and enlisted. My brother had to sign my release since my parents were dead, which shows I was just a kid. I didn't know it at the time, but what we had enlisted in was the V-12 program, which we called "Victory in twelve years." It turned out it wasn't quite twelve years. All of sudden I'm shoved off to Notre Dame. I was there from June to October, then I went to Parris Island. I remember distinctly my

drill sergeant. He was a big tough guy, but he was good. He made men out of us . . . made Marines out of us. From there I went to Quantico. We were almost through with officer training school and an instructor from The Citadel came and talked to us. In this speech he said, "I want to tell you something. Any lieutenant is expendable, but a good enlisted man is not." I thought to myself, in my wisdom at that time, I'd rather be a good enlisted man than a lieutenant, so I got out. Then I volunteered for reconnaissance, not knowing what it was.

Kemp: E&F/2/29

[Henry Kemp was from South Carolina. He had just turned twenty-two at the time of the invasion and was a First Lieutenant.]

I volunteered in 1942 for Officer Candidate Reserve. They had a whole lot more candidates than they could use, so they sent me back home. I was at the University of South Carolina a whole other year before they needed me. On July 5, 1943, I was sent to the V-12 school for two semesters.

We went to Parris Island to boot camp. I believe we were the only officer's candidate school to go to boot camp. Following that we were sent to Shapely [Lejeune] to a holding detachment. . . . About this time was the Battle of Tarawa, and there became a great shortage of cannon fodder—better known as second lieutenants. So they sent half of the instruction staff from OCS at Quantico down to Lejeune. We had the same course of instruction.

Wanamaker: F/2/29

[Ike Wanamaker enlisted in the Marine Corps in 1942, immediately after his junior year in high school. He was from Toledo, Ohio.]

I just thought it would be a good outfit to be a part of. Well, I'll tell you one thing; they were all volunteers. I felt if I was going to get in the armed services, I wanted to get with guys who wanted to fight, not the guys who were there because they had to fight. So, that was my reason.

DeMeis: K/3/4 &22

[Paolo (Paulie) DeMeis was from Brooklyn, New York. He was given the choice of being sent to a state juvenile facility or joining the military. Recruiters often waited in the backs of courtrooms in those days. He joined the Marines at fifteen and spent forty-one months overseas. He returned at nineteen and had been part of three major campaigns with the Fourth Marines regiment. He was known as the Bazooka Kid.]

I had gotten in trouble and had gotten ninety days to find government employment or I was going to go to reform school. So, I tried to join. The Coast Guard was the first stop. They laughed at me. They said, "Are you a relative of Tony Martin?" and I said, "What do I got to be a relative of his for?" "Well," he says, "he is the only guy they took this week and he's a singer." And so I said, "I know who he is. I got to be a singer to be in the Coast Guard?" I went on down the street to where they have the Army and Navy recruiting. The lines over there were around the corner. Then I went over to the guys [in line] and I said, "Is this where you enlist?" They say, "Yeah, why?" I said, "I had ideas of enlisting, but . . . " and he says, "What, you don't like to wait in line?" I said, "Wait in line . . . I thought they were giving out free turkeys or something." He says, "Well, if you don't want to wait, go across the street. It's the Marine Corps there.

There's no line." So that's where I went. There was no line, and I walked in there, and there are some sergeants, and they said, "What do you want?" I said, "What do you mean what do I want? I want to enlist!" He says, "You gotta be pulling my leg," and I said, "No, I'm ready to enlist." He says, "Well look, first you have to go through a physical. Second, before I even let you go through the physical, you have to go through a written test." So I had to take a written test. He said I did all right on it, and he says, "How old are you kid?" I said, "I'm twenty-nine." He said, "Come on, what's your real age." I said, "Seventeen." He looked at me and said, "You got a birth certificate?" I said, "Yeah, I'll bring it when you want it. I don't have it on me." He would be amazed if they knew the truth. Anyway, he said, "You level with me. Tell me what you're doing here, and I'll go to pass for you." I was fifteen that November. My sixteenth birthday was in January. For boot camp I went to Pendleton.

Whitaker

They were drafting left and right, right out of high school, and I knew that and everyone was aware of it. I was going to turn eighteen years old on March 13, 1944, and I was going to graduate in June of 1944. That meant that I would be drafted and most certainly be inducted into the Army should I stay in high school and graduate. I got myself off to Albany, New York, which was fifty miles away, and offered myself to the Marine Corps, took a physical, and they accepted me as a volunteer. They gave me papers to have my parents sign because I was only seventeen, and I came home and presented these papers to my parents and the lid came off. My father had a fit, my mother had a fit, the principal of the high school got into it, and I was just beaten down. I finally threw up my hands. There was nothing I could do. They weren't going to sign, so I was probably a little sullen for the next six months, but that's the way it was. Sure enough, I graduated in June of 1944, got drafted, got on a bus, went to Albany. While I was standing in line waiting to take my physical for the United States Army, I ran into the Marine Corps sergeant that had interviewed me three or four months earlier, and he recognized me. Asked me what happened to me, and I told him my parents wouldn't sign, and he says, "Do you still want in?" I said, "I'd love to." He said, "Well, get in here." I stepped in his office and said, "What about the Army? I'm about to be sworn in," and he more or less said, "To hell with them, I'll take care of it." There was another kid with me under the same circumstances. The Marine sergeant gave us both a ticket to the YMCA for a room and a couple meal tickets and told us to get out of there. He would take care of the Army and [told us] to be back in the recruiting station the next morning at 7 a.m. to be sworn in the Marines. They were taking two a day. By nine o' clock the next morning, I was on the train to Yemassee and had been sworn into the United States Marine Corps.

Oh, I was a victim of the movies. There were some great Marine Corps movies. Some of my friends that I admired had gone in the Marine Corps. The Marine Corps had a certain allure to it. We all know about that. The Marine Corps still has it today. It was an attractive alternative to a young and patriotic and stupid kid like myself. . . . I remember getting off the bus down there and there was a sign hanging across the road. It was like a canvas sign and we, ya know, there was a DI screaming in my face, all our faces, not just me. The sign said, "Let no mother ever say that her son died in combat for lack of training." I remember looking at that sign and thinking these guys are really serious, and that sign is announcing that this is going to be tough. It was tough. It was discipline, and conditioning, and pride, and confidence. The way they held out the emblem until the very last day, practically, of boot camp . . . it made just becoming a Marine special and it never leaves you.

Tremblay: 1st Arm Amphib.

[For George Tremblay, Okinawa was his third Pacific landing—a hardened veteran at the age of nineteen. Tremblay is very short and well built. Knowing this will improve the next two stories. His town's movie theater had a stage, and new recruits went before the whole town for a send-off on Friday nights. Dressed to the nines, Tremblay had assumed the recruits would go home before shipping out. That was not the case.]

It was in the summer of 1942 and just before we left for Parris Island we were on a stage and we were sworn in. Right from there we got on a train and went to Parris Island. Well, we got off the train there dressed in our suits and all that. I had a bow tie and tan jacket and slacks, saddle shoes, and argyle socks. So when we lined up, straight in, facing the drill sergeant, and he said, "Answer when you hear your name called." I answered, and he said, "Tremblay, come over here son." [Pantomimes someone looking up from a piece of paper and makes a beckoning gesture.] So, I walked over and he says, "Face this way." [Indicates towards the front.] He puts his arm around me and says [Pantomimes putting arm around someone's shoulders.],

"My, my, now look what we got here." Several hours ago I was a hero, ya know, and from there it went . . . [Indicates thumbs down.]

There's one more story to tell, about bayonet practice. I played a lot of ball in school. [At Parris Island] you had to run through sand and bayonet a dummy. When you'd run you were supposed to yell, why I don't know, but I couldn't. A whole platoon waiting, saying, "Come on, Tremblay, the whole platoon's waiting." Finally, I got so mad, tears in my eyes, and I went screaming at that dummy and lunged and . . . missed, [laughter] and I'm lying there. I'm just lying there, and the DI says, "Okay everybody, back to the hut . . ."

Whitaker

You asked a question about the most memorable experience in boot camp. I remember thinking, ya know, boot camp is terrifying. You've gotta approach it mentally because a lot of what they do to you is mental. I remember a threshold, it was like an emerging, an awareness that they were not going to kill me. At least [not] on purpose, because they needed me to go someplace else and kill Japs before I got killed. They certainly weren't going to kill me on Parris Island. But they're going to make it appear like they were trying to kill me. Once I caught on to that, life became more enjoyable and endurable.

White J: G/3/29

[James White graduated from high school at sixteen and had completed two semesters of college when he enlisted in Nebraska. He was wounded on Okinawa, which was his only invasion.]

Yes, I remember at Parris Island they herded us into an area where they showed us a film of Peleliu. That was a pretty rough film. I'm not sure that it's ever been on television. It showed a lot of casualties. Some in the process of being hit . . . but this was in full color. They showed us Tarawa and we saw Mount Peleliu. . . . Well, it was designed to shock, and it did.

We had two corporals and a PFC. Had a real tall, bony corporal named Pike, and I don't remember the other corporal's name. It ended in "s-k-y." We had a PFC named Russell. He was medium sized, well built, and tough. They were brutal to us, as they were supposed to be. Mid-week in the third week, they did their job on me. I had the longest day of my life, before or since. After that, they could make me feel pain but they couldn't hurt me. Know what I mean?

Chaisson: G/2/22

[Born in Canada, James Chaisson was married and a thirty-four-year-old PFC when he landed on Okinawa. He had already proved he was above the ordinary. He organized boxing aboard ship and ran the ship newspaper en route to Guadalcanal. He was then chosen to be part of the Underwater Demolition Team that was an advance party prior to the invasion. He received the Navy Cross and Bronze Star for his actions during Operation Iceberg. He wrote a song to the tune of *The Battle Hymn of the Republic* that captures the torments and humor of boot camp. He sent the song home for safekeeping, and it was later placed in a scrapbook. He and his wife had a code that enabled her to figure out where he was, and this is included in the scrapbook along with many timely articles and mementos.]

18 Day Blues by James Chaisson

Oh, we came to Parris Island and they shaved off all our hair.
They took away our "civy" clothes and left our backsides bare.
They jabbed us up with needles and they didn't even care,
But we still go marching on.

Chorus:
Hogan's goat is still a virgin,
Hogan's goat is still a virgin,
As compared to 2-5-9.

They assigned us all to a barrack and they made us swab the deck,
And if we missed the corners there our DI gave us heck.
They gave us extra duties until we looked a wreck,
But we still go marching on.

In the morning at 4:30 "hit the deck" is what we hear,
And we "hit the sack" at 10:00 p.m. without our usual beer.
Through the day, our Drill Instructors keep us standing
    on our ear,
And we still go marching on.

Most of us are known as boneheads and the rest are known
    as clowns.
They drill us hard from dawn till dark and break our arches
    down,
But you should see us hit our stride when we hear chow call
    sound.
Then we DO go marching on.

We've learned to strip our rifles and to put the parts all back.
We've learned to scout the enemy and how we should get back.
We've learned field sanitation, what goes in a transport pack,
As we go marching on.

The Sgt. say "By left flank march!" and we do a "right oblique."
We look like a "Chinese fire drill" much to our DI's dislike.
As a reward for our stupidity we take a ten mile hike,
And we go marching on.

Now our feet are one-half blistered and our gut has disappeared.
Our faces they are sunburned and the skin's all off our ears.
We wouldn't be a boot again in one hundred million years,
But we still go marching on! Hogan's goat is still a virgin.[9]

Sams: 1/3/15

[Orphaned from the age of twelve, Bill Sams was raised by a half-sister in Georgia. He worked at a clerical position at Parris Island after boot camp. He saw the likelihood that he would be replaced as a typist when women joined the Marine Corps. He worked at getting himself assigned to artillery and was a Sergeant by the time of the landing on Okinawa.]

To begin with, we were at Camp Lejeune, North Carolina, and it was the last weekend before we were going to the West Coast. We got paid on Saturday morning. At the same time that we got paid . . . in North Carolina at that time, you had to have a coupon to buy any alcoholic beverages above beer. So we had our . . . me and my group, Paul Foster and I think Frank Goetz, and I don't know . . . one or two more. We got our pay, which wasn't much, and our coupons and we went into Jacksonville.

The big city of Jacksonville, North Carolina, downtown, consisted of the courthouse, post office, and one restaurant [then] bar. No, the bar then the restaurant. The bar did not have anything but lukewarm beer. They had a jukebox. It had only one record on it. The name of that was *Under the Double Eagle,* and if you didn't like *Under the Double Eagle* you were in bad shape because it played over and over and over, wide open, top volume. Well, we wore around in that place a while.

With this coupon you could buy your booze, such as they had to offer, which was mostly rotgut of some description, but we had no place to drink it. You could not drink it downtown in Jacksonville. They'd put you in jail. We couldn't take it on the base. We found this wooded area, very swampy, down by a branch. I won't say it was a creek, just a branch bottom. Before we got there we went in this one restaurant. That's where my friends departed from me a little bit. We all ordered a half fried chicken as they did back in those days. We ate that and we ordered a steak, and we ate that. Then I ordered me another half fried chicken and that's when my buddies left—left me in the restaurant by myself. I finished the chicken up. You didn't get but two or three pieces. It was not a great big deal. I met 'em out on the street and we got our booze. As I said, you couldn't drink it on the street. I don't know what they expected you to do with it. We found this wooded area and there was an old log down there and a stump or two. My memories say that we had a case of Dr. Pepper, hot Dr. Pepper. We went down in the woods with the mosquitoes and sat down on these stumps and logs and began to drink whatever it was we had with hot Dr. Pepper chasers. We got that job finished up about dark or so and came stumbling out of there.

We decided we might as well get back down to the second front, what we referred to as the second front. It really was. I'll explain what the second front was. It was a row of beer joints right down U.S. 17, across the highway, across from the entrance to tent city, at the time, which I think now is Camp Butler or some big outfit. At that time, it was tent city. That's where everyone wound up who was fixing to go overseas. That's where we were staying. We decided it was about time to get on down there around the second front 'cause the entrance to the tent city was right across the street. So, we go in there. We have done drank up all the stuff we had. It's getting about dark and we were thirsty again. All that man . . . Oh yeah, I was telling about what the second front was. It was some building, very, very temporary, made out of slabs. Slabs are the outside bark of a tree. When they put it through a sawmill, they saw the slabs with bark off the outside, square it up and saw lumber. They had nailed it up and that was the walls.

In the second front, in these beer joints, they were two or three feet off the ground and sand all around, like everything else there. Somebody would be sitting in there drinking. A Marine would stand up, wasn't anybody in there except Marines all fixing to go overseas. If they weren't mad, they were something—scared. One would stand up and say, "Anybody in here want to fight?" Somebody would look him over pretty well and say, "Yeah, I believe I'll take you on a little bit." They would go at it. Knock, feet, beating on each other. One would get in a good lick and knock the man down and hit him up against the wall and knock the boards off the side. Later on in the night, the man, the owner, would get a hammer and hammer them back on there. They would be halfway knocked off.

We were in one of the joints on the second front. There, to the best of my memory, were four or five of us. Whoever's turn it was would order a jug of that wine. A quart of that old wine, bad wine, peach . . . I'm not talking about no . . . I'm just talking about wine made in Carolina somewhere. It was terrible. We had some paper cups. One quart would fill up our paper cups, and that was a round. We had several rounds of that. In the door came an old friend of ours who had just come from Quantico. We had been with him up there. His name was Alfonzo Twenty-five. His last name was Twenty-five. We were going to celebrate meeting up with him again. He had just joined the outfit somewhere. So we had to have another round of that wine. Winds up we drank all the man had. Then it's getting on up ten, eleven o'clock, everybody was in pretty rough shape. We started out the door to go on back to our tents.

As I have said before, it was about four feet off the ground, had some old steps there. Paul Foster never saw the steps, never saw the four feet, he just step down and fell flat right in the sand. Well, he was in rough shape. So, Al Pearson and I got him up. He got on one side and I got on the other. Got him under the arm. He couldn't walk, and we just drug him more or less. His feet were trailing behind us and we had him under one arm each. We went on, went in the gate, they let us. . . . It was a wonder they didn't call the MPs when we got to the gate. We were in bad shape! We went a ways down a gravel road. It was rough gravel. Every now and then Paul would grunt—couldn't talk— he just grunted some kind of grunt and would get his feet up, and I'm going to say he'd buck on us. He'd throw us all over in a ditch. We just were maneuvering. We get over there and get him back up, and [we'd] go on down the road again. After awhile he would holler, grunt, and carry on, and over we'd go again. That happened several times. In the meantime, Pearson broke his thumb, but we didn't know that until the next day. End result we finally got over there, got Paul in his bunk, little ole cot.

The next day, I needed me something. I was going down to the PX [post exchange] and get me some cold buttermilk. I decided I would stop by and see if I could get Paul anything. His tent was right behind mine. He was lying up there with his eyes closed, looking like a corpse, and I asked him, "Paul, can I get you anything?" He grunted and threw up and I'm not going to go into all that . . . just a green rope that's all it was. I looked down at his feet. He still had what was left of his shoes on. I discovered what was probably his problem when we were trying to get him in. With his feet dragging it had worn the top of his shoes off, dragging behind. And it had worn down his toenails. His toenails were worn off. The top of his shoes . . . [laughing] I imagine it was smarting on him. That's when he would throw us all in the ditch. He had worn the top of his shoes off and old toes were sticking up there, all bloody, the toenails gone. That's how we got back that night. He just laid in his sack all day. I didn't do much for him.

Early the next morning the train was backed in, ready for us to load all our equipment. We had already loaded all our equipment, guns and equipment, on flat cars of a freight train. We got together and put what Paul had in his sea-bag. Got his stuff ready, whatever he had to take, just like the rest of us. We just took him, cot and everything, and marched down to the train. Went right on the train with him; him lying stretched out on that cot. He didn't know where he was, in the Blue Laguna, or where he was going, and it didn't matter to him because he was deadly sick! That's about the story, he woke up down around New Orleans somewhere, about two days later.

Schlinder: K/3/22

[Ray Schlinder was from Illinois. He enlisted in 1943 at the age of twenty.]

I had always wanted to be a machine gunner in combat. I had never been in combat before. We got out of the trucks and some big gunny sergeant said, "All you riflemen over here (points out in front of him), all you firemen here (points in another direction then points behind him), all you machine gunners over here." I thought to myself, "Well if I'm going to be a machine gunner I better make my move." Finally a machine gunner.

I was assigned to this one squad leader and his name was Bill Enright. He ended up being my mentor and one of the greatest men I ever met. We get assigned to the tent. I introduce myself and he introduced himself and he was from Gary, Indiana. I was from Milwaukee. Well, we were buddies already. We were neighbors. I said, "Bill, I wonder if you'd do me a favor?" He said, "Sure." "When I go into combat I would love to be a number one machine gunner." He said, "That could probably be arranged." I said, "But I haven't fired a machine gun yet." [Laughs.] He gave me this little book, about four pages, and he says, "I want you to learn every word in that book. You've got forty-eight hours." In an inspection you had to be able to break a machine gun apart. He says, "And I want you to tear that machine gun apart faster than anybody else in the squad and I want you to be able to do it blindfolded." I had a memory that wasn't worth too much, but I tell you what, I learned every word in that book 'cause I wanted it pretty bad. I could take it apart and put it back as fast as any man had.

Honis: 1/3/29

[Don Honis had two older brothers, one who landed at Normandy, and one on Iwo Jima. As the youngest child in the family, his parents did not want him to join the Marine Corps. He was short and so thin he could not pass the physical. The recruiter had him go across the street and eat as many bananas as he could hold, which was a common practice. When he returned, he weighed enough to pass.]

(Chuckles) This is really funny. . . .A bunch of us for Christmas, a bunch of us, well we didn't . . . we had to be back Christmas Eve. We went on liberty to Wilmington, North Carolina. Got a room and we started walking the streets, and of course it was full of uniforms. Army, Marine, Navy . . . and we did spend a fair amount of time at the USO, an oasis. In Wilmington we did step into a bar and there was a huge fight going on. We said,

"This is ridiculous," so we found a liquor store and bought some very low-grade booze and had a party up in our room. It was the Brunswick Hotel, in Wilmington. There were five of us, and three out of the five were killed on Okinawa. I have a picture of the group.

LOVE DAY

ICEBERG IN THE SUBTROPICS[1]

As the battle for Iwo Jima raged some eight hundred miles from Okinawa, the Sixth Marine Division began the journey to its own battle. The embark records show that the Marines left Guadalcanal in the early part of March.[2] They stopped in Ulithi, and many went to Mog Mog (a chain of islands about halfway between Guadalcanal and Okinawa) for warm beer and assorted activities. Some decided the beer was not worth the trip and stayed aboard, where several of the veterans mentioned seeing the USS *Franklin* limp into port. The trip to Ulithi was not only about rest and relaxation, however. It was also a rendezvous spot for the U.S. Fleet. The number of ships that assembled there amazed all of the men who were interviewed. One veteran recalls being aware that this contingent was not even the entire U.S. Fleet, which made it all the more awe-inspiring. From this meeting point, the Task Force was 1,375 miles from its destination. By the time they reached Okinawa the supply line for the invasion force would be more than five thousand miles long—the distance back to Pearl Harbor.[3]

The troops were told their destination after leaving Ulithi, although many still had no comprehension of where Okinawa was located. They did understand that it was Japanese soil, though. Many had already heard

enough about other island invasions to have a mental picture of what
was in store. The trip was tedious, but for the most part the weather
was good, allowing the troops to stay on deck for games of cards and
visiting. This is when the officers, the noncommissioned officers
(NCOs), and the old hands began briefing the youngest Marines on
combat. All of the veterans remember getting up early on invasion
morning. Many disagree about whether they had the traditional steak
and eggs breakfast—whether this is because they were nervous or
because the meal varied from ship to ship is unclear—but some remember not eating at all, and some recall feeling that it would be their last
meal.

The sight the men beheld as they came from below deck to topside
was overwhelming. More than fourteen hundred ships lay in wait for the
invasion. As he looked out on the sight, a Japanese soldier remarked to
his comrades that, "It's seventy percent ships and thirty percent ocean."[4]
Another Japanese veteran, Yoshinaka Yamamoto, recalled his shock that
morning as he watched with his binoculars. He stated, "For the first time
in my life I saw ships coming out of ships. They would get to shallow
water and start moving on their own." He continued his description of
his amazement at U.S. landing craft: "I had never thought of that idea. I
was stunned. I said, 'My god, what kind of enemy do we face?'"[5] Aircraft
roared overhead; people shouted; guns exploded. It was a chaotic and
frightening sight. By the time the Marines went over the nets and into the
crafts waiting to take them ashore, they had grown used to the noise of
the naval barrage. The bombardment of the island had begun days
before. By March 24, 1945, military communiqués mention naval action
around Okinawa.[6] James Chaisson, who was a member of an advance
Underwater Demolition Team, remembered that Green Beach, the
beach he was to land on, worried him during that first observation in late
March because the Marines would be required to climb a retaining wall
in order to get to land. By the time he landed that April morning, however, the Navy had destroyed the wall and the Marines walked right onto
the island.[7]

The invasion began with little resistance. Medical teams waited
with nothing to do. Only twenty-five people died the first day, predom-

inately from two kamikaze attacks. Units that had planned to go ashore on L+2 (L-Day, plus two) or later were on shore by the first afternoon. The troops felt relief, disappointment, and confusion. Col. Alan Shapley, who commanded the Fourth Marines, later described their utter disbelief at the unopposed landing. "My third day objective was to take the airfield. By 10 o'clock that morning [they were there] and then I just had to stop because I didn't want to get out of phase with my logistics."[8] Adm. Richmond Turner telegrammed his boss, Adm. Chester Nimitz, "I may be crazy, but it looks like the Japs have quit the war." Nimitz was not so optimistic. He wired back, "Delete all after crazy."[9]

The Tenth Army split the island in two. The Marines went north while the Army headed south. The resistance to the north was scattered. Ernie Pyle wrote about the troops' boyishness at this time—riding bicycles and horses they found, and adopting animals—yet snipers were a constant menace and civilians were an unknown element. Then the Marines hit the Motobu Peninsula and the twelve hundred foot–tall Mount Yae-Dake. They ran into "Udo's Force," so named for its commander, Col. Takehiko Udo.[10] This largely guerrilla operation, entrenched in the mountain and supported by artillery, took a heavy toll on the Sixth Marine Division.[11] In particular, the Fourth Marines saw heavy combat.

It was a time of distressing news for the troops. During this push north, President Franklin Roosevelt died and Ernie Pyle was killed in the field. Bill Sams and the gun crewmembers of the Fifteenth Artillery moved directly across from Ie Shima to lay a barrage when the Seventy-seventh Army Division landed. Ernie Pyle had just left the First Marine Division, and was with the Seventy-seventh on Ie Shima. Bill Sams remembers that very soon after he had finished this support barrage he heard on the military radios that Pyle had been killed. News actually arrived pretty quickly to the troops. Radios such as the SCR-300 were backpack-sized, and units could easily communicate with each other. Tanks often had AM radios that got Tokyo Rose, and troops in support units received mail frequently, if sporadically, during the campaign. Most of all, "the word", whatever it might be, traveled quickly among the troops.

Despite these emotional setbacks, by the middle of April the Motobu Peninsula was secured and the Sixth turned north. On April 20, 1945, General Shepherd announced the end of organized resistance on the northern two-thirds of the island. The Marines had secured 436 square miles in Japanese territory.[12] The division rested and rumors circulated. One rumor had the unit being sent back to Hawaii. The salts knew better, for rumors also flew about the battle in the south and the Army's lack of success there.

The Marines had survived the unprecedented landing on April 1, 1945. The ones who had fought on the Motobu Peninsula had seen the face of combat, yet the real struggle was still to come. Colonel Shapley later stated that Okinawa was the toughest campaign for his regiment.[13] Over those three months, his troops suffered more than 110 percent casualties.[14]

LANDING DAY MEMORIES

Chaisson

> We got ashore on Green Beach One, and before you knew it, we had taken and secured Yontan airfield area. We were on our way north. It was just, ya know, a great experience . . . and standing up instead of lying down.

Jones: HQ/2/22

[Thomas Jones joined the Marine Corps in 1942. L-Day was his fourth landing. By this time, he was one of the most senior lieutenants and was the battalion liaison officer.]

> I knew I was looking at something that had never happened before in the history of the world, and will never happen again. The largest armada ever assembled by far—larger than anything else, including Normandy. . . . Normandy didn't need that kind of naval armada 'cause they only had twenty-seven miles of water to deal with. We had twenty-seven hundred miles of water between us and home. I was aware of it as being historic.

You couldn't help, when you're in a lagoon, miles across. Where we staged was Ulithi. Our armada was so big, with fourteen hundred and forty ships, that half of them had to stage in Leyte Gulf over in the Philippines. We couldn't get them all in a place like Ulithi. Our section of the operation was staging in Ulithi. The other section was staging in the Philippines, and we all came together. I think there was a forest of ships everywhere you looked. When we got to Ulithi and, of course, when we finally landed off the beaches of Okinawa there was a forest of ships. They extended as far as the eye could see.

Fitzgerald: E/2/22

[John "Jack" Fitzgerald, a lieutenant, joined the Twenty-second on Guam. By the time he reached Okinawa, he was considered "an old salt."[15]]

We were scared to death, to tell you the truth. Then, when we got to shore, there was no resistance . . . no resistance. We saw no booby traps. There were no heavy beach obstacles and there was some enemy smoke, harassing stuff. Dick Pfuhl said the colonel called and said, "How is it?," and he [Pfuhl] said, "Send in the PX."

Sams

There has been much written about us getting there, loading and leaving the Canal and going to Ulithi, and all that good stuff. You've read it, and so have I many times over the years, and there's no need to elaborate on that because you're familiar with it as we were by this time. So, we'll just go on to early morning on April 1. If we had the breakfast . . . I don't recall us having the breakfast they always said we would get before getting ready to going ashore, which would be steak and eggs, but it didn't happen to us on that LST [landing ship transport]. I can assure you that. I can't recall exactly what we had but it wasn't that. It was probably bully beef, something like that, and potatoes. At daylight they summoned all the chiefs of sections up topside with our binoculars and compasses and what have you, to identify our landing beach. We could see a little bit better from up there. There was a lot of smoke, a lot of confusion, you name it. It didn't do too much good. About seven o'clock, to start with, our guns, our 105s, were loaded in a DWUK, D-W-U-K or something like that. It had wheels on it but it would go in the water too. That's what we were loaded on. We loaded them down at Guadalcanal. We had a hundred rounds of ammunition. No, we didn't either. We didn't have a hundred . . . I forget now. We didn't have that much ammunition. We took only six men. It might have been a hundred rounds of ammunition, I think. We took six men and me. Being Gun One, I was in the bow of the LST on the [gun] ramp chained down. When they opened the doors I was looking right down at that water, four miles out to sea. We had a black man . . . Army . . . these were Army DWUK's. Where they came from, God only knows. There was a black man [who] was our driver. I've never seen anyone more scared than he was. He liked to turn white. Anyhow, he eased that thing down that ramp and we went into the water. When it finally settled down the nose came back up. I thought it was going to sink before we got ten yards from the LST. The nose finally came up, and we turned on all the bilge pumps because we were knee deep in water at that time in this DWUK.

First time I had a chance to look around, I looked and all I could see was solid steel. What I mean is solid steel ships, three hundred and sixty degrees around me. The compass bearing that I had taken when we were topside earlier was of absolutely no value, as the little compass we had—the needle—would just spin around and around. There was so much metal until it attracted that needle, and we couldn't tell where we were going. I had absolutely no idea where we were. We paddled around out there, almost sinking at times. What I mean by that, on the sides of this DWUK were only about four inches above the water line. Scary, yeah, it was scary. Eventually, sometime during the process, I passed under what I think was a battleship and they cut loose a broadside of sixteen-inch guns and almost sucked me out of the water. Well, this old Georgia boy, he didn't know which way to go but he did the best he could. We finally got us a direction and headed for the beach. As I say, we left off the LST at 8 o'clock in the morning. We started toward the beach, and I guess got a half-mile out from it, and we hit a coral reef with one side. It turned up sideways. I thought sure as God it was going to sink right there. I got all the men up on the topside, best I remember. We threw some excess stuff over the side to lighten the load. Eventually we saw some guy, I guess he was some Navy personnel, running around on that coral reef in about knee-deep water. We got his attention eventually, got him over, and asked him to pull us off that reef, dislodge us from it so we could go on in. He backed up and threw us a line or cable, and we tied it on, and I told him, "Just ease us up on there." You know, he eased us up on there, wide open, and snatched us up on there. God knows we didn't turn the rest of the way over and go down in the drink [ocean], but we made it.

Eventually we got up on in. It got up along noontime, twelve or one o'clock, something of that nature. I eventually found the battery, my outfit. They were in a rice paddy, in a holding position, nobody . . . well they were just there, assembling let's say, getting regrouped. I wasn't the only one who got lost. We got regrouped, and when I saw everybody I was mighty proud to see them. I jumped down off the top of that DWUK. That was about the only way to get down. It didn't have any ladders or anything. You jumped down off of it, I guess. When I did, my feet straddled a little rice terrace in this rice field . . . a terrace where they maintain their water in this rice field at certain times. My left foot on one side, my right foot on the other side, and I popped both ankles. It didn't break them but I thought to God it had. Down I went. That was as hurting a hurt as I have ever known. But at any rate, we made it on and got together, and eventually got assigned some gun positions late in the afternoon.

Joralemon

All I remember is walking, finally getting up on deck, and I just remember that was when everything . . . it was a beautiful day, beautiful sun-shiny day, clear sky. The weather was just perfect. That's when I was awed. When I looked around, for as far as the eye could see were ships—ships of all kinds and descriptions, I mean from battlewagons to whatever, landing craft. In addition to that, of course, all of the gunfire from the battleships sitting out there, with a noise that is hard to duplicate. [Chuckles.] It's resounding. It shakes everything and so forth. From that, all the way down to the 20-millimeter and 40-millimeter on the antiaircraft, all the way down to the planes. All that going off at one time. That's spectacular.

Then all the activity. Planes zipping in and out. You could hardly follow the whole thing. I remember one plane. I thought, "Oh jeez, he's dropping a bomb," but what it was was just a fuel tank. I had been in convoys in the Merchant Marines, and that was a lot of ships, a hundred ships or whatever. That paled by this thing that was there. It was unbelievable. Unbelievable scene . . .

Well, the first thing that we did when we got off . . . some say its fear and so forth. I don't know, I think it winds up to be anticipatory. I mean it's something. You build this thing up and part of it may be fear, but its more apprehension. You say to yourself, "Don't think . . . I'm not going to die." I think an awful lot of people feel that way. "It's not me. It's someone else." They let the thing down and you go out there expecting whatever you have seen in the movies and it's not there. It's just like business as usual. It's a funny feeling. I don't know how to describe it other than it's almost a disappointment. It's like, "What are they talking about?" Then all of a sudden you say, "Thank God." You think of what you're getting out of, and thank God.

White, W.: G/3/29

[William "Red" White was from Pennsylvania. He had finished high school, and by then young men were being drafted. They could no longer enlist. He made arrangements to join the Marine Corps.]

As near as I can recall we went in about eleven o'clock. The event I recall was Red Wilkerson went down the nets carrying a can of peaches. I never heard where he acquired this prize. Since he only had two hands things got complicated, and in the end he still had the peaches but he dropped his rifle into the ocean. We razzed him unmercifully about this, but when you think about it, there were a hell of a lot of rifles but only one can of peaches, so maybe his priorities were right after all. I remember we dug in. Whitaker and I were in a hole together. They announced a bunch of Jap parachute troops were coming, and be ready for an attack. Later this was called off, as the night fighters shot them all down but one plane, and I believe they landed and were promptly wiped out. The first day primarily consisted of good news where we were.[16]

McConville: L/4/15

[Joseph McConville was born in County Down, Ireland, and came to the United States as a boy. He was on Guam and was augmented into the Fifteenth when it was formed.]

I was busy praying, to tell you the truth, because we knew we were going to land on a piece of Japanese territory, and we figured it was going to be hell to pay. We had heard reports, the news coming from Iwo Jima. Iwo Jima was in full swing at that time. I was aboard ship. We pulled into Ulithi and probably the greatest armada, something like twelve hundred ships were amassed there. Everywhere you looked were crafts of all sorts and descriptions. Aircraft carriers, battleships, cruisers, destroyers, APs, LCIs, LST's, LCMs [all different varieties of small ships and landing crafts]; they were all out there. Thousands and thousands.

We got mail when we were in Ulithi. Here I got a letter from my mother because I was worried about John, [brother] because I knew they were catching hell on Iwo. I got a letter from my mother saying that she had a letter from John saying he had been wounded, but he was all right and back on Guam. In a hospital on Guam. I was very happy. I knew he was alive.

Niland

We were one of the first ones, yes. [To go in on L-day.] We had steak and eggs, yes. I was scared stiff because it was the first time I had done that. I didn't know what to expect, but I knew I had to do it. So I thought what I'd do when I got there, and I did what I had to do. It was frightening, yes, but on the other hand, I felt proud being a Marine, being a man. I saw an enormous collection of ships, vessels. The Royal British Navy, the United States, they were all over the sea and everything was blasting simultaneously. It was frightening. I have never been so impressed in my life. It was impressive.

Nothing . . . there were very little resistance [from] the Japanese defensive positions. Very little. A machine gun here, a rifleman there, but nothing. Another thing, incidentally; I'm Irish and have light skin, and the day before we sailed I took off my dungaree jacket to play cards. I won over five hundred dollars, and I'm not a good card player because you can read my emotions in my face, so I figured I was a dead man because it was the only time I've ever won. I went to the post office and mailed it, but the ship was sunk so I never got it anyway. Anyway, when we got to the beach I was more worried about my sunburn than anything else.

Moore: HQ/2/29

[Glen Moore was from New Jersey. He tried to enlist in 1942 and was told that all enlistments were frozen. He was later drafted after he requested it from the draft board. At twenty-one, he was "an old man" going into Okinawa.]

When we were finishing our training on the "Canal," we had trained as a division during the final week. The marks given by the observers were high for all regiments, but we were told that the Twenty-ninth Marines received the highest scores, and for that reason were held in division reserve on April 1st (L-Day). Our Twenty-second and Fourth Regiments were in the first wave and had the objective of securing Yontan Hill to the left and North of Yontan Airport. Waiting aboard ship to land, we heard the unbelievable reports coming back from our brother regiments that there were no Japs in sight. About 10:30 a.m. we were given the word to land the Twenty-ninth. We joyously found out that their reports were correct, and we moved up to secure Yontan Hill, and the Fourth and Twenty-second were working their way across the island with very little resistance. We kept thinking that this was a Jap trick and all hell could break loose anytime. It never happened.[17]

Wilkins: A/I/29 and H/S/3/15

[Claud Wilkins was from Henderson, Tennessee. He graduated from high school and was then drafted.]

On Love Day, First Battalion, Twenty-ninth Marines were not supposed to go in until Love plus three. So we were sitting there not even ready. Twelve o'clock, eleven o'clock, the middle of the day, on Love Day, "Get your gear ready, were going ashore." They were already where they thought it would take three days to get. We actually landed about two or three that day.

Chaisson

On the way up from the landing to Hedo Point, which was the very north end of the island, there is a little episode that you could, might be interested in hearing about. . . . My wife Pearly . . . I, of course, would correspond with her. I would do anything I could in the letters to alleviate her worry. So one of the things I remember writing when we were in that little town of Nago . . . we were securing some caves and ran into a bunch of rolls of cloth, real fine white linen cloth, that some storekeeper, I suppose, had hidden in a cave. So, you can imagine how careless it would be to take white sheets across, over your foxhole, in combat, but we weren't too conscious of the danger we were creating. So I took a sheet of that white cloth and I covered my foxhole, lined it with it. Then we were laughing about sleeping under sheets, big deal. So I wrote that to my wife and told her she didn't need to worry. We were sleeping under white linen sheets and everything was great.

Wanamaker

The kamikazes were coming in and attacking our ships. Of course, the ships were all shooting. Now, the sky was all bright. It looked like a big Fourth of July, all the tracers and big shells blowing up there, and we were actually more in danger at that time of shrapnel in the air than the Japanese, because they were all hiding. . . . Yeah, the first, the second guy who got off the ship, they just loaded themselves down with ammo. They made ammunition available for us just before we landed, and you could pick out as much as you wanted, and hand grenades. A lot of guys just loaded themselves up with ammunition. Then it got so heavy they couldn't carry it because of all the weight. Then you'd look back and you'd see a trail of ammo along the road. (Chuckles) Of course, they still had enough to take care of themselves. They just realized that they had a lot more than they could carry and they were just dumping it.

McKinney: F/2/4

[Thomas McKinney looked so young that, on Guadalcanal, they separated him and made him an aide because they though he was too young to be overseas. He was almost eighteen and Okinawa was his first invasion.]

We had set in just about where Camp Schwab is now. We had a security line clear across that end of the island. It's not very far across up there. We were searching people coming and going. Very few people were coming and going. We figured well, hell, we've already fought our battle. Were sitting up here big, fat, and dumb. Then every now and then when things got quieter up in our area, you could hear the dull roar going on towards the south. We knew that the Army, the Twenty-fourth Corps, had run into it. There was talk among some of the older men [who] said, "Don't let your gear get too far from you because we

are going to get into it. We are going." But then somebody started a rumor that we were going back to Guam, get brought up
to strength, and get ready for the operation, the invasion of
Japan. The older men laughed and said "Uh huh." It didn't take
very much longer for the officers to put the word out to start
looking towards your gear. "Get your gear ready and don't get
too far away from it," and all these things.

Then all of a sudden we started seeing Army. It turned out
they were from the Twenty-seventh Division. They came up
and they were looking over the area, and where they were going
to put their people. Old Corporal Doris, we called him Dew-
lolly, he was from Alabama. He said, "There's our replacements, guys." The next morning the word came down that
we're moving south. The Third Battalion would be going first
because they were the farthest north, so they marched down so
they could get to the trucks. They loaded 'em on the trucks and
they went south. Then all of a sudden here comes an Army con-
voy coming up . . . they . . . their troops. It was the first time that
I had seen military vehicles with tarps on them. Their troops
were inside those trucks and they didn't want to talk to us. They
didn't want nothing . . . and they said, "You're going to get your
butt kicked, Marine." We said, "Well you doggies can't do it."
We all went south. We formed up, oh down . . . just about
where Yontan airfield was. It was made sure we had three days
of rations, three days of units of fire, all the grenades you wanted. At this time, we could really hear the cannon and see the
flashes. We knew that trouble was coming.

WAR BECOMES REAL

Sugar Loaf Hill, ya know, that was (sighs) what, I guess, that is what Okinawa is all about. I think I said in Tennozan just because I was on Sugar Loaf, I don't . . . I never felt that the guys who weren't on Sugar Loaf did anything less than I did. Because everybody had their Sugar Loaf.

—Dick Whitaker

Samuel Hynes explains in *The Soldier's Tale: Bearing Witness to Modern War* that the history of a war, its myth, is very different from what troops experience in combat. Their reality, he concludes, is in fact what war really is. "The myth of war tells what is manageable, the soldiers' tale in its variety, tells the whole story."[1] Veterans believe that there are many realities in combat. Combat brought out the best and worst in them and those around them. The best can only be understood when one realizes just how deplorable conditions could be, and that men still did normal and amazing things.

The worst can only be partially understood by those never exposed to the "point of the spear."[2] The realities of war are, in fact, unique to each person. However, some common elements exist in battle. They are the threads that make stories similar. The next several sections explore some of those common realities of war.

Most troops who face an enemy bring with them preconceived notions about who that enemy is. Many of these ideas are completely exaggerated, and the soldiers believe that the enemy is superhuman or, conversely, animalistic. At some point, often when in close contact with a foe, combatants realize that the enemy is more like themselves than they had imagined. This is often disconcerting to those in combat. Additionally, many men mentioned the respect they gained for their enemy, although that did not dispel their hatred.

The Marines on Okinawa, unlike others who fought on Iwo Jima, had to contend with the reality of exposure to civilians. The added burden of killing women and children, or possibly being killed by them, became a deep and abiding fear. J Glenn Gray, in *Warriors,* explains that men who are able to fight an enemy without compunction may be wracked with guilt over those he did not intend to kill.[3] Observing the horrific and senseless scene of old and young Okinawans killing themselves left the Marines saddened by the futility of such loss of life. They understood that the civilians were behaving in this manner because they had been convinced through Japanese propaganda efforts that the Allies would torture them if they were taken captive. On the southern end of Okinawa, many people (military and civilian) were compressed into a small area. The reality of what war does to noncombatants when they find themselves on a battlefield was ever present.

War is chaotic and the Marines who were on Okinawa remember that chaos. They also recall how difficult functioning under combat conditions was for extended periods of time. Random death, constant fear, and assault on the senses left the troops terrified that at some point the realities of war would seem banal. They grew brutal and numb because they had no choice. Most chose not to step over the line and lose their humanity. War, however, taught them what a fine line there was between remaining human and becoming completely savage.

The Marines of the Sixth learned how big a flea could be when you are infested, how to be afraid of rain because you might drown in your foxhole, how similar rice looks to maggots, and how dry socks could be more important than a place to sleep. The Marines learned they could sleep standing up, or not sleep at all, for extended periods of time. They learned they could eat next to a rotting body and only be disgusted about having to fight the flies for their food. To their dismay, they discovered that their comrades died trying to go to the bathroom, and that a letter could mean far more than food. In fact, food mattered very little. They learned that the hardships of war do not only involve mortars and machine guns.

Those in combat came to understand that wounds were reality, that the best you could hope for was a "million dollar wound": one that would send you home, neither in a box nor maimed for life. They saw friends wounded and killed in every way imaginable. They heard young soldiers cry for their mothers as they died. They also saw some become so emotionally wounded that they screamed, tried to run away, drooled, soiled themselves, or did nothing at all.

Troops eventually dealt with the ultimate reality of war: They might not return alive. Gerald Linderman, in *The World Within War,* examines the many stages of combat that soldiers move through. Many start out with a sense of hopeful optimism and dream of heroism. They eventually move to the pragmatic realization that they are completely out of control. As Dick Whitaker explained, "Doing anything can get you killed, including doing absolutely nothing."[4] By June Lt. Col. Victor Krulak, G-3 for the Sixth Division, recorded low battle readiness for the Sixth. Casualties were not the only reason for the decline in effectiveness, but also the prolonged exposure of the troops to the realities of combat.

White, J.

> I think I got immune pretty early. Not immune but immured, 'cause I saw a lot of people. . . . I saw three actually get hit at the moment. I was watching them at the minute they were hit, and numerous right after. I'd hear something, look over, and see somebody fall or something. I remember the first dead Japanese I saw. That was kind of a shock.

Brining: H/3/29/Sixth Med. Bat.

[Donald Brining was drafted in 1943. He was from Bradford, Ohio. He was selected to be a Corpsman, went to Great Lakes for naval boot camp, and then went to Balboa hospital for medical training.]

> They had a company of Marines went off the edge of the airfield back in the ridge and hills there, and they got pinned down and they had some casualties . . . second day. So I went in to bring out the casualties, and on the way in there was a Marine sitting against an old building, a cane building, and his leg was shot, so I stopped to bandage his leg up. He had his M-1 lying

with him and he says, "Doc, don't move." [I] laid the rifle on my shoulder . . . (Chuckles, then chokes up, head down.) He fired three times. The Jap fell . . . went right between my legs. Didn't think too much about it until I got back to the outfit and got to thinking. A bayonet's about that long. (Indicates with hands, maybe two feet.) Didn't see him coming. Seemed too close. That got to me (visibly shaken). That's the only time ever that a Jap got close to me.

Sams

Lacey: When you . . . you are writing in May and it's obviously during the battle of Sugar Loaf time. In one of your letters you write, "I've got a ring side seat but it's not a pretty sight." Were you looking down into Naha and Sugar Loaf?

Yes, that, but also about fifty . . . well just a short distance from my gun pit. I could walk up on this ridge and look out over Bunkner Bay . . . later in the afternoon when the kamikazes would come in, I could stay right up there and have a ringside view of what was happening out there. There was so much fire in the air, so many tracers, that sometimes you'd lose sight of the kamikaze, you know what I mean?

Manell

You can see pictures in the papers . . . you see pictures at the movies or on television but they can't possibly . . . the maggots, the smell, the terrible stench . . . like a flame-thrower hits a person it smells like a lot of burnt hair. An ugly smell. Guys have been lying around in the sun for a couple weeks. They have a sweet smell that's something terrible. Once it gets in your nostrils it stays there for a couple weeks. These things you can't possibly get across. I saw a picture, the other day, of a guy that his guts hanging out in his arms trying to hold them in. That happened more than once. You can't possibly put that agony . . .

THE OKINAWANS

Under Japanese rule, it's kind of tough to be an Okinawan.
—Nansei Shoto, War Publication

The Okinawans were a docile people of small stature who were faced with an unenviable situation. Whether they were considered to be "like Go pieces, in a game of Go," as often referred to by former Okinawan Governor Masahide Ota, or caught between the hammer and the anvil, their situation during the war was miserable. At battle's end, one-third of the native population had persished. The Japanese military had told the Okinawan civilians to go south. They were thrown out of their hiding places as the Japanese retreated, and took those caves for themselves. Very little consideration was given to these noncombatants by their Japanese overlords. A lone exception to the normal disregard that the Japanese reserved for the Okinawans was exhibited by Rear Adm. Minoru Ota on June 6, 1945, shortly before Japanese naval headquarters on the Oroku Peninsula was overrun and Ota and his staff committed seppuku (ritual suicide). No other description better reveals the Okinawan's plight:

> Since the enemy attack began, our Army and Navy has been fighting defensive battles and have not been able to tend to the people of the Prefecture. Consequently, due to our negligence, these innocent people have lost their homes and property to enemy assault. Every man has been conscripted to partake in the defense, while women, children and elders are forced into hiding in the small underground shelters which are not tactically important or are exposed to shelling, air raids or the harsh elements of nature. Moreover, girls have devoted themselves to running and cooking for the soldiers and have gone as far as to volunteer in carrying ammunition, or joining in attacking the enemy.[5]

The fact that a Japanese officer would admit negligence makes this passage especially important. Historically, the Japanese admit no fault in

World War II. Also significant is his comment that the men had been conscripted. This is not to say, as Ota points out, that some Okinawans were willing participants. Like all civilians who have been fed wartime propaganda, the Okinawans had unwarranted fears that accounted for their initial resistance to the invaders and the large number of suicides. Many Okinawans made it clear that they felt they were fighting for their lives against barbarous Americans who would rape women and eat children. Once the civilians discovered the Allied troops did not intend to harm them, they surrendered and again became extremely docile. The naval military detachment established to support the local population commented on their passivity regarding the Japanese Army, attributing it to "great shock and fright," but added that from the point of capture on they were docile and cooperative.[6] Rear Admiral Ota also described the particularly horrific move south for the Okinawans:

> This leaves the village people vulnerable to enemy attacks where they will surely be killed in desperation. Some parents have asked the military to protect their daughters against rape by the enemy, prepared that they may never see them again. Nurses, with wounded soldiers, wander the battlefield aimlessly because the medical team had moved and left them behind. The military has changed its operation, ordering people to move to far residential areas, however, those without means of transportation trudge along on foot in the dark and rain, all the while looking for food to stay alive.[7]

Other accounts regarding civilians support Ota's claims. The naval personnel responsible for their relocation during the battle explained that the Okinawans had been living in caves and were terrified to come out. Even at the battle's beginning, "seventy-five percent of their homes were found destroyed, two-thirds having been burned. They were covered in lice and unclean, starved, and injured from bombing, shelling, and bullets."[8]

One of the most riveting stories regarding the civilians of Okinawa is that of the Himeyuri Student Corps, composed of schoolgirls. Schools in Japan, including Okinawa, had been militarized in the early forties. Conscription, activation, and intensive nurses' training began late in

1944 in all-female schools. The First Okinawan Prefectural Girls School and the Women's Division of the national Okinawa Normal School made up the Himeyuri Students Corps. These were the most admired girls on Okinawa.[9] When the battle began, the Himeyuri girls, numbering roughly 225 and ranging in age from fifteen to nineteen, were used as nurses' aides in the Japanese military hospital.[10] These privileged young ladies usually did the most menial, and often the most dangerous, work. Thoroughly indoctrinated, most would have had it no other way.

By May 30, 1945, the Japanese had already lost seventy percent of their forces stationed on Okinawa.[11] At this point, they abandoned the Shuri-Yonaburu line and headed south. The military also abandoned these young women. Medical units were deactivated and the girls were left to their own devices. Pushed out of the caves, they moved south unprepared and unprotected, which exacerbated their losses as they tried to find family and safety. By the end of June, just twenty-one remained alive. They have become a symbol on Okinawa of what the civilians endured. Explained Setsuko Ishikiwa, "My classmates died one after another."[12]

The conclusion to Admiral Ota's telegram to Tokyo exhibits unique understanding of what the Okinawans had endured. He expressed his concern for a people the Japanese had done little to protect:

> Ever since our Army and Navy occupied Okinawa, the inhabitants of the Prefecture have been forced into military service and hard labor, while sacrificing everything they own as well as the lives of their loved ones. They have served with loyalty. Now we are nearing the end of the battle, but they will go unrecognized, unrewarded. Seeing this I feel deeply depressed and lament a loss of words for them. Every tree, every plant is gone. Even the weeds are burnt. By the end of June, there will be no more food. This is how the Okinawan people have fought the war. And for this reason I ask you to give the Okinawan people special consideration this day forward.[13]

The Americans who landed on Okinawa had been briefed regarding the Okinawans, but they quickly surmised for themselves the Okinawans' pitiful situation. U.S. troops tried to look out for them as best they could. In *The Last Chapter*, Ernie Pyle wrote that the Okinawans were "obviously scared to death, shocked by the bombardment, and that after a few days when they realized that they would not be hurt, they came out in droves to give themselves up."[14] He concluded that the Okinawans' real befuddlement occurred when they realized not only that the propaganda concerning the horrors of the Americans was incorrect, but also that part of their intricate invasion plan included enough supplies to feed the civilians.[15] This is not to suggest that all American encounters with the Okinawans were benign. Many Okinawans were caught in the crossfire of war, and, as in any war, some troops were not always compassionate to others when assessing their own chances of survival.

The survivors of the Battle of Okinawa remember the Okinwans with pity and regret. Many remember a specific Okinawan they encountered. Others are now amazed at the indifference the war fostered in them. Most have a firm conviction that they did what they could for them, but often the Okinawans were just in the way.

Buchter: H&S/29

[Norris Buchter had been delivering ice and working on fishing boats before he enlisted. Okinawa was his first landing.]

> We're casually walking because there was really no resistance. . . . We weren't marching . . . walking . . . I don't know if it was that particular day or the following day. We got up quite a way. I'm not too sure how far up it was. . . . It was past that little island, up there . . . that island. Then it, the road, was up on the hill, and as we were going up the road we looked out at the water and here was this Okinawa girl, washing her clothes. She was completely nude 'cause she had taken her clothes off and she was washing them as well. She was, of course, startled and so were we. We guys were amazed at this thing. We just stopped and got out of line and whoever was in charge, an officer, said, "We'll take five or ten, you guys." I had my camera, and went down and took a picture of her. She was a little bit nervous at first, but when she realized we weren't going to bother her at all, she relaxed a bit. We couldn't speak to her,

couldn't communicate, and I think that lasted ten to fifteen minutes. She's still washing her clothes and had no . . . is completely nude, and that didn't bother her at all, so we went back on the road and continued on.

Someday . . . I'd like to get a copy of that picture for you and maybe find that lady. Going up in that area and talking to people, and having the picture . . . maybe somebody will recognize that lady. I've always wondered what happened to that lady.

Niland

I felt sorry for them. I was too young to get into philosophical processes, but I came from a middle-class Irish Catholic family. We didn't have any money, but we loved each other and had customs of normal families. When I saw these people I knew that they were different. They lived differently, but they were close families. Being distraught, blown up, mistreated . . . women, babies, wounded. I felt terrible . . . terrible. I wondered about my own family . . . my own family.

Gillespie: K/3/22

[Ray Gillespie spent much of the last year of his life trying to find a little girl who haunted him. He contacted Japanese, Okinawans, and Americans, but died without any answers. This is a poem he wrote.]

The Little Girl by Raymond Gillespie

Two days of war are recorded here,
Showing death, along with man's fear.
Okinawa in the year Forty Five.
You'll meet people both dead and alive.

The firefight was short and swift,
Taking place in a stream below a cliff.
A little girl took our quick surprise,
As I ordered firing to cease and subside.

A higher ranking Sergeant took no heed
Of my order to leave the little girl be.
His first round missed, going astray.
His second shot tore her intestines away.

My complaint to the Lieutenant in command
Brought a tart reply and a sharp reprimand.
The platoon moved on; she was in my care.
Her chances were slim, no better than fair.

On a path toward a road lying west,
I carried the child being gentle as best
While very high on a hill to my right,
Someone followed, well out of sight.

Was it enemy? Did compassion restrain
A warrior from putting lead in my brain?
Or were they parents or relatives above.
Following in fear, but driven by love.

Big brown eyes caught sight of my tear
As I repeated, "You're all right dear."
My language she could not understand,
But near the road she touched my hand.
She was taken to a hospital down on the bay.
Two of my friends died the next day.
Lieutenant, he lost his sight.
And that Sergeant. He caught a bullet that night.[16]

Buchter

As you said, from Sugar Loaf down we were squeezing them.
A lot of the Okinawans wanted to get out of there. They would
try to go up through our lines, and quite often we would let
them through, but after awhile we knew or we found out . . . we

found out, or realized later on, that the Japanese were dressing like Okinawans and they would go up through, and that's how they got in back of our lines. Unfortunately, then, we had to shoot them. That's when a lot of the poor Okinawans got killed. They were victims of war. We felt bad about having to do it, but we were protecting our own life. Survival of the fittest.

McKinney

We had been on the road. We were traveling with tanks. The big thing was get north . . . get north, take the ground. We were three or four miles ahead of any other American units. We got up to this one area, and the tank commander and Captain Homegrain decided we had gone far enough . . . that it was time to set up the night defense and get with it. So we did. We set up the perimeter. F Company was on the left side. Easy Company was on the right side. It just happened that there was a road that ran through the perimeter. My machine gun section that I was with . . . we were on the left hand side, and my friend Dallas Newman and his section was on the right side of the road. We set up the watches and everything, the reconnaissance people, which Lou Adams was part of . . . we knew they were out in front of us. Long about two in the morning . . . we knew the pebbles started hitting the dirt in front of us . . . we knew that somebody was drawing our attention. It turned out that it was Lou Adams and the recon people. We passed the word to hold your fire, and Lou and his people come in. Right away we get them in the holes, and they passed the word that we were going to have company. He said the Japs had all these people back down the road, down there, and they were getting ready. They were going to come down that road hollering and screaming and run over us.

Things got quiet and we kind of doubted, then all of a sudden we could hear . . . I guess thirty minutes after we got the recon people in . . . about 2:30 or so. We could hear the Japanese coming down the road. They were talking. You could hear them. I guess the Japanese soldiers were driving the people, actually forcing them to come forward. It was just about 3 o'clock when all of a sudden the sixty mortars throwed up a star shell. Lord behold, there was all these people on the road down there and they broke into a hard run straight at us, and the word came: Commence fire. Well, Dallas opened up with his machine gun. I wasn't on the gun . . . [it wasn't] our gun that was doing the firing. I wasn't privileged to do that. All of us were on the line using our rifles and all, and when it was all over, it lasted a good three minutes. After it was over it got dead quiet. Recon got ready to go out. Captain Homegrain forbid it because of the danger out there. The star shells went up and you could see the bodies lying all over the road. Along about four, maybe something a little later, we heard this little voice crying out there. Lou Adams came up and said, "Some of them are still alive." He heard it about two or three times and Lou says, "I'm going." Lou went. We passed the word, "Don't fire, Lou's out there." Lou went out, and next thing you know he came back and he had this little boy. It kind of made all of us feel kind of bad because, hey, a lot of our people had brothers and sisters at home about that age. After it became daylight, the boy was taken care of by the Corpsmen, and he was evacuated.

The tank commander said that those bodies will have to be moved off of the road because his tanks don't need to grind them up underneath their treads. Us infantry people and the Two team (intelligence team) . . . we went down, and we didn't have to search the civilians because civilians never carried anything of interest to us. We helped move all the people off the road. The Two team turned to and started searching the Japs. We found that one of them was a major, two of them were captains, and the rest of them were all enlisted. They were all from the Japanese Twenty-second Infantry Regiment, if I'm not mistaken, out of the Twenty-fourth Division. We did recover some maps from them. None of the maps had real good information about what was on top of that mountain, and what we were going to look at when we got up there. But we did find them. It was a grisly mess, I'll tell you.

Chaisson

I said, "That woman is still alive." I could see her stomach. Then old Daniel said, "You stay the hell away from her. That damn woman is booby-trapped." I said, "Hell." I go over and take a look anyway. I went over and stuck my foot under her hat and lifted her hat up, and her eyes were just that big, ya know, and she's still alive. Japs . . . and wherever we went we were killing people, but this woman was by herself right in the mud. Daniel thought she was booby-trapped. I pursued, determined [to see] that she was alive, so I picked up her hat . . . sure enough. Came back [and said] "Well, she's alive alright." That's how casual we were.

Honis

In fact, there was this one night . . . it was a moonlit night, and I had . . . (of course they fired flares all night) and I'm . . . I don't recall what time it was. I see a couple [of] figures coming across the valley floor. I could also tell that one was very old and one was a kid. They came right to the bottom of our hill and started up. I was not going to throw any grenades, or I'm not going to fire at them until I'm absolutely sure who they are. I yell to them in Japanese to stop. They did stop and . . . but what they did is they went down half way, and then there were some Nip spider holes, and crawled in there. But I still said to the other guy, the ones I was in lodge with, that these were civilians. The next morning it got light and they started off back down the valley floor. We went down and grabbed them because guys on the other hill would kill 'em. There's always somebody who would shoot them. It turns out the guy, the man, the adult, was seventy-five years old and blind, and the girl was about eight years old. She had a few . . . had caught . . . had maybe gotten scratched and they got infected on her hands. That seventy-five-year-old was so terrified, and it was amazing he was so strong. He was scrawny. He was strong as an ox. He was afraid and, of course, the girl was terrified. A Corpsman came up and sprinkled some sulfur powder on her wounds, she—the guy completely relaxed. The guys gave him a cigarette and all was well. Nobody got hurt. I saw too many dead civilians. I didn't want to add to it.

Baird

Well, they were pretty nice people, but they was afraid of us. In the fire company it got kind of quiet. I ran into a little boy, maybe twelve years old . . . some of 'em were questioning whether he was Japanese. Ya know, well, I didn't know any Okinawan, and I asked him, "What are you?" He surprised me. He pulled out a little blue book, about like the kind I had in grade school, and he began writing in the prettiest hand you ever saw. I am a schoolboy. I finally found out later it said I am schoolboy. It saved his life.

McKinney

Second Battalion . . . we were below Naha moving, . . . not too fast or anything, but we were moving. I don't know if it was in the first platoon or what, but the first platoon saw a woman turn and run into a cave. The word came down and said, "Get the Two team down here." So, we formed and went down to where it was. Already there was three or four Marines were down there. They had a civilian, who later on it turned out to be the chief of police . . . the former chief of police from the city of Naha. He had surrendered. They had . . . well, Johnny B. was there too, and a couple other people. They were trying to talk to this woman. She would only come out of the cave just far enough that you could see her . . . just barely see her. She was Japanese. The chief of police had talked to her and asked her, "What all do you have in there?" She told them she had her entire class of all girls from the Naha Primary School . . . were in that cave and had been in there somewhere over sixty some days. She said she would not surrender until a Japanese general, which would have had to be Cho or Ushijima, had come down and told her to surrender. She wouldn't surrender. The chief of police . . . he told her that "the Americans are here and I have watched them for over a week and they are very generous. They will not kill you, they will not kill the girls, they will not rape the girls or nothing, please." They were begging and pleading for her to come out. So she said, "Wait and let me go in and talk." She went back into the cave, and while she was out of sight a couple Marines moved up pretty close . . . either side of the cave door. Hoping if she came out far enough they could grab her, then get the children out. Evidently, when she went back in there she must have told the girls that we had forced the chief of police to tell them lies and everything. She came back out . . . had two little girls that came out with her . . . they came right to the entrance. We waved at them and everything and the little girls waved and looked up at her. She turned her back on us and took the two little girls and went back into the cave. She had said, "I don't know." That's all she said, and she went back into the cave.

Lord the . . . she hit that bomb. That's what we figured there must have been . . . a five hundred pound bomb buried in the floor of that cave. She hit the nose of it, evidently with a mallet, and the whole top of that hill . . . it wasn't a real big hill . . . the whole top got up and I swear it turned around and then fell back into place. Dirt and dust just flying and coming out of that cave, what was left of it. The cave was almost completely sealed, and by estimates [we] figure that there was in the neighborhood [of] thirty-two little girls in that cave with the schoolteacher. She had destroyed them all . . . they would have been taken to the civil affairs people and found a home for them real quick. The mayor and the chief of police were both flabbergasted. They were both crying. To think, there went thirty-two Okinawan girls that would have helped to repopulate the island and everything else. There was quite a few misty eyes among the Marines that were there. . . . To think so strongly of their religion, which was the Bushido, that they would kill the children instead of surrendering them and take a chance on letting them live a real good life. . . . From then we moved on . . . all of us had the same feeling. That these people aren't for real. Life is so cheap that they would destroy it rather than give it up and take the chance that they would live, and survive, and prosper later on.

The caves were burning out. The hard part is there were an awful lot of civilians in those caves. That was their final refuge. There was nowhere to go. They were hid in there. In our *Sixth Division History* book there is a picture of a huge cave on the southern end of Okinawa . . . where we were taking caves out of that cave. Civilians had been in there. Some of them had been in a month or so. They were almost blind . . . light . . . the sun and all. I don't know who found the cave. Everybody was around there. We started down into it and started helping the people come out . . . the Japanese soldiers . . . there were Japanese soldiers in there also, and they were hollering at them and all in the back. The Okinawans knew if we were there . . . the fight was over. They let us take them out. We had to carry, physically carry, people out of there, they were so weak. From malnutrition and all. We got 'em. I don't know . . . there must have been three or four hundred people came out of that cave in the day and a half that we operated there.

Whitaker

The Okinawans volunteered to retreat with the Japanese. So as this island got narrower, the density of the population increased. It was Japs and Okinawans and kids and old people and ducks and dogs and cats . . . ya know . . . everything (Chuckles) was being smashed in together. And it's hard to sort them out when you're the attacking force. You can make some very serious mistakes as a Marine if you don't treat them all as enemies until you've had a chance to sort them out. So, I'm sure a lot of civilians were killed, especially at night. Despite all the warnings and leaflets, they would try to come through the lines at night, and, ya know, that's the worst thing in the world to try . . .

Here again, that happened on Oroku. It was no one I knew. And as I said, we were converging . . . there were other units. One day we'd be next to George Company, the next day we'd be next to Easy Company, and I even think at times we got close to the First Division. Anyway, we were going through a small village and there was some guys ahead of us. One, a small group of guys were screwing around a house. We asked them what they were doing and this guy said, "There's a great samurai sword." This guy's trying to get it out and he's afraid it's booby-trapped. So, he's throwing a little piece of rope in and trying to hook it. Anyway, he finally gets this thing hooked and drags it out the front door. And it was a beauty. Then the sword case is just inside the door, so this guy walks in, picks up the sword case, and blew himself up. It was the sword case that was booby-trapped.

Miller

They were friendly people, nice people. We were unusually cruel to them, which they did not deserve 'cause the Japs were cruel and they did not need us on their backs either. But they had slant eyes. We were very anti-slant eyes. Guys would say, "There goes a slant-eyed chink, pow, pow . . . there goes a slant-eyed pig, pow, pow." We were not the most charming people in the world.

Drago: 1/3/22
[Joe Drago was from Boston. Okinawa was his only campaign, and he was wounded on Sugar Loaf.]

One afternoon I observed interpreters talking to civilians. We're at a fork in the road, and from what I could see there was a crowd of them at the foot of the road that led down to where, I have no idea. They were being told not to come out at night. It was dangerous. We would be set up along the road. Further, earlier that day, we had confiscated two wagons loaded with women's clothing, wigs, etcetera. So possibly enemy soldiers disguised as women and try to infiltrate our lines. Settling in our foxholes . . . set up the machine-gun. Around midnight a sole figure came down the road from our left, the direction where the civilians were. It was an old man, without a doubt. We held our fire and passed the word down the line, "Hold your fire, a civilian." No matter . . . he never got fifty feet down the road when he was shot.

About an hour later there was literally a parade of civilians heading our way. They were tightly bunched together, also from our left. We were the first to encounter them . . . almost pitch black out. In spite of the darkness my vision was acclimated enough to discern they were old men, women, and children. Ed Yahara, my squad leader, and I left our foxholes and jumped onto the middle of the road with our 45s drawn. Ed instructed one of our men to take over the machine gun and cover us. What transpired next resulted in a bloodbath of huge proportion. Someone in the middle of the crowd panicked and started running away from us. Suddenly bullets went flying by, narrowly missing our legs. Ed and I emptied our 45s into the fleeing crowd, ran back to the foxhole, took over the machine gun, and traversed to the left and slowly brought it right, and left again.

Throughout the night, chilling screams, moaning, crying. We reacted by firing more rounds wherever we thought the sounds were coming from, to still them, stop their suffering. We had not a clue if there were any enemy in the crowd.

When dawn came, [we] left our foxholes, observed the carnage strewed about the road. . . untold numbers . . . women, old men, children. My guesstimate, in the hundreds. Our officer told us to remove the bodies off the road as the tanks would be coming through. Forget it. We never touched them. Let someone else do it. That incident was never mentioned again throughout the rest of the campaign, or years afterward. However, I've often wondered, was any report ever made of this incident, by any in authority? Guess not. Looking back, I guess you could describe it as a massacre.

Years later, during our reunion, Albuquerque, New Mexico, NHK Japan TV [Japan's PBS] were there to interview veterans of Okinawa. They handed out questionnaires. One item related to contact with civilians . . . shot, maimed, and so forth. I mentioned this to Jim Day, recipient of the Medal of Honor. "How should I answer this prior to the on-camera interview?" He asked me, "Does it bother you, what happened that night?" "No," I said. "Then screw them."

So, I related what happened. They were horrified. Couldn't believe what they were hearing. Did I have any remorse, guilt, regrets? "Not at all," I said. Needless to say, an hour's worth of interview was whittled down to a few seconds in the final cut. Win some, lose some. I have to admit, I often thought, "Would someone out of the past accuse us of war crimes . . . the massacre?" Scary.[17]

Pierce: WPNS/29

[William Pierce was making his first landing at Okinawa; however, he had served stateside prior to joining the Sixth overseas.]

Well, on the southern end we were put up on a ridge. Our particular [group of] ten or twelve of us . . . and told to guard this spot where the road came down. Every night a Jap would come through, or two, and what if we didn't get him the guy on the right would get him. We would go out in the morning and inspect every cave and hole that was out in front of us, because someone could have come there during the night. We had a war dog with us this one day. The dog went into the cave and sniffed in the corner, and we kind of readied the rifles, and we poked around, and the Japanese got up and he was in a brown uniform. No hat on, but the hair gave it away. Someone said, "That's a girl." Well they got her back and took her back to the ridge where we are, and a couple of these guys form Alabama and Georgia, they stripped her down. Put her over a helmet . . . they bathed her with the soap and washed her nice and clean, and put her in the pup tent and kept her there for four days. Then they got tired of her, or we were going to move somewhere. So they got her out, mudded her up, put her clothes back on, and marched her down the hill and said, "Sir, we just captured this Japanese soldier. It's a nurse." But they used her for four days . . . dirty Marines.

We let them alone, but our thoughts were that we wouldn't touch her, because to us she represented filth. God, who would want to go in the tent with that thing? Why would anybody do that? But these guys did. What are you going to do though? If there were eight or nine . . . say if there was ten of us on that hill, probably seven of us wouldn't go near that woman.

Kraus: E/2/15

[Stephen Kraus, from Brooklyn New York, enlisted at eighteen. Okinawa was his only battle.]

Well, a friend told me when he returned to Okinawa for the fortieth anniversary. They took a tour and they stopped the bus. The tour bus driver was really Okinawan. He had a very good education . . . He was there for the anniversary with other Marines. He got to this spot. Like I said, this tour was very good. They had stopped and they got out. He says, "Boy, I've been here." It's been years and there is a lot of growth and everything. [He] started to work his way, and he got to a spot and he starts sliding. He says, "Ya know, I was here forty years ago on this spot." He remembered he had a flamethrower on his back and he was trying to get himself in position to get . . . (Points upward.) there were pill boxes [caves] up there. They were causing a lot of trouble. He crept forward and finally got the aim in the cave and . . . well, he did his job.

As he is looking around there is another cave beside it, and he decided he'd better hit that cave too. Pillbox . . . no I think it was a cave. Anyway, he got over there, got all in position and tried to fire and nothing happened. He couldn't understand. This thing [the flamethrower] worked perfect all the time. He checked the injector, he checked the pressure, he checked the fuel, he checked the igniters . . . nothing. The sergeant came and said, "Move on." He moved on. The job was done. But that certain cave . . . over the years he often wondered about that cave. He thought, "A lot of Marines may have gotten killed because I didn't do my job." As he's looking around, the Okinawan [bus driver] from this reunion worked his way over. Oh, by the way, the first cave he found black and dark burned out area. The second cave, he gets over there and there are no burns or anything . . . nothing. He is looking around. He's looking for something.

All of a sudden, the Okinawan from the tour bus, the tour bus driver, says, "Hey mister, are you looking for something?" He says, "Yes, but I will never find it, I believe."

He said, [The Okinawan] "When I was a little boy, I was with missionaries. They saved a lot of children in this cave. They told us that we would be safe and God would take care of us . . . it's amazing."

MADE IN JAPAN

> *"The Japanese fought a lot of the war with the heart, not their heads."*
>
> —Don Honis

Many people today cannot understand the vehemence with which the troops who fought in the Pacific express their hatred for the "Japs." Although in the past fifty years many veterans have embraced the children of their former enemies, others retain an almost visceral dislike for the Japanese. Many Pacific veterans, for example, will not buy a Japanese-made car. This same level of animosity is not seen in veterans of the European Theater. In recent years this prejudice has been attributed to racial attitudes, but this conclusion is too simplistic. Germans, with some exceptions, fought like Americans. Both sides in the European Theater observed an unspoken code; sometimes that allowed for humanity to exist, even in war. The Pacific War did not often follow a similar pattern.

Although race cannot be discounted as a reason for the differences in how the war was fought in different theaters, other factors were far more important. Pearl Harbor may have been reason enough. A sneak attack, such as the one on December 7, 1941, gave license to violate accepted standards of behavior in war. War against Japan was always a "win at any cost" campaign. "For the troops it would be about avenging the event a thousand-fold."[18] Another explanation for the extreme brutality of the Pacific campaign comes from the extreme conditions under which the troops fought. Heat, mud, and disease, along with

hand-to-hand and cave-to-cave combat, made combat especially brutal.[19] The enemy's way of fighting became all too familiar, and often all
too close.

Still, Samuel Hynes, war correspondent and author, has explained
the most important factors that led to the animosity between the
Japanese and the Allies. His conclusions are as valid today as they were
then when he wrote them in the midst of the Pacific conflict. After
returning from the battle on Guadalcanal, he explained that Marines
saw their enemy differently than they saw themselves in "two funda-
mental, fearful ways."[20] First, the Japanese fought with no regard for
their lives. They were suicidal. They fought to kill, or to be killed. This
proved dissimilar to the French, Germans, Italians, and Americans who
fought with an appreciation for the concept of living to fight another
day. The devaluation of individual worth was so alien to Western values
that it made the Japanese seem subhuman to American troops. The second crucial difference was the perceived inhumanity or lack of compassion that the Japanese often exhibited. Whether it was regarding
Nanking or Bataan, rumors of Japanese brutality were evident. As combat in the Pacific progressed, Allied troops came to believe that the
Japanese would adhere to none of the "rules" of war.

A member of the First Marine Division tried to explain this brutality by quoting Eugene Sledge. He addressed the end of innocence and
the development of the hatred that American troops had for the
Japanese:

> Understand, in Gene's first book he relates on page 148 finding
> three Marines that were wounded and on stretchers that had
> been captured by the Japs. He states, "The bodies were badly
> decomposed and nearly blackened by exposure. This was to be
> expected in the tropics but these Marines had been mutilated by
> the enemy. One man had been decapitated; his head lay on his
> chest. His hands had been severed from his wrists and also lay
> on his chest, near his chin. In disbelief, I stared at the face as I
> realized that the Japanese had cut off the dead Marine's penis
> and stuffed it into his mouth. The corpse next to him had been
> butchered, chopped up like a carcass torn by some predatory

animal. Many Americans are not aware these things happened, and as a result do not understand the bitterness that remains."[21]

The troops who landed on Okinawa had all heard stories, and some had witnessed similar scenes to the one Sledge described. These experiences ensured that both sides would not compromise but would practice total war.

Many of the troops also regarded the Japanese with something akin to respect. They were good soldiers, one hears repeatedly; courageous, insistent, and unrelenting. Many veterans grudgingly admit that they were a formidable foe. Ernie Pyle encountered this schizophrenic attitude toward the Japanese. The Pacific troops told him "by the dozens . . . how tough the Japs were, yet how dumb too; how illogical, yet how uncannily smart at times; how easy to rout when disorganized, yet how brave. I became more confused with each story."[22]

Today most veterans concur that suicidal tendencies were Japan's greatest weakness. Their willingness to waste assets ultimately became a liability. Gerald Linderman writes in *The World Within War,* "As the war proceeded, Americans increasingly regarded such incidents as exemplifying weakness rather than a strength."[23] Many still shake their heads and say they just cannot understand why the Japanese fought the way they did. Some have spent the last fifty years trying to understand.

Never before in Japan had nationalism been raised to the status of religion as it was before and during World War II. The military took this new religion and mixed it with the existing folk religion (Shinto) and the ancient code of the warrior (Bushido). They developed an institutionalized religion, different from past religious states because it required sustained nationalism and mobilization of the populace.[24] By World War II Japan's tradition of nationalism was some fifty years old. The Japanese population had come to believe that to die for their country was a selfless act that truly sustained the state's greater good.[25] The Japanese accepted war as positive for Japan and for Asia. This deeply held national concept was an important contributing factor to the brutality that resulted, since the Japanese military had not operated in this manner in the past.

In previous military involvement with Europe in the twentieth century, Japan had played by the rules. In both the Russo-Japanese War of 1904–1905 and in World War I, the Japanese military had behaved in accordance with the accepted courtesies of war. The Japanese treated combatants and prisoners as agreed upon by international law, and in accordance with their own Imperial Japanese Army order, which declared that prisoners of war "shall be treated with a spirit of goodwill and shall never be subjected to cruelties or humiliation."[26] Although the Japanese did not formally ratify the Geneva Convention in 1929, Foreign Minister Shigenori Togo did pledge in 1942 to fulfill its requirements. Furthermore, Japan's Emperor Hirohito proclaimed that his soldiers should treat prisoners of war as "unfortunate individuals" whose situation merited "the utmost benevolence and kindness."[27] By 1941, however, attitudes had changed too much to follow the codes that had previously seemed reasonable. By the beginning of World War II, the Japanese had begun to stray from these codes as they fought for their Emperor. Their lack of benevolence toward even their own troops became legendary. Americans came to expect even worse treatment.

Pearl Harbor was the first whisper of what the Pacific campaign would be like. These two latecomers to the war were fighting for limited resources, and Japan seemed to be intent on threatening the established status quo in the Pacific. Pearl Harbor can perhaps be seen, as suggested by historian Akiria Iriye, as "Asia's revolt against the West."[28] Still, most Americans had no comprehension of where Pearl Harbor was, nor did they understand the diplomatic wrangling that had been going on between the two countries. The attack, then, was condemned as unprovoked, and the commonly held perception was that the United States had been unfairly deceived. This unprovoked attack was an example of how much the Japanese cared about "fair play." "Americans detested the Japanese the most," concludes historian Paul Fussell, "for only they had the effrontery to attack the United States directly."[29] It was the first lesson to the Americans regarding the new Japan, and they quickly learned that, in the war in the Pacific, there would be no rules.

Americans entered the war accepting and expecting specific codes of behavior in combat. They understood that these codes, both written and unwritten, enhanced their chance of survival, and for this reason they tended to adhere to them.[30] The Japanese exploited this American assumption early in the Pacific campaign. They understood that their enemies were fighting under certain premises and exploited U.S. soldiers' and Marines' preconceptions on the battlefield.[31] The Americans' proclivity to help the wounded, even their enemies, is one such example. Often U.S. units were drawn out of cover to retrieve the wounded, only to be slaughtered as they did. Many Corpsmen were lost trying to assist wounded Japanese. Other forms of deception were used by the Japanese, and they quickly changed the traditional rules of combat in the Pacific campaign. Setting booby traps, speaking English to draw American troops out, and sneaking into foxholes at night to slit throats were all tactics that Americans perceived as unfair. By the end of Guadalcanal, American patience was lost. The Japanese had breached the rules, and if no quarter could be expected, none would be given.

The troops who fought on Okinawa were aware of all of this, even before their landing, although no official word had been released to the public regarding war atrocities. By 1942, in training facilities and boot camps, draftees watched films about Japanese battle tactics. Similarly, stories were carried from soldier to soldier, Marine to Marine. By early February 1944 the public knew of the tragedy of the Bataan Death March. American hatred for the Japanese had firmly been sealed.[32]

Ernie Pyle wrote that he had quickly realized the Pacific campaign was a different war from the one fought against the Germans, with regard to the extreme hatred of the Japanese by Americans. "Shortly after I arrived I saw a group of Japanese prisoners in a wire-fenced courtyard, and they were wrestling and laughing and talking like normal human beings. And yet they gave me the creeps, and I wanted a mental bath after looking at them."[33] Much has been made in recent years of the issue of race and U.S. attitudes toward the Japanese. Although it is impossible to discount it entirely, this explanation may be overstated. Samuel Hynes has concluded that hatred like this cannot be

explained "as simply the feeling of the soldiers of one race for the soldiers of another. No doubt that is part of it."[34] Most of the veterans, in
fact, discount the race issue. They hated the Japanese, they insist, simply
because the Japanese were so brutal. This trait made it easy to dehumanize the enemy, which is crucial to executing a war.[35] It became convenient to promote the idea of the Japanese as subhuman because of the way
they treated enemy combatants, noncombatants, and their own troops,
and because they exhibited no apparent fear of death. The developing
conviction that the Japanese could not be human because they cared
nothing for human life led American fighting units in the Pacific to be
"almost twice as likely to feel that it was necessary to wipe out the enemy
nation" as their European counterparts.[36]

Another contributing factor to the American assumption that the
Japanese were inhuman was their willingness to die. Germans, like
Americans, understood the concept of living to fight another day.
Richard Bush, Medal of Honor recipient, explains it best: "It is difficult
to fight an enemy when they want to die and you want to live."[37] The
Japanese repeatedly proved that they were willing to fight to the last
man. Americans admired fearlessness and bravery, but eventually they
began to see this willingness to die as a weakness rather than a strength.
This weakness led Americans, in time, to dehumanize the Japanese even
further. Eventually, no limits existed on either side, although Marines in
the Pacific sometimes held back in combat, fearing that it was degrad-
ing them.[38]

Since racial attitudes cannot be totally overlooked, it is useful to
examine American propaganda of the time to see how often the
Japanese were portrayed in a less than flattering light. It is also inform-
ative to recall the names that the Marines called the Japanese, in order to
understand that the two enemies did see themselves differently. The
prejudices were mutual, which is why the Japanese were able to convince the people of Saipan and Okinawa to commit mass suicide in front
of the advancing U.S. troops. Tokyo's leaders convinced the Japanese
people that Americans were barbarians who would rape their women
and kill all civilians with little thought. The Japanese easily believed this,
as their soldiers had used these tactics in China and Korea. Why should
their enemies, when victorious, be any different? Propaganda dissemi-

nated to Japanese soldiers on Guadalcanal warned that the Americans on the island were not ordinary troops, but were instead Marines. Marines were a "special force recruited from jails and insane asylums for blood lust."[39]

Lemuel C. Shepherd/ Commanding General, Sixth Marine Division

You've got to instill in your men the will to kill the enemy to the point—perhaps because they are heathens, so to speak—that killing a Jap was like killing a rattlesnake. I didn't always feel that way in Europe about some poor, German family man, but I felt with a Jap it was like killing rattlesnakes.[40]

Fitzgerald

Well, they were fearless. They were clever and devious. They were well trained, I thought. They used the spider hole to their advantage behind our lines. They used the trees. They were excellent at night. They fought mostly at night. Their equipment didn't match ours, but they still shot between the eyes. Ya know, they said they had bad eyes. They were accurate. But, above all, was their devotion, their tenacity, to their cause and they just didn't give up . . . didn't give up.

One incident . . . we found one . . . he must have been a Jap Marine . . . his arm was off almost to his shoulder and gangrene had set in. A Corpsman tried to put some sulfer in, and this and that, in our OP [operation post] there, and he spat right in our man's face. Just spat right in his face . . . just didn't want any help. I didn't see any afraid or surrendering. They fought hard for their country. . . . I think their brutality stems the tide. Their whole culture cultivates brutality at that time. What they did in China in the rape of Nanking . . . what they did in Manchuria. One of my high school teammates and friends went through the Bataan Death March. I think the Japanese have a whole history, beginning in the thirties. I don't know what they did in the war with Russia, but there's a history.

Buchter

Of course, when we were home as civilians you hear the war propaganda . . . war material . . . it builds up in you. Hate the enemy. We hated. But there were a lot of things that they did that caused a lot of hate. Of course, when you go over there your job is to kill the enemy. Some guys didn't go over there, but had a desk job. Even to this day, I still have that feeling . . . I think if they could have been nicer people to our prisoners . . . to our prisoners who were helpless guys . . . and they beheaded them and cut to pieces with knives. Unnecessary cruelty . . . that's why though I never really witnessed that, but I knew. To this day, my biggest hate for those people is that they just treated our prisoners so badly. We did not . . . well we did, because of course we didn't want to take any prisoners either. Of course, our officers wanted to take them and screen them, and find out what they knew, and sometime then they didn't get very far to the back.

Brining

Yep, [I] had a forty-five and a carbine. On the line, I had three grenades. [They] wanted us to look like Marines. "Cause the sight, the kit, and the backpack on your back gave you away. . . . Well, first, you understand, the first operations they pulled over there . . . I'd say in"42 . . . the doctors wore the Red Cross badges, and the Corpsmen, and they had eighty-five percent casualties. Hard. The Japanese did not honor the Geneva Convention, where in Europe some of the Germany Army did.

Sukowatey: C/3/29
[Edward Sukowatey was from El Paso, Wisconsin. He enlisted in 1942 and was in the Marine Corps for thirty-nine months.]

The Doc came over and I can remember saying, "Doc get down, get down, they're shooting at you." The Nips had their machine guns. He didn't get hit. This is so amazing, it's unbelievable. The

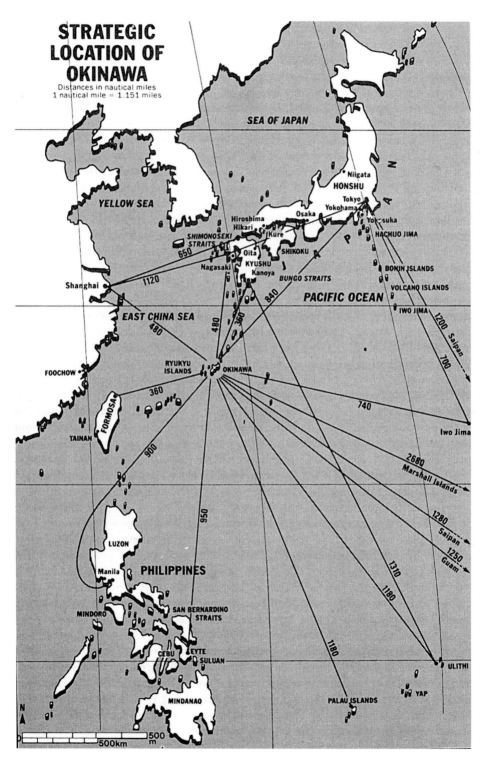

Gow, Ian. *Okinawa 1945: The Gateway to Japan.* "Strategic Map" Golden House, London. 1986.

Explosion following a hit on the USS *Franklin* by a Japanese dive bomber. 19 March 1945.

時は迫れり！！

沖縄　日本　ガ島　比島　アッツ　ボーゲンビル　グァム　サイパン　ニューギニア　アドミラルティー　マーシャル　タラワ

The message of this American propaganda leaflet dropped over southern Japan was clear: Time is running out. The Japanese had been defeated in a succession of island assaults, and now the Allied juggernaut was about to invade Japan.

From James Chaisson's scrapbook.

Southern tip of Okinawa. *U.S. Marine Corps*

OKINAWA, START TO FINISH

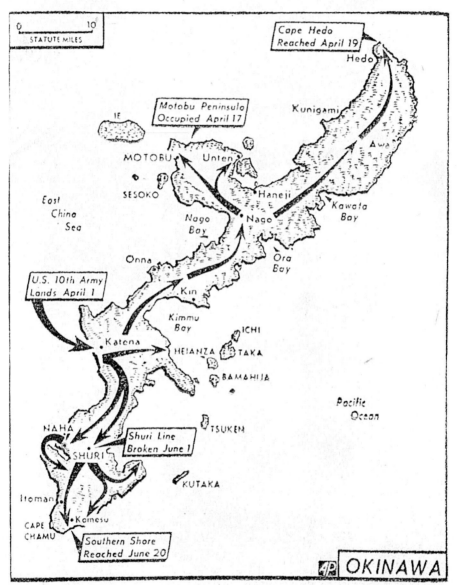

Scrapbook, James Chaisson, "Okinawa Start to Finish" 1945, Battle of Okinawa Museum, Okinawa, Japan.

With Yankees on Okinawa

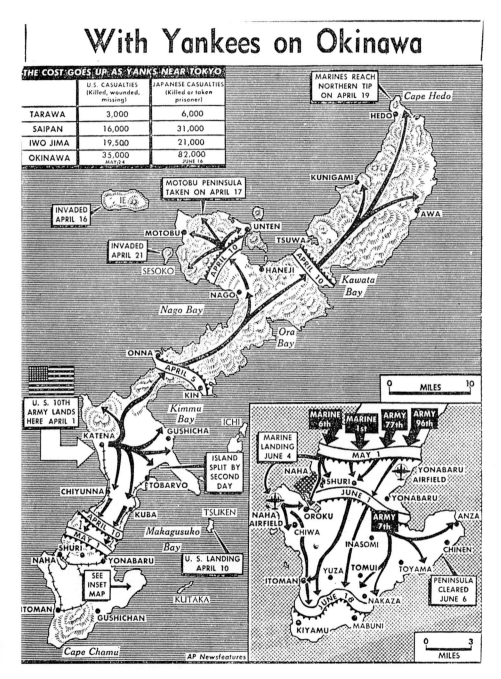

THE COST GOES UP AS YANKS NEAR TOKYO	U.S. CASUALTIES (Killed, wounded, missing)	JAPANESE CASUALTIES (Killed or taken prisoner)
TARAWA	3,000	6,000
SAIPAN	16,000	31,000
IWO JIMA	19,500	21,000
OKINAWA	35,000 MAY 24	82,000 JUNE 16

MARINES REACH NORTHERN TIP ON APRIL 19

Cape Hedo

HEDO

KUNIGAMI

AWA

MOTOBU PENINSULA TAKEN ON APRIL 17

INVADED APRIL 16

IE

MOTOBU

UNTEN

TSUWA

APRIL 10

INVADED APRIL 21

SESOKO

HANEJI

Kawata Bay

NAGO

APRIL 10

Nago Bay

Ora Bay

ONNA

APRIL 5

KIN

Kimmu Bay

ICHI

U.S. 10TH ARMY LANDS HERE APRIL 1

KATENA

GUSHICHA

ISLAND SPLIT BY SECOND DAY

0 MILES 10

CHIYUNNA

TOBARVO

TSUKEN

Makagusuko Bay

KUBA

APRIL 10

MAY 1

SHURI

NAHA

YONABARU

U.S. LANDING APRIL 10

KUTAKA

ITOMAN

SEE INSET MAP

GUSHICHAN

Cape Chamu

AP Newsfeatures

MARINE 6th · MARINE 1st · ARMY 77th · ARMY 96th

MAY 1

MARINE LANDING JUNE 4

NAHA

SHURI

JUNE

YONABARU AIRFIELD

YONABARU

NAHA AIRFIELD

OROKU

CHIWA

ARMY 7th

ANZA

INASOMI

CHINEN

ITOMAN

YUZA

TOMUI

TOYAMA

PENINSULA CLEARED JUNE 6

JUNE 18

NAKAZA

KIYAMU

MABUNI

0 MILES 3

Scrapbook, James Chaisson, "With Yankees on Okinawa," *Hackensack (NJ) Record* 51, no. 14.

Okinawa Landing, April 1, 1945. U.S. Marines calmly walk out of their landing craft and wade ashore onto a beach that shows no sign of the Japanese garrison on the island. This was a deceiving introduction to a campaign that required bitter fighting later on before the Leathernecks could rest. *U.S. Marine Corps*

Implements of War, Saipan, March 7, 1945. At the harbor on Saipan, in the Marianas, numerous ships are loaded with the vast quantity of supplies that are necessary for the coming invasion of Okinawa by the Marines and solders of the U.S. Tenth Army. *U.S. Marine Corps*

Ernie on Patrol, Okinawa, April 8, 1945. Columnist Ernie Pyle (third from left) trudges along with First Division Marines on a patrol in the interior of Okinawa. A short time later, the noted writer was killed by Japanese machine-gun fire on the island of Ie in the Ryukyu group. At the time this picture was made, Ernie selected the Marine at the extreme left, PFC Urban Vachon of Laconia, New Hampshire, as the typical illustration of the characters used in the Mauldin cartoons. *U.S. Marine Corps*

Tanks for the Buggy Ride, Okinawa, April 1945. Herded atop a tank, Marines are rushed to the town of Guga on Okinawa to take over before the Japanese get the same idea. *U.S. Marine Corps*

Smoke Grenade, Okinawa, April 1945. This Japanese smoke grenade was captured by Marines on the Motobu Peninsula on Okinawa. *U.S. Marine Corps*

Bottle Grenade, Okinawa, April 1945. Empty sake bottles filled with type 88 powder and equipped with a safety fuse and detonating cap served as blast grenades for the Japanese. Thousands of these bottles were found in caves on the Motobu Peninsula. *U.S. Marine Corps*

Knight of the Bath, Okinawa, April 1945. His rifle in easy reach and his constant companion on the alert, Marine PFC Fred Muscard of Springfield, Massachusetts, lathers up for a once over at Motobu Beach, Okinawa. The Doberman pinscher, Lux., and his handler are members of a Marine Corps War Dog Platoon.
U.S. Marine Corps

Frontline Action, Okinawa, May 4, 1945. On this ridge two miles north of the city of Naha on Okinawa, Marines battled strong enemy forces for forty-eight hours before the position was captured. Here amid shell bursts and rifle fire, the Leathernecks prepare for the drive on the town. *U.S. Marine Corps*

Cavern Post Office, Okinawa, May 9, 1945. Post office of the First Engineer Battalion was established in this Okinawa cave to protect the precious mail from devastation by enemy air raids. *U.S. Marine Corps*

Cabbage Mine, Okinawa, May 1945. Among the booby traps discovered on Ie Shima when the Marines of the Second Marine Air Wing went ashore was this mined cabbage head. The Japanese had cut the heart of the cabbage and left a fragmentation grenade, pin pulled and head down, in its place. Marine ordnancemen uncovered the trap before it caused damage. *U.S. Marine Corps*

Direct Hit, Okinawa, May 1945. This Japanese gunner was a menace to the Marine advance on Okinawa until a direct hit left him and his weapon in this battered pile. *U.S. Marine Corps*

The Fight for Sugar Loaf, Okinawa, May 20, 1945.
Intense enemy fire kept the Sixth Division Marines
from removing their wounded during the battle for
Sugar Loaf Hill on Okinawa. Tanks were pressed
into ambulance service as shown here.
U.S. Marine Corps

Swamped, Okinawa, May 27, 1945. A bulldozer snakes a 155-millimeter "Long Tom" rifle
from a water-filled position on Okinawa. Persistent rains gave comfort to the defending
Japanese. *U.S. Marine Corps*

Death at Shuri, Okinawa, May 29, 1945. First Division Marines cautiously pick their way through the bodies of Japanese soldiers who were killed while defending the entrance to Shuri Castle on Okinawa. *U.S. Marine Corps*

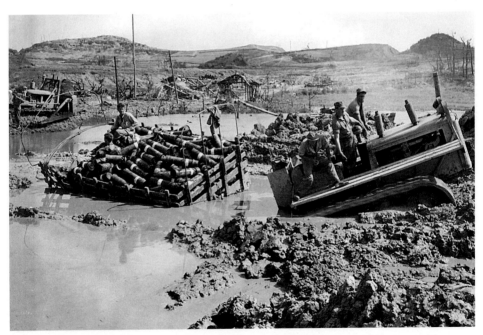

Okinawa Mud, Okinawa, June 1945. A tractor was required to rescue this ammunition trailer from this mud hole where the water and mire was waist deep. The heavy rains turned low places and fun positions into small swamps. *U.S. Marine Corps*

Beyond Naha, Okinawa, June 4, 1945. Having fought their way into Naha, capital city of the island, the Sixth Marine Division emplaces its artillery amid the rubble of the city to shell the Japanese beyond the town. This 105mm howitzer has just sent another of its projectiles into the enemy lines. *U.S. Marine Corps*

Jim Chaisson at the Sixth Marine Division Memorial in Quantico, Virginia.

man dressed out and bandaged up a good portion of a company of 250 men and didn't get hit, wounded, killed. The Nips would make a point to kill or wound Corpsmen first because they knew they were dressing us, and they loved to see us suffer.

Niland

You know, I talked to a group on Memorial Day and I mentioned that. I said the thing that they should remember is . . . the Japanese had never lost a war. They had beaten England, France, Germany, Russia, China, and they thought we were these . . . soft. They had all their best forces on Okinawa because it was a battle for the Japanese Empire, like one of our states . . . like Hawaii. They would have kept that at all costs. The people who fought on Okinawa were young boys, not all men. I was eighteen when we got there. We were just young boys. We came from middle-class homes with middle-class values. We were good people. We beat the best fighters in the world. I'm telling you we beat them. We beat them. They are afraid of the United States Marines to this day, and the only thing they resent—that they regret—is that they lost. That's all. We beat them, and before you even ask the question, it's still sixty years later and I still despise them today.

Edward "Buzzy" Fox: G/2/22

[Buzzy was a self-professed "jock" and played sports for the Marines. He was one of the many who was transferred to the front in 1944–1945. He was a replacement on Okinawa.]

I don't know whether I would be as courageous as the Japanese were . . . with all the fifteen hundred ships out in the bay firing at them . . . napalm bombs and noise . . . everybody dying . . . no food. It seemed like it was hopeless. Yet, they were still fighting. I said to myself, "If I was in that position, would I be that tough?" I don't think I would be. Oh, I admired them, as much as you can admire Japanese. We're not supposed to like them but . . . I found I liked them . . . I never got hurt, so . . .

[Buzzy thought, at the time, that the Japanese were incredibly brutal. His "liking" has come after working with Japanese contemporaries on WWII projects later in life.]

McKinney

They were good, tough fighters. An example is when General Ushijima decided to move south . . . the wounded that was in those caves . . . and all begged and pleaded to go. So many of them could not go . . . legs were gone . . . in real bad shape. When General Ushijima decided that he could not defend Shuri Castle and that line up there any longer, he ordered everything, everybody [to go] south. The poor wounded that was there were receiving little or no medical attention whatsoever anyway. Those that were really bad there . . . medical people gave them a shot, and killed them. A lot of the wounded did not want to be killed that way. Without arms and legs they tried to crawl down that road going south. They had a good five or six miles to crawl. Weeks later when we finally got into that area we found, I don't know, hundreds of them with arms and legs off, laying out there, and it was obvious that they had tried to crawl. The stumps of their legs and all were still bandaged up but covered with mud and everything else. They had crawled through it. They had tried it. They were bound and determined to go. They died along the way.

General Ushijima and General Cho . . . I had all the admiration for them in the world except that I thought they were stupid . . . sit there, knowing the battle is over and know they're going to lose all those men . . . what's left of them . . . and decide to fight to the end, and then go and put on their ceremonial clothes and sit out there and let a man with a sword chop their heads off, when they could have lived and done some good for their people telling them how the Americans had treated the people. That we weren't the killers and rapists that they all preached against us.

They could have saved an awful lot of their men. But they didn't do that. They chose the big bad Bushido. They lost their man. Cho and Ushijima supervised one tremendous battle. For eighty-two days they really operated, they really held us back, and they extracted an awful lot of casualties out of us. They could have saved an awful lot of their men, but Bushido threw them off the track. They blew it; that's all I can say for them.

Rittenbury

I could tell you plenty about the Japanese, and none of it good. They were barbaric, they were cruel, they were inhuman. This is something else that might be a little off color, but you can delete it if you like. We sent out a patrol one night to illustrate what I said about their inhumanity. The patrol didn't come back . . . thirteen men. Our scouts found them the next morning on that little railroad that ran down towards Naha, and they had killed all thirteen of them and dragged them up and put their heads on the railroad tracks, and a Japanese soldier had defecated in each man's face. We didn't take any prisoners from then on.

On the other hand, a lieutenant told me one day . . . he had his jeep; we were at Okinawa . . . he said, "Chicken, come with me. I want to show you what your fellows did last night." [Chicken was often the nickname for the youngest in a unit] I rode with him in the jeep, and we came to a little wooded area and there must have been over a hundred dead Japanese, some with their feet . . . legs still in their foxholes, some with arms shot off . . . disemboweled, and all dead. Like I say, there was at least a hundred there. What really got me when I looked in the faces of those Japanese . . . I couldn't get rid of the hatred, because of our young boys. But they're all young boys, seventeen and eighteen, just like me. The thought came to me that they have a mother and a girlfriend, and they're here because of Hirohito and the warlords of Japan. The politicians send you to war. The lower ranks fight the wars.

Carne: C Company, Tank Co. Sixth

[George Carne was born in Nebraska. He had completed four years of college and was twenty-two when he enlisted in 1943.]

When I went into the Marine Corps, I had a college education . . . relatively well educated. The first thing you got was their psychology. I said, "It's not going to get to me," but it did get to me, and they taught me to hate. I got over it though . . . I got over it.

Miller

He came up and he's just there. He hollered, "Banzai." He had a grenade and a samurai sword. In order to ignite a Jap grenade he . . . (Makes motion of hitting something against head) pops his helmet and his head went off. All my people started laughing, "Ha-ha-ha, made in Japan." (Laughing) Because that was a slur—anything that was cheap and no good was made in Japan.

CHAOS

"In combat there is only one person who can help you and that is God."[41]

—Gen. Lemuel C. Shepherd Jr.

If one has a serious conversation with a veteran, the word chaos is soon mentioned. Again and again, veterans describe battle as chaotic and surreal. Troops in battle are assaulted by far more than the machinery of war. They are assaulted with conditions that are noisy, dirty, constantly changing, and obviously terrifying. J. Glenn Gray, in *The Warriors*, concludes that the assimilation of "intense war memories to the rest of my experience is difficult and frightening."[42] War and its chaos are so removed from the noncombatant's realm of understanding that those who have lived it have difficulty explaining its affects or coping with it.

The senses are continually attacked. At night, illumination shells often expose an enemy that is far closer than ever imagined. The constant, graphic sight of the wounded, dead, and dying is, even after fifty years, hard to describe to a noncombatant. The combat-altered terrain gave the battlefield an almost moon-like appearance. The smells of a battlefield—corpses rotting, excrement, unwashed bodies, and smoke from weapons—all mingled to create an unimaginable stench. Equally disorienting were the noises: Grunts as flesh met flesh, machine guns, artillery, "screaming meemies" (a Japanese missile that struck fear into the Marines because they could not tell where it was coming from), shouts, and cries. Don Honis recalls being wounded, arriving back behind the lines, and being amazed by the quiet.[43]

On Okinawa, the rate of attrition was another element that added to the chaos. William Manchester describes one Marine company: "Meissner's company went up the hill with 240 men and came back with two."[44] This kind of attrition rate is recounted time and again. Moreover, during the fiercest fighting on Okinawa in May and June, leadership continuously changed as officers and NCOs were killed or wounded. It meant that replacements were thrust into units with no combat experience, and they changed the dynamic of established units who were loyal to each other and knew what to expect from one another.

In addition to this chaos, veterans mention and seem resentful about how little they knew about what they were doing. Troops were told neither the names of the hills they were taking, nor the planned objective. They fought entire battles with very little idea of what was happening more than a few feet away from them. This, they argued, added to the surreal quality of what they were doing. The Marines on Okinawa quickly grasped the concept that what was happening to them was completely out of their control, which is the ultimate example of chaos.[45]

The attack on the senses, limited information regarding the situation they were fighting in, and the altered terrain all made combat chaotic for the troops. The loss of control of their situation, attrition, unavoidable changes in leadership, and the ever-shifting mission took chaos to unimaginable levels. Veterans agree the reality of combat is that it is unreal.

Pesley: F/2/22

[Ed Pesley was a pre-Pearl Harbor Marine who was selected out of the ranks on Samoa and commissioned. By the time he reached Okinawa he had spent three years in the Pacific. Pesley's account demonstrates many of the chaotic aspects of a battle.]

The three hills were in our way. The first one was . . . Colonel [Woodhouse] called it . . . Hill One. The second one was Hill Two, and a little bit further up, the third one was to the left and was called Hill Three. The operation was to take Hill One, then Hill Three, and then all assemble and take Hill Two. . . . Hill Two was Sugar Loaf.

Colonel asked if anybody had any questions. We said, "Yeah, why don't you order the hill numbers in the order they're going to be taken? Hill One on the left, then Hill Two on the right, and Hill Three the fore one." The Colonel said, "No, I've already given the regiment my attack order. It's going to be Hill One, Hill Three, and then Hill Two." When he finally got finished with the summary he asked if anybody had any other questions. Some young captain said, "How 'bout that hill numbering . . . what can we do?" He said, "All right, the heck with it. We're going to call it like this: Hill One on the right, Hill Three on the left, and the fore hill is going to be called Sugar Loaf." It got the hill name right there when he gave his attack order.

We did take Hill One and Three. Hill Three was on the left and that . . . of course, inland Hill One . . . was close to the coast. Hill Three was inland and we were ahead of the First Division, which was off to our left. Hill Three was very difficult to take. In fact, one of my platoons was on Hill One and success-ful. Hill Three, they were being shot up from the rear and from the side. There were very few people left that were still in fight-ing condition because they were being attacked hard from the left side.

So, when [it] finally got dark, we still hadn't taken Sugar Loaf. Then battalion executive officer Major Courtney came over and said, "Well, okay, we got to go over there." He thought I had people on Sugar Loaf because we could see people running around. We could see them, too, running around, but they were all looking at us. They were all Japanese, not our troops. (Chuckles) If they had been our troops they would have waved at us to come on up. Anyway, he said, "You've got troops up there so let's go join 'em." It was dark and our flares start to fire and light up the area. It got so that the flares were really loaded. They were so bright that finally the major said, "Okay I'm going to get the thing sorted. Our attack situation is going to be, when the flares stop, then we'll attack. Maybe we'll have some safety in darkness."

So anyway, we all got lined up in platoons, and the next flare went off and died, and we took off. The major's leading us right straight up the line, up the base of Sugar Loaf. Then, on the base of Sugar Loaf he says, "Okay one person was shot on the way going up there, and it came from Sugar Loaf." You could see a flash coming out of the hillside. So anyway, the major said, "Take off." So we all took off and got on top of the hill. So there we were, pretty well spread out, and we didn't realize they were on the top of the hill until they started throwing grenades at us, and we started throwing grenades at them. They were coming up the far side of the hill and we were on top. The major said, "Pes, we're out of ammunition. Go back and get some." I took off and one of my officers, [who] had a platoon on the left side [that] was pretty well shot up, said, "Pes, you'll never make it by yourself. I'm going with you." We took off, and as we're coming around Hill Three going back towards our . . . the battalion command post, people start jumping up and trying to shoot us. They were the wounded of our platoon who were shot up and still alive. They thought we were the . . . good thing they recognized the voice when we hollered in.

Anyway, we went all the way back to battalion . . . going two, three hundred yards back. Told the colonel what was going on and so he says, "Okay, I just got a load of ammunition from regiment and it's on that tank over there." It was just loaded. He says, "Is there anything else you need?" I said, "Yes, there's so few of us up there . . . maybe about ten or fifteen left up there." He said, "Okay, I just got twenty-two reinforcements from regiment . . . " I said, "Yeah we'll take them." So, they came out of the boondocks there and joined us. I told them to get on top of the tractor.

The officer who had left with me got on one side of the tractor, and I got on the other side of the tractor. We could talk to the driver that way. Anyway, it was loaded. We drove up to the base of Sugar Loaf. I tried to see where that path was that we had gone up Sugar Loaf [earlier], but I couldn't see it. So I told the driver, "Keep going, keep going, keep going." As soon as I saw where the road was not a road . . . the trail going up the hill . . . I told him to stop. As soon as I said, "Stop," he dropped the ramp, and the ramp tumbled down and threw some of the Marines off. (Chuckles.) Some of the ammunition fell out. I wanted the people to pick up some hand grenades . . . the boxes . . . and take them up the hill. It looked to me about twenty feet past the trail as I recognized it, but he wouldn't back up because he said that he had dropped some ammunition on the ground, and ammunition would explode if he backed up any. So, that added a little bit more to our run, [carrying] cases of hand grenades up to the top of the hill.

Then we got to the top of the hill. The tractor took off. By the way, we got to the top of the hill with a case of ammunition. Each one of the cases was banded with a metal band, and there we are on the top of the hill trying to get this thing . . . with bayonets . . . trying to chop the metal bands. Each hand grenade was wrapped in an individual container that you had to unwrap the strap around it . . . so . . . of course not making noise. Then every once in a while the Nips would throw a hand grenade way up and get to the reverse slope of the hill where we were with those ammunition boxes. So every once in a while you had to dodge before you and the hand grenade would go off, and you'd go back to work. Then we passed out ammunition . . . people came back, took turns to get their pockets full of ammunition . . . grenades mainly. There I was trying to dig a hole for my foxhole. Start digging a hole and a hand grenade would land near it, so I'd move over a little bit. I bet I tried five or six different places before I decided, "I'll dig right here and fix a foxhole." A couple of times a grenade would land where I was digging and I would just jump away and let it explode.

After everybody got loaded, the major said, "Let's clean out the top of the hill so we can get some rest." We wandered a long line on top of the hill going forward, and before long the hand grenades were exploding in back of us. They didn't realize . . .

we'd moved forward. There they were, coming up the hill a whole line in front. They would throw the hand grenades at us. We started pulling the pins and throwing them down on them, and they were screaming, and tumbling, and full of dust and everything, and one of our grenades . . . we had a case of grenades . . . smoke grenades. Four or five [smoke grenades] went down there with the Japanese and, of course, blocked our view. So, the smoke coming up [from flares] . . . I referred to before we started our attack. Our flares were landing way back there so we could see columns of Nips coming towards us. I said, "Call artillery." I had [no] radio man with me, so I called artillery. "Put it out there five hundred yards," and they were coming forward, and I was dropping it down "four hundred yards, three hundred yards, two hundred yards." When I got down to one hundred yards, the colonel back there on the phone would say, "Hey, some of those rounds are going to land right with you if you lower them a hundred yards." Anyway, it finally got quiet enough that we could go dig in. Then during the night, boy . . . in the hill itself . . . I remember when we were unloading the tractor . . . eye level . . . I'd swear somebody was shooting an automatic weapon at the tank and hitting the tank. I stopped a way, and he stopped, and I went back and grabbed another box of ammunition and took off. During the night up near the top of the hill there were some holes, facing the rear, where we were coming from. They'd holler at us, "Hey Marine, you're going to die! You're going to die by morning." They knew enough English to holler a threat like that at us.

Oh, I guess about twelve o'clock the major got killed, so that put me in command then. I would run back and forth between places. People were pretty well positioned and . . . there were always less than fifty up there. Oh, I guess about two or three o'clock, the colonel he said, "It got pretty quiet up there." I said, "Yes, there weren't very many left." He said he got the company from another battalion and wanted to know if I could use them. I said, "Sure." So, I talked to the colonel until they got back to Hill Three. Then it was close enough that I could hear their radio somehow. The frequency weren't . . . each unit had its own frequency on the radio . . . so, well, he got in front of Hill Three when I could hear Lieutenant Fincke . . . another unit, spouting off . . . wanted word on how to get to the top of the hill. So, I could see the action back there. So, I told them where to go. The flares were lighting the activity back there and I could see him, so I told him just to keep on coming straight up. Then they found the pathway and started coming up leading the way. As soon as they came up near the top where my foxhole was, I hollered at him and he jumped in with me. No . . . just before he did that, the Nips in our left rear started moving up on the clearing with a mortar. I could see the flashing coming out of the area. It took about ten . . . twenty seconds and it landed right on the hill. Landing there. Fincke called at the same time. Then he recognized us and says, "Machine gun, come up here." He was ten feet from us, the machine gun, and he came up there and he was telling them to start fire. He was saying, "To the right," and I was saying, "Down, down," trying to get them to the area where the flashes. Twenty seconds later, three rounds of mortar landed right at the machine gun and killed all the machine gunners and Lieutenant Fincke. I told the colonel what had happened. He said, "Okay, let's see if the rest of the people were injured or not." An officer ran up to the hole where I was . . . I'll think of his name . . . I just forgot it. He said, "I was with Lieutenant Fincke who just got killed here. I was his executive officer." He stayed in the hole . . . in the hole with me, and called back that he got the command back with the company.

They came up the hill . . . that's right . . . when Major Courtney got killed. I got wounded . . . a hand grenade. It bounced into my left . . . right side. I thought it came from the front, and it came from the side, and I turned away from where I thought the sound was, and I [turned] right into it . . . the chest, the throat, and everything. My arm was all right, so I threw my last grenade. Anyway, it got Lieutenant Roe. Roe is the lieutenant who came in and said Fincke had gotten killed. I told him how . . . where our men were, and he . . . as the men came up . . . he told them which direction to go to. When they got to the top of the hill . . . and at daylight he sent a tractor up to pull the wounded out of there. The tractor came to the base of the hill. I let everyone know the wounded should go down. A few of the wounded were unable to walk. A couple of the

Marines got them to the edge and let them roll down. The trac-
tors pick them up and put them in the back, and then they said,
"Any more?" I was going to go too. Captain Roe was taking
over. A couple of shots came out of the hill below us, into the
tractor. So, I said, "Yeah, okay, crank it up." The hand-cranked
tailgate then dropped down. When they got it up about three
feet, I jumped up . . . out and bounced down the hill, and landed right on the wounded.

Andersen: H&S/29

[Nils Andersen was from Brooklyn. He enlisted in 1943, right before his
seventeenth birthday. Okinawa was his only military engagement.]

As I have been told, one or two Marines had gone into a cave
and there were Japanese in the cave who fired on them. They
began yelling for help and that they were wounded. Several
Marines, individually and in groups, attempted to get to them,
only to be wounded or killed. So I held back a bit as eight other
fellows volunteered. It's really something how the enthusiasm
that a lot of us Marines had . . . and they jumped down in the
hole and there was a repeat of that . . . with the firing and the
yelling and the screaming, and all those guys were hit or killed
also. (Sigh.) So I was in wonderment as to what we were going
to do, and Captain Petri says, "Blow 'em up." We looked at him
and he said, "BLOW 'EM UP!" One Marine says, "But the fellas down there are wounded." He says, "We can't get 'em out.
Blow 'em up." We brought over some of the Marines with ban-
galor torpedoes [a tube that is packed with explosive that can be
connected end to end and pushed forward to clear mine fields
or tactical barriers] that just blew up that hole. The Japanese, we
found out later, had many, many entrances and exits to these
caves and underground barriers. But we blew up those Marines.
(Pause.) Another case of devastation.

White, J.

Lacey: Tell me about your Sugar Loaf, which was Charlie and Half
Moon.

We had several of them, but the main one was Half Moon. After that, we assembled back on Charlie Hill where we left. I'm not sure if it was early in the morning. (Pauses.) I'm not exactly sure when we got on. Well, let me continue. There were twenty of us left. I'm not sure . . . they might not have all been killed or wounded . . . might have been some that were just lost and mixed with other outfits. But there were twenty of us left with a sergeant as a company commander. The company had landed with two hundred and twenty-five April 1, and we had some replacements also.

So, we were down to twenty men. We went back to the back of the lines, a short way, in reserve. After a couple days there we got relieved and went back to where we waited for them to come south. The sea wall. We had several hills where we had a lot of people hurt, but that was the main one.

Niland

I think it was about seven o'clock at night. I can remember the slugs from a nambu machine gun smashing into the deck right there. I was lying there, right on the hill, and I could feel these things thudding into the ground right where my head was! I don't know how they ever missed me. (Chuckles.) I remember thinking, "My God, what's a young kid from Boston doing in a dump like this? Are you crazy?" So, finally they called in naval gunfire and everything, and they got stopped. Well, we had to take these people back to Regiment. They were wounded, so they improvised. We didn't have stretchers, so they improvised stretchers from shelter halves and branches of trees. That was one of mine. So, we picked these guys up and take them back. So, we're going back and its raining cats and dogs. So we're going back. It's probably a mile and a half, two miles. It seemed like twenty miles. Nobody knew what the password was. I mean, no one had any idea. So, we're going back and people are asking, "Give me the password." We don't know the password. We were getting shot at by American soldiers, Marines, Japs, and God knows who else. We were taking casualties carrying the stretchers. So this fellow I had in the stretcher . . . I was so concerned about him in the beginning. He had been hit in the head . . . his skull is in half . . . I could see his brain pulsing. I'm saying the first half-mile or three-quarters of a mile, "Don't worry buddy, just hang on, we'll get you there." Of course, he started to moan and the farther we went the louder he got: "Ohhhh. . . . " I became less sympathetic with every step. (Chuckles) There was one of the knots from one of the branches sticking into my shoulder, and the pain . . . oh my God. So instead of saying, "Don't worry buddy, we'll get you there," I said, "Shut up you son of a bitch, or I'll blow your head off." But we got them back.

We had a whole compliment. Two hundred and eighty people, or something. By the time we were finished, we were down to twenty-five people of the Twenty-five, Twenty-six. The Twenty-sixth had been wounded and returned to duty. This is not the original company, but we had tremendous casualties and replacements. The replacements . . . the Marine Corps was desperate for replacements . . . there was no one at the time, so they had cooks, and chaplains' assistants, and buglers, and all kinds of people coming. Kids right out of boot camp, and they weren't trained, as you know.

Schlinder

I landed in his foxhole. Here was this guy, a machine gunner . . . I don't want to mention his name . . . reading the Bible out loud. I said, "Hey, I thought you were an atheist?" He looked at me kind of funny. I said, "But don't stop; I am listening to every word." He kept on praying.

Baird: B/1/22

[Tom Baird was from Jellico, Tennessee. He enlisted in 1942 at the age of seventeen.]

They blowed that bridge down, and we had to go up about a quarter of a block and cross. I was carrying that ninety-pound tank [Baird was a flamethrower]. The riflemen got in there and

were up to their ankles, but I got in there and was pretty nearly up to my knees. I worked and worked and got three-quarters
of the way across the river. My platoon sergeant came back and
said, "Hey Tom, do you want me to throw you a rope?" I said,
"Yeah, I've gone as far as I can go." He [the sergeant] made me
so mad. He laughed. He even laughed that day, and I felt like
shooting him. He said, "About the time I throw you that rope,
here comes a Japanese machine gun," and he said I came up out
of there quick! Here I had said I was done and I couldn't go any
farther. He said, "You came out of there with a wake!"

I come across some records . . . after that year . . . about two
or three months later, and I counted that we had lost fifty-eight
men those three months.

Tremblay

We'd get new people. I talked to this one kid and he was pasty.
He had brand new dungarees, brand new shoes, brand new
everything. I said, "Where's your helmet? Where's your rifle?
What outfit are you with? What's wrong with you?" He said,
"Sir," (Mimics looking around and points to himself, making
fun of the young man saying "sir") "when Okinawa started I
was still in high school . . . " They were finishing their boot
camp training on that sand, right there.

Terry: F/2/29

[Howard Terry was from Nashville, Tennessee. He ran away and joined
the Marine Corps in 1942, at the age of fifteen.]

Just before we entered the lines near the southern tip, we had
walked for many hours carrying all that machine gun ammo.
We were so damn exhausted, someone suddenly sat down by
the side of the dirt road. Then is when the platoon leader came
running down the middle of the road yelling, "On your feet, on
your feet! I will court martial every damn one of you!" Those
155-milimeter shells were going over our heads about room
high and exploding about five hundred to one thousand yards
in front of us. No one paid any attention to him. Very quickly,

Sergeant Warner ran up to him. I just happened to be about ten feet away and heard him say, "Calm down, calm down . . . these guys are too damn tired to go into that hell up there right now. Give them a break . . . they know what they're doing and when they get up there, they'll get the job done." He didn't say any more after that. About ten minutes later, one of the guys stood up and off we went. We sure as hell got the job done. That was the rainy night that I spent in that water-filled hole all alone. Water above my waist . . . no sleep that night at all. That was the night I saw a head pop up in front of me. I blew it away, and the next morning I found to my dismay it was a little boy with a surrender ticket in his hand. I have to tell you that has bothered me all my life, however, I know there is nothing I can do. Had I known that was a little boy, I would have pulled him into that shell hole with me and protected him. To have to live with that has been some little bit of hell.[46]

Fox

I could smell the salt water. I knew it. I went down and saw the bloody clothes on the beach . . . shoes. . . . The poor Japanese guys were swimming for it. I guess they couldn't go any further.

Whitaker

Oh, chaotic is putting it mild. It got surrealistic. Strange things happened. Japs would stand up in the middle of fields with their hands in the air. Japs would dress as Okinawans and try to get through the lines. Okinawan civilians would suddenly go crazy and try to do something really stupid. Japanese soldiers did stupid things and as we, the Marine units, kept going south, the island keeps getting narrower. So we all kept getting closer and closer together and, as I say, it was sort of surrealistic. I remember one day when there was a whole gang of us . . . we were on the top of a large cliff, and there was a cave in the face of that cliff. There were Navy ships going up and down the shoreline, broadcasting in Japanese, telling people to come out of the caves and surrender. At the same time, there were guys,

Navy guys, on the ships with rifles, shooting at the Japs on the beach. We were up on the top of the hill pouring napalm down the vent holes of these caves and igniting them with white phosphorus grenades. There were Okinawan casualties all over the place . . . Jap casualties all over the place. It was just chaotic. That only lasted a couple of days. Then the word came that it was . . . over.

Fitzgerald

Well, the word came down to raise the flag, securing the operation. The two company commanders are Crane of G Company . . . Gunner of E Company. We're the assault companies. They are both class of Notre Dame of 1940, which is interesting. Neither one wants to do it. Why take this last hill and get somebody killed? Frank says, "You do it, Hyme." "No, you do it Frank." So they drew straws and George Company lost. So that's how they became heroes . . . flag raisers. They don't like to hear that. (Chuckles) . . . Last summer I told Dan Derescheck, [Bronze Star recipient from G Company] I said, "You're a great Marine, Dan, but your company commander didn't want to raise the flag. He was afraid he'd lose some men."

Manchester, William: E/2/29

[William Manchester is the author of *Goodbye, Darkness: A Memoir of the Pacific War*, *American Caesar: Douglas MacArthur 1880–1964*, and numerous other books.]

On Sugar Loaf, in short, I realized that something within me, long ailing, had expired. Although I would continue to do the job, performing as a hired gun, I now knew that the banners and swords, ruffles and flourishes, bugles and drums, the whole rigmarole eventually ended in squalor.[47]

White, J.

There's all kinds of war, and about five percent of the participants in a war are actually on the "point of the spear" . . . what

I named mine [his memoir]. Most members of G Company, not all, but most members of G Company were on "the point of the spear." And that's something about war . . . a lot of men never went overseas, or if they did they might be somewhere in England in a corner bunk with a stove the whole war. To them it was just time deducted from their lifetime. For most of us . . . I can hardly say it was a memorable experience, but it was one that had a lot going on.

WAR'S BRUTALITY

> *"I always felt war was very simple; you either kill or you get killed."*
>
> —George Taylor[48]

The war in the Pacific did not involve passionless killing. A mutual animosity between the Japanese and Americans existed and could be characterized as "brutish, primitive hatred."[49] After Pearl Harbor, William "Bull" Halsey, commander of the Pacific naval forces for the United States, declared that by the end of the war, "Japanese would only be spoken in hell."[50] As part of the preparation for war, as preparation to kill their enemies, leaders of both sides convinced their troops that atrocities would be committed against them. This was important to the process of dehumanizing the enemy. Conversely, disregard for humanity can also lead to atrocities.[51] The frequently cited story of the young lady, stateside, who received a Japanese skull is one example. *Life* magazine highlighted her on its front cover; she was writing her soldier a letter with the skull beside her on the desk. This picture reflects the degree to which U.S. citizens had come to see the enemy as something that must be destroyed.

The troops on Okinawa were exposed to all the elements that would make Okinawa excessively brutal: Knowledge of past atrocities committed by the Japanese, belief that the Japanese were different" than they were, and sustained combat under difficult situations. There were "unit dentists" (those who removed the teeth from dead or almost dead Japanese), but most of them were ostracized, and most officers discouraged such behavior.

There were also very few prisoners who made it behind the lines, in part because U.S. troops on Okinawa feared the Japanese prisoners' trick of booby trapping themselves and then surrendering. This tactic had killed many of the troops who tried to accept surrenders, and it made them reluctant to take such a risk. They also did not take prisoners because of the difficulty involved with turning the prisoners in behind the lines. However, the most often cited reason for not accepting surrender from the Japanese was that, because the Marines knew there would be no mercy from the Japanese should they themselves be captured, they felt the Japanese earned the same degree of respect. Most veterans remember few individual acts of brutality, but recall, instead, that war is just intrinsically brutal.

Niland

> We went there [to the front] . . . and American soldiers on stretchers, and they had been mutilated by the Japanese. I had never seen anything like that. Like I said, I came from a Christian family, and I saw that and it changed me. I became . . . not immediately . . . it wasn't a complete, instant metamorphosis . . . but I became just as bloodthirsty as the Japanese. We all did, and I think we became better at the game than they were. I know we did. We knew they had lost the war. They were arrogant . . . had contempt for Americans. We became better at the killing game than they did. We really did.
>
> We showed no mercy. We never took a prisoner. We couldn't leave them there, we couldn't take them with us, and we couldn't send them back. So we interrogated them and we killed them. It may be a terrible thing to say, but it's the truth. One fellow called me, distraught, devastated with guilt at the number of Jap prisoners he shot. This is sixty years later, and I told him, if it makes him feel any better, that a lot of other people did the same thing. We had to. There was no question. Survival. We killed prisoners. That was it. That's why we beat them. We became better than they were.

Fitzgerald

My gunnery sergeant came to me and said, "Lieutenant, some of our guys are collecting Japanese ears and teeth and wearing them on their gun belts." I held a meeting immediately and told them if I saw one man again [with such items] I would follow the Articles of War and court-martial them, because we are not tolerating that! Another incident that happened in the Guam campaign was observed by the Third Battalion, which was commanded by Claire [Schlishler]. [Marines] picked up, near the end of the campaign, some Japanese prisoners. [Prior to this story] . . . the Third Battalion had found a Navy pilot, during that period, strung on a tree and crucified.

They brought the [Japanese] prisoners in to be interrogated and . . . now this . . . I wasn't there now, but they said that the troops were lined up in the road, and the colonel started haranguing the troops that these are the murderers of that Navy pilot, and this and that. Adding rage . . . and several of the troops jumped up and gunned the prisoners down.

Several of the officers, led by Lt. Hugh Crane and a couple others, went to the colonel and told him that they were putting him on report. They went to the brigade commander immediately, General Shepard, and Colonel [Schleicher] was relieved immediately of his command . . . . It wasn't tolerated by international . . . by the rules of engagement, or the rule of humanity. We knew it. We were basically civilian people at heart . . . knew that this was wrong. Some of the kids who practiced this were just adolescents, young impressionable guys, who just didn't know any better. They had to be stopped.

Joralemon

I will also have to say, from what I know and what I saw, that the Japanese weren't entirely alone in that. There was always a certain segment . . . I think that's probably true in any military organization . . . that were kind of rough themselves. Some of the things they did . . . things like taking their teeth out and all that sort of stuff. It wasn't the prevalent thing, but there was enough of it . . . not towards the Okinawans . . . oh no, no . . . it would be towards the Japanese. That was the thing, tit for tat. That was the thing. That was the prevailing attitude, anything goes. It's fight, no quarter taken, no quarter given. That was basically . . . that was the basic philosophy. Nobody would expect you to surrender. We know they're not going to, you know, and we don't want to surrender to them.

Miller

A lot of men came into our platoon as replacements. A lot of men came in the squad, and you never got to know their names before they were dead. I remember one in particular when we were on that Hand Grenade Ridge. I put him on the point over . . . I was on the extreme left flank . . . I put him out about ten or twelve yards further. He didn't have a shack-up mate, and he was out there by himself. One reason I put him out there was so I would have some kind of warning . . . for selfish reasons. I would have some kind of warning if the Japs were coming, because we fully expected a counterattack. But it never happened. The next morning, bright and early, I don't know which happened first . . . the Jap coming up in my hole, or him . . . must have been him. He got out of his foxhole and stepped on a mine and blew himself to smithereens. His arms and legs were just sticks . . . our platoon Corpsman . . . we started out with two and had one left . . . he was a damn good man in combat. He took care of a lot of people. He came up to see this guy. He was a basket case. We put him on a stretcher and two of us could carry him, he was so light. Half of him gone . . . he was all black. Johnny wanted to take him over here to this other place behind the lines. Maybe thirty yards behind the lines more or less. We're on the front lines. We're not on the front lines . . . we are where the Japs are. We are carrying him back to the area because Johnny had called for a half-track or tank to get him. Like I said, he was really a basket case.

I laid back there with him, keeping flies off of him, and this kid who I never knew his name . . . we only had him a couple days as a replacement . . . he was telling me about himself a little bit. During the conversation, he kept wanting to know would they let his parents know that he had been hit? I said, "Well, they won't let them know." He wouldn't believe me. He kept thinking they would send them a telegram or a letter saying that "your son has been wounded," which is exactly what they do. My parents got a letter like that . . . I didn't know it of course . . . when I got hit. He was really worried about it because his brother had just been killed on Tarawa, and he thought this might be bad news and they wouldn't be able to handle it. Well, then he died so they had [lost] two sons.

I stayed back there with him while he was on the stretcher, and I kept brushing the flies away, trying to make him comfortable any way I could. The First Marine Division came up with green troops, green and clean, to relieve us. (Scoffs) Relieve us . . . shit. One of the First Division kids was on the ground right near us, so he asked him, "Do they let your parents know." "Oh, yes they do, they let your parents know." I thought I would shoot him! After all this lying I had been doing, here comes this punk! So, anyway, this kid got transported back but he didn't live much longer. Sometimes I'd get these kids in . . . hell, I didn't even know their names and they were dead.

McKinney

They gave up, and I kind of thought it was cruel of us anyway. We had one battalion of flamethrowers and tanks working with us. They were Army tanks. The tanks were being used to burn them out. They burned out I don't know how many square miles of weeds and brush, and that Kunai brush that stood eight, nine feet tall. It wasn't unusual to be working along the edge of a field and have the tanks come up. We pulled back real quick.

The flamethrowers went to work, and out of the fields would come. (Chuckles) We didn't have the term "crispy critters" back then, but here would come individuals . . . and two or three Japanese soldiers at a time, on fire. Their clothes were burning and they were doing their damnedest to get them put out. Running towards us without a weapon, that we could see . . . and our men broke down then and they would help them. They would knock them down and roll them to knock out the flames and then stand them back up. Make them take their clothes off. A lot of them were burnt horribly. The Corpsmen did everything they could to help them. That went on for, I don't know, about a week, a week and a half.

PEST AND PESTILENCE

Damn fleas don't bite so much when your ass is in water up to your armpits.

—Lenly Cotton[52]

Civilian observers might only see war as bombs and bullets. For the troops, war's reality is far more complex. Pests could be as much an enemy as the Japanese, and for the Marines on Okinawa, the weather also contributed to making life almost unbearable.

In April, when the Tenth Army landed on Okinawa and they began heading north, they encountered many abandoned homes. The Tenth discovered that the homes had straw mats (tatami mats) on the floors, and troops quickly took them into their foxholes. They soon discovered, however, that those mats were swarming with fleas, and in short order they had infested everyone. Veterans begin scratching themselves almost immediately as they recall this pest. Fleas gravitated to the waistbands of their trousers and to the seams of their clothes. The veterans all agreed that the fleas could not be killed easily, and many laughingly recall sitting around and picking fleas off one another. By the end of spring the military provided relief, spraying the island from planes and killing the insects.

As it did in most places stateside, April began cool on Okinawa. Bill Sams wrote home in early April about how the island reminded him of Georgia in the spring.[53] Many remember it as a pleasant surprise after the torrid heat of Guadalcanal. Nights could be uncomfortably cool in a foxhole.

May brought movement south and constant combat. It also brought rain, of the kind one only sees in the Pacific. The skies open up and the rain seemingly never ceases. The veterans remember it being cool rain, the kind that gets in you're a person's bones and wears them out with continual exposure. It became very difficult to accomplish anything. Eating, sleeping, moving supplies, getting aerial support, all became next to impossible. Veterans talk about the physical exhaustion of trying to maneuver in knee-deep, churning mud, about not getting food because supplies could not be brought in, or about having to carry it in hand-over-hand. Tanks stopped, mired in the mess. Troops stripped to their skivvies, and even discarded their boots. General Ushijima used the driving rain and darkness at the end of May as cover to retreat farther south.

By the end of May the rains had subsided, but an unbelievable mess had accumulated. The earth turned into a churning pit. The refuse of war appeared everywhere. Proper sanitation became next to impossible. Meanwhile, most of the heavy fighting occurred in May, which left exposed bodies everywhere. A Japanese student nurse recalled trying to hurriedly bury bodies, only to have the graves blown up and the bodies reexposed.[54] At least one hundred thousand people were dead by this time. The smell was horrific, and eating became difficult because everything smelled and tasted like death. James White in *Point of the Spear* recounts a story of hunting several years after the war and coming across a rotting carcass, instantly transporting him back to Okinawa.[55] The smell of a hair permanent had the same effect on George Niland after the war.

All of this carnage only attracted more pests, rats, maggots, and flies. James Chaisson related a story of sleeping in a cave one night and feeling a rat climbing up his trouser leg. He was in a predicament, afraid to swat at it for fear it would bite him. He was equally fearful of shooting the rat with his pistol, as such an action might create a firefight among his sleeping, trigger-happy comrades. He had no choice but to lie there until the rat had finished investigating, turned around, and left.[56]

Although rats and the fear of snakes (the dreaded habu, a pit viper similar to a rattlesnake without the rattle, which few of them saw alive), caused moments of discomfort, nothing was as distasteful to the Marines on Okinawa as the flies. All veterans' accounts mention the green flies of Okinawa. Eugene Sledge's book, *With the Old Breed*, contains the most famous, yet each has a similar story and a visceral dislike for flies. They watched maggots feast on the bodies of Japanese and Americans alike. Tomiko Higa in *Girl with the White Flag* told of stopping at a creek for water, and the entire creek was filled full with maggots because underneath the water's surface were dead bodies.[57]

Those maggots turned into green flies, larger than American houseflies and impudent in their slowness and persistence. They swarmed on anything revolting, and then tried to land on the troops, tormenting them with images of where the flies had last been. Bill Sams recounts a story that occurred on the southern end of the island when they were brought some hot rations. One of the items they received, raisin bread, resulted in queasiness. Something that earlier would have been considered a treat now went uneaten by one and all. All of a sudden raisins bore too much resemblance to flies. Others recalled that rations containing rice were another item quickly passed over. Maggots came to mind too readily for them to enjoy a meal of pork and rice. Cooks in the rear echelon, concludes Sams with a shake of his head, could never understand.[58]

These realities of war went beyond the expected toils or terrors to make every day miserable. Veterans see these seemingly minor realities of combat as the ones that can create the most horrific nightmares.

Moore

> Another story involves our jeep driver, Jim Baker, from Jackson, Tennessee. The mud was deep enough to stop our tanks but somehow, through all this knee-deep slop, he got our ammunition, rations, and water up to us. We commended him and asked him how he got through. He drawled out, "Oh! Shit guys, this is nothing to the mud we have back in Tennessee."[59]

White, J.

The rain . . . that you'd lay there and shiver, and the water would absorb body warmth, and the immediate area right around would get to where it was almost comfortable, but then you'd have to move. So, it was impossible to sleep. If there was time you weren't actually being shot at, you could dig a hole . . . on end of one corner of the hole, so you could kick a grenade if you had the time. If you were a real good engineer or architect, or whatever they call . . . a civilized engineer (Chuckles) . . . a drain towards that hole so it was easier to bail out. The bottom of those holes, the surface, was pretty uneven. In fact, you dig kind of a recess of your hips and buttock, ya know, to make it a little more comfortable.

McKinney

Ohhh, you haven't lived until you have gone through fourteen or fifteen odd days of twenty-six-hours-a-day rain. Raining so hard that it sounds like somebody is beating on your helmet with a hammer. You stay wet twenty-four hours a day. You can't eat because you open a can of chicken and noodles . . . you eat four cans before you ever decide to throw it away. It will fill up with water as fast as you can eat. Your clothes, your equipment is wringing wet. You go anywhere, you try to protect your weapon to make sure it is safe, not water logged or anything. You operate the bolt as many times as you can, every now and then, to make sure there's no mud, no water in the receiver. You have a foxhole at night. You don't lay down because you would drown. You can sit . . . you can sit up in the corner of the foxhole, but you don't dare lay down . . . you had a hard time walking. We got rid of our leggings because they were a nuisance, really. We got rid of our leggings, but we would tuck our trousers into our socks . . . pull our socks up over our trousers. The mud and all went right down into your boondockers . . . a constant squishing in your shoes. You were coated with mud. It was hard to tell . . . the Japanese uniform was brown, a brownish tan look. Here we are wearing dark green, then all of a sudden we are all looking brown too, from the mud. You couldn't dig in it because you took two shovels out and two fell back in. Even the tanks . . . there were times we needed the tanks real bad . . . they couldn't get up to us 'cause the roads were so muddy . . . so tore up they couldn't get to us. The six-bys couldn't move because they bogged down because they make their own mud wall as they go.

Long: I/3/29

[Ken Long enlisted at the age of seventeen, in 1943. He was from Minnesota.]

During the middle of May 1945, I Company of the Twenty-ninth Regiment was moving to the Half Moon Hill area adjacent to Sugar Loaf. I spotted some personal items on the ground that had been discarded by Okinawans, and one of the items was a rice straw mat, which the natives used as a mattress. I thought it would be ideal for me since it rolled into a small cylinder and could be easily attached to my pack. It was about 18–24 inches wide and about five feet long. Heavy rains had just begun, and the mat would fit nicely in our foxhole as a little protection from the damp ground. My foxhole buddy and I used it for two or three nights before we were overwhelmed by the fleas, and it wasn't until my squad leader told us to check the seams on the inside of our trouser legs that we got rid of them completely, as there must have been hundreds of them lined up under the flaps of our seams waiting patiently for another meal.[60]

Whitaker

It's one of the few things about my hundred and one days on Okinawa that still bothers me a bit. As we moved toward the southern end of the island, the Japanese military and the Okinawan civilian casualties spiraled upward. There were bodies everywhere. The stench was incredible. The bodies were rife with maggots, and maggots mature into huge, ugly green flies. Those flies became more and more numerous. The minute you opened a can of cheese or a can of pork and beans it would be literally covered with flies. If you made coffee, your canteen cup would have a hundred flies *on it* and *in it* before you could get it up to your mouth. They made an eerie buzzing sound. They would light on your face and crawl into your nostrils, your mouth, and your eyes. They were everywhere. And so, while we were trying to sustain ourselves with rations and liquids, those horrible, dirty, aggressive, revolting, disgusting, green things were ever present and ever relentless. They wanted to eat what we were eating, and they wanted to eat us. They already had a taste for human flesh. Every single Marine was acutely aware that those green flies had just recently been transformed from maggots to flies in the rotting body cavities of dead Japs, unfortunate civilians, or perhaps even from some buddy who did not come back from a patrol or was cut off in a firefight and became an MIA [Missing in Action.].[61]

White, J.

There were times that we had a lot of dead bodies lying around, mostly Japs, but a few Marines when we couldn't get to them. Flies would feast on these cadavers, and they'd also lay eggs which would form maggots. I became somewhat of an expert on maggot development. Flies on Okinawa, as I recall, had . . . they had a green body, a little bit larger than a housefly. They were persistent. They would get on your food and you almost had to pick 'em off.

Now the C-rations we had in Okinawa were a lot better than the ones we had in training in North Carolina and on Guadalcanal. They had a number of heavy flavors. They had two cans. One can had crackers, a drink mix, maybe coffee, maybe lemonade, a little toilet paper, maybe a three pack of cigarettes. Then the heavy [can] had like pork and beans. They had various flavors. One of them was pork and rice. I was unable to eat that pork and rice because I could not look in that can with those white grains with that gray meat. I would look out twenty, thirty feet from me and this body with gray meat working with maggots. I couldn't believe that rice wasn't moving, and I tried to get some other kind of heavy other than that.

Honis

Every bite of food you took tasting death. That [is the one thing that] in all the movies and everything they cannot photograph . . . the smell. The smell was overwhelming all the time. You just lived with it. Some guy said he opened a can of rations and took a bite and it tasted like, ya know, dead bodies. It isn't in the can, but it's in the air. That's the one that really annoyed me. You got over it . . . when I think about it, over the island there had to be trillions of flies. They were big . . . they call them the Blue Bottle Green fly.

WOUNDS

> *"I got two Purple Hearts for Okinawa, but that just means I was too stupid to duck."*
>
> —Dan Dereschuck

As shocking as casualty reports can appear, it is important to realize that as late as World War II more troops died of illness than of wounds.[62] Although the troops spent much time, especially at first, worrying about their personal safety, as war progressed they became increasingly numb to what was happening and their level of fear often decreased. Somehow being wounded or killed still seemed accidental and random. Hynes concludes, "War is men shooting at each other; but their wounds, when they occur, don't seem as straight forward and as intentional as that."[63] Wounds are shocking to those who suffer them, and shocking to those who witness them. From their exposure to wounds and death, the troops began slowly to comprehend their own mortality, perhaps not fearing it as much as accepting it. Veterans now recount the day they feel that they faced death, and that every day since has been a gift. In reality, after a time, the apprehension about wounds often grew greater than the fear of death. Both eventually evoked little emotion.

Casualties become a reality of war very quickly, and the troops learned instinctively to determine the severity of their wounds. Even when they were wounded themselves, some often accepted its fatality and encouraged medics to help others.[64] Many secretly prayed for the "million-dollar wound", one that would send them home neither maimed nor killed, yet by Okinawa those were few. Instead, most were patched up and sent back to the lines, or they returned to their units on Guam to prepare for the invasion of mainland Japan.

The effect of being exposed to battle casualties cannot be overlooked; it had a lasting impact on the Marines of the Sixth. Every veteran relates a story about another badly wounded comrade or someone's heroics to save a wounded Marine. Buddies tried to plug holes in their friends with their hands, some tried to put their intestines back inside of themselves, and young men close to death looked to other young men for one moment of peace in the insane world they had both shared. It is understandable then that more often those who kept diaries in wars recount the tales of dying rather than the tales of killing.[65] It is also understandable that they took away unobservable wounds, emotional wounds that might reappear weeks or years later.

White, J.

I was trying to get to another hill. The platoon leader, a Gunnery Sergeant Quatrone, had gone to this other hill where there were these two platoons of G Company. My platoon, the Third platoon, was on a hill slightly behind and over to the left. So I kind of . . . not necessarily to charge, but nobody else was doing anything . . . so I was going to get to this other hill and find an officer who'd know what to do, 'cause we were in a precarious position there.

There was a hillside, kind of a real sheer hillside, and there was kind of a gully right next to it. It had a little water in it, and there was a dead Japanese lying across it. He may have been the reason. He may have been the dam that caused the water.

Anyway, I went up in this building where I could have straight shot to go across this valley to the hill. I got myself in shape. Ya know . . . made a gut check, ya know, then stepped up out of the gully. At that time a man named Warren Lowe . . . I didn't know his name, then I found out later . . . got hit in the elbow and the gut with a bullet. He started screaming, so I hesitated there. A Jap shot me . . . both legs. I was able to spin around and get back in the gully, or halfway back in. He sprayed me twice more with bullets . . . with dirt from the bullets . . . before I got back in the gully. So I started crawling up the gully, heard a noise, and Gunny Quatron was running towards me from this other hill. He ran past me, and I guess the same Jap that got me got him in the right side, back to front. He took off like a scaled cat. Never saw him again. I got back to where the rest of the platoon was, and they pulled me back up into safety. We had a Corpsman with us. He bandaged my legs. I was bleeding pretty good. I wanted to have some morphine to kill the pain. My right calf felt like a Charlie horse. He said, "Naw, you're liable to pass out, and you may have to walk out of here."(Chuckles)

We were up there . . . there were four of us, I think it was, that were wounded. After a couple hours they either threw smoke grenades or shot some smoke up there somehow, and four of them put me on a poncho and hauled me back to company headquarters. Then from there I got put on a four-by that had two racks of stretchers. This is getting towards probably dark, and they made it into Sixth Division Hospital . . . Sixth Medical Battalion Hospital . . . which was in the southern part of Naha or somewhere in Naha, in a building that hadn't been destroyed, and I was lying there on the stretcher and looked down and I was lying in a pool of blood. The man on top of me, in the stretcher on top of me, died on the way. I don't remember who it was. I got some whole blood and began to feel a lot better. Didn't have the effects of the loss of blood, ya know. [The] next day . . . I also got some morphine, which doesn't work on me. I get . . . I wasn't even sleepy, and it doesn't kill pain. I got moved into a room in this hospital, this building that had been used to conduct sewing classes. There was a poster on the wall, a Singer sewing machine poster. I don't remember if the verbiage on it was in Japanese or in English. Then that afternoon we got taken out to an LST, and then lying on a tank deck was like the scene from *Gone with the Wind* . . . laid out stretcher-to-stretcher. I'm not sure if they moved the LST or what. Anyway, put us over the side of the hospital ship *Relief* by crane. They hooked lines over the stretchers and you got lifted over the side. It was good duty from then on.

[In James White's memoir, *Point of the Spear*, he elaborates on the treatment he received aboard the USS *Relief*. He ran into a nurse who obviously did not understand conditions on Okinawa, and she made remarks about his personal hygiene. "Front line service is not a nine-to-five proposition," White recalls.][66]

Schlinder

Getting to Sugar Loaf . . . the word came that General Shepherd said we're taking that hill no matter what the cost. He was referring to Sugar Loaf. So it's sometime after midnight on the night of the fourteenth, about a half an hour or so after Major Courtney made his charge up the hill with seven or eight guys. He got the Medal of Honor. At midnight, moving up Sugar Loaf Hill, was a sight I would never want anyone to have to see (Long pause, as Mr. Schlinder composes himself). There must have been ninety dead Marines . . . we had to step over them. It wasn't a pretty sight. We got on top of Sugar Loaf. I get flat all the way over to the end.

I was on the top of Sugar Loaf so that I was looking all the way down. It couldn't hold another person. I was in a slit trench, and I set up towards the south. I was in there, firing away and throwing grenades, and I see two Nips out in front of the machine gun maybe sixty yards. I always wondered how far I could throw a grenade, because I used to be a catcher when I was kid. I let it rip and fired it away. I didn't get it all the way, but I nicked them both. I wonder what happened to them? Anyway, we're going . . . shortly later I feel something hit my leg. Of course, it's like daylight. I looked down at my leg and there is grenade, a Jap grenade. You're trained not to worry about it, not to think about it, to just reach down and toss it over the side (Makes a motion of covering his face), cover your face, and pray a lot. There was so much stuff flying that I'm not sure if it was a dud or if it went off. The thing that I can say is, I was thankful it didn't go off and I still had two legs. Then in about half an hour, a guy who I had never seen before stuck his head in and said, "Hold you positions. We'll be moving in twenty minutes." I said, "Don't you worry, I won't be doing any dances. I'm hanging right here."

It must have been three, four, five o'clock in the morning . . . whatever time it was. Here came the squad leader. He leaned over and said, "Hey, the number one machine gunner on the other gun was hit." He was New Hampshire, and he survived, I found out later. "He's hit at the other gun." I said, "Where abouts is he?" He told me. (Schlinder points off to his right) I said, "Okay, I better see if I can go help him." He said, "Okay." I got up out of my hole like a pushup, and I had just got in the push up position when a knee mortar hit right here (Holds his right hand up above his ear, two feet.) A piece of the knee mortar went down through my right lung. It ended in my liver, and it's still in my liver today. I thought I had gotten hit by concussion; I had been hit by concussion before. It kind of knocks the wind out of you. I was kind of getting my breath, but this concussion was a little bit different. I felt the warmth down here (Points to his side), something real hot down here (Mimes opening his shirt). I see a hole in my chest about the size of a silver dollar, and I thought to myself, "A guy could really get seriously hurt if he stayed out here any longer." The thought came to me that I'm out here pretty far . . . we took that hill . . . we're pretty forward. We lost lots of men. Some guys were never picked up.

I think . . . I remember shooting a deer right in the heart, in Wisconsin. It ran a hundred yards before it fell dead. I got hit, not in the heart, but pretty good. I decided I'm going to do the same thing . . . stand. You should have never stood up, not on Sugar Loaf. But an act of contrition . . . the man upstairs said zigzag on the top of the hill, and when I got to the back I dove over . . . rolling in this stuff, and I yelled for the Corpsmen. The Doc came over. I said, "I need some help." He said, "Ray I'd like to help you but I'm out of everything. I don't have anything." We all carried a first aid kit on our belt (Points to his back around the belt). He took that off and he stuffed it in the hole in my chest. That's what saved my life. He stuffed me in a hole underneath, on the backside of Sugar Loaf Hill. He said, "Keep your head low. If they come over the top, you and me will go." (Points upward) So I lay there all night, until ten or eleven o'clock the next day. They were all praying for these amtracks to get through, about eight or nine of them. They'd get hit 'cause the Nips had them zeroed in beautiful. The next morning, whatever time it was, an amtrack got through. He was probably thirty feet from me. I thought, "I have to get on that thing right now." What I found out is, I was more dead than alive; I had just about run out of soup. I was lying in the amtrack in and out. I saw the guy next to me had got hit in the gut with a grenade. He was calling for his mother, in fetal position. Ted, who had gone to camp with [me], was dying. I thought I was in bad shape until I saw all my buddies. Terrible. They got me to the Army hospital; that was the closest on. They operated on me.

[The part of the story that Mr. Schlinder does not relay in this interview is that when they got him back to the hospital, he was triaged into the dying pile. However, a Corpsman who knew him pleaded on his behalf, and he was operated on.]

Honis

We were dueling back and forth most of the day with Nips. We attacked one of those holes that the Japs had, down over the railroads and up a hill, and then the hill dipped down to another elevation. Grenades are flying back and forth. We set up our machine gun and we were firing at any Nips that showed themselves. It didn't take too long before we ran out of ammo. Then, they started zeroing in on us. So, then they were really chewing us up because we're getting fired at from Sugar Loaf, with mostly rifle fire. Then, they were hammering us so much with artillery and mortars they were able to set up some automatic weapons. Well, a fellow from G Company, Barney Wright was his name . . . a Nip threw a grenade in his foxhole, with some other guys. He reached down. He was sitting up in the hole and the grenade was at his feet . . . he reached down to toss it back and it exploded. Lost his feet and his right hand. We had to get him out of there. He was from Lancaster, South Carolina. We put him on poncho and started out, and a nambu opened up on us, and I'm the rear man. First, it's kicking dirt on me, but then one got me in the left leg and down I went. (Chuckles) I'm thinking of Barney, though, because I'm looking at him from my position as we're taking off, and his feet . . . his feet were such a mess. We had bandaged his hands but his feet were un-bandaged. I felt bad for Barney because I let go of the poncho and his feet hit the ground. So, I rolled down the hill to the rail-road tracks. Johnny Coughlin, the Corpsman, was there.

He had a bunch of wounded down there. Bandaged my knee and gave me a shot, and then, of course, there was a little defilade there. Again, while I'm down there, a bunch of Nips come out of a cave on Sugar Loaf and they had fixed bayonets, and the bayonets are gleaming in the sun. There was a melee going on. Anyway, they put me on a poncho and carried me back to the CP [command post]. Then they loaded up this amtrack with wounded. There was fifteen or twenty of us in there. Heading back, there's a lot of artillery coming in but they stopped the amtrack. Barney Wright, the one I was carrying out, was going into shock. So they had to stop and get a needle of plasma in him. We stopped long enough to get the needle in his arm. The shrapnel was bouncing off the side.

The amtrack, itself, is like a slaughterhouse. We're bleed-ing, of course, and the blood is just sloshing from side to side. Both guys on my left and right are bleeding on me. They had upper body wounds. We get back to the battalion aid station. They drop the ramp and immediately they have people helping those that needed help. Then a shell came in . . . we heard a shell come in, and now it's just about getting dark, and that shell landed. It was a heavy caliber one, at least a hundred and fifty millimeter, or a 1-5-0 . . . that's about a ninety-pound shell . . . rocks, dirt, shrapnel flying all over. Fortunately, I was upright . . . I didn't have time to hit the deck, but all it did was hit . . . Well, that's the last time I saw Barney, but he survived . . . It was like . . . it was surreal. It was surreal and with a shot of morphine . . . a little bit in a fog . . . added to the surreality of it. But looking in the deck and that blood sloshing, every time we'd hit a bump, it was just unbelievable . . .

When they stopped to give Barney the needle . . . we were . . . I . . . there was so much artillery landing around us, it was amazing. They were screaming in, landing, and bouncing off the outside. I didn't think about it at the time, but I've thought about it since. If one round had landed in there . . . there were fifteen or twenty guys, plus the crew. It would have killed a lot of people. Anyway, when they put me in that ambulance back at the battalion aid station it's dark. I couldn't tell what kind of lights they had. It's pitch black out. I was taken aback at the silence all of a sudden. It was so quiet. After all that melee, that noise I had left. Again, the whole thing was surreal. Then I went to division, and the usual paperwork and re-bandage. I ended up in the 168th Field Hospital. I don't know exactly where it was on the island, but I'd say, oh, maybe another five miles.

Andersen

Sergeant Hickins, he had gathered a number of us Marines together to ask volunteers to go back up onto Sugar Loaf Hill. He said, "Back up on to it, so we were there and around there." This was (Sighs) after that major battle by a couple of days, and he stated to us that Marines take care of their dead, and there were a lot of Marines on and around Sugar Loaf Hill that needed to be buried. He said, "It was important that we get up there now, at that time, because some of them had been hit five day previously or so and were disintegrating. Some of them might be melting into the ground." I thought that was quite a statement. So, we were ready, but he picked us out by "you, you, and you." It was PFC Jack deLeeuw, PFC William Lockwood, and

Private Grenade, spelled that way like grenade, and I thought that was unique that a Marine should have that kind of name.

We went up to the area, and proceeded to go over Sugar Loaf and down into the reverse slopes and the valley beyond. We had in our mind an ulterior motive to pick up some souvenirs while we were there, so that when the Seabees came up to, or close to, the lines with their trucks loaded with eggs and meat, which we considered steak, we could trade off some of the souvenirs and receive a good meal for the day, because we were into C-rations and K-rations.

Lockwood and I had paired off. Before starting to pick up the dead and bring them back on the reverse side of Sugar Loaf Hill, where Graves Registration could come and pick them up to be brought back further to the rear and identified and on the way to be buried, Lockwood and I spotted a hole. He or I looked in, and there were some dead Japs inside, and spotted five nambu machine guns. We thought that was a find, to find them in such a condition. Right next to the hole was a dead Marine, and he was about twice the size of his normal size, I suppose. His clothing was split and, of course, he was turning black and green. Where he was not split he had a hole right in the seat of his pants, right in the asshole, and looked to me on that immediate investigation that he had been hit right in the ass. The bullet went right up through his body.

I took his rifle and started to open up the cave wider and it stunk, the smell coming up out of that! Since the hole was larger, I decided that I would now enter the cave. There were numerous ones like this throughout Okinawa. I couldn't take the smell. I went in headfirst (Coughs). So, I came out and went in feet first, took a deep breath, and entered the cave. Making my way over towards the machine guns, there were three dead Japs there, into near skeleton remains, the clothes hanging off of the remains. The skin lying almost like a pool still attached to the skeletons, in a pool beneath the bodies. As I was making my way over to the machine guns, I stepped onto the skin and slipped, like one sliding on a banana peel. I fell into those three dead Japs, and what I wasn't lying on came down over the top of me. What a feeling. I got up and away from them and picked up the machine guns. Brought them out too. These are portable machine guns, easier to carry than our heavier, air-cooled and water-cooled machine guns. Brought those out onto the side of the hill, breathing in heavily because of the smell that I just experienced and taken in. I was covered with maggots and parts of their flesh and skin, and what have you.

Then we proceeded to start to pick up the dead. Since most Marines carry ponchos with them to the backside of their belt over their buttocks, folded, we picked the poncho and tried to get a fellow onto the poncho. It was not that easy. So, we picked out the most recently killed that were still whole. They had already started to turn green . . . the skin onto the hands . . . the skin of the hands, were now coming off somewhere around the wrists. It looked like they were wearing surgical gloves. We rolled this Marine on and proceeded to go through . . . mortar shells and small arms fire, machine gun fire, and we had to weave our way, crouching low, taking this body up to the top of the hill and to the other side. We were doing this one after another, and the bodies were, as we were picking and choosing, they were getting more decomposed . . . picked up a hand and proceeded to pull, and the hand came off into . . . the whole arm came off into . . . at the shoulder . . . came off into Duluth's hand. He immediately began to throw up. We were feeling the effects now. Our orders were to seek out a major who had led a reverse banzai charge with fifty men.

We had picked up a litter and we put Major Courtney onto the litter. He hung over the edge of the litter. He was too long, too tall. We made the decision to break his legs under him and compact his body so that we could run through the enemy shell and machine-gun fire. This is what we did, and we brought him onto the other side of Sugar Loaf Hill and set him apart. We were stacking these fellows up neatly as we could, which would be like lining heavy wood onto a pile, logs if you will. We laid down four Marines and the three Marines on top of them, and two, and then topped it off with another Marine. So they were pyramid style; we started to build up quite a few of these piles. In all of this, there was no thought in my mind that this was so terrible that I would turn my back onto it. I was of the frame of mind, and I'm sure the others were too, 'cause none of us spoke hardly at all while we were doing this, and then we [wouldn't] speak of the fact of how terrible a experience that we were having, or that we couldn't take it or any of that stuff. We were following what we're directed to do. We were continually doing this, and then we were getting to the point where these pieces, these people, these Marines were not in whole body form. So we suggested before we started that we put a body onto the litter, or canvas, or poncho that we were using, and it consisted of a head, torso, two arms, two legs. If they didn't match we'd do that anyway, and Graves Registration could sort out the pieces later. So now that was what the process was, to gather the pieces together and to bring those and stack them up also.

We were at this a number of hours, and were hungry and decided that we would start to look around the area for food. Of course, we were not going to seek anything around in that area, so we left the area and went further back, a little bit further north. Found a cache of food, a dump of some kind, and something to eat. Then we went back to the business of picking up the dead.

Ya know, in all times, all those years since this incident until 1986, forty-one years later, I never told anybody about this. Or any of these war stories. In 1986 I was invited to be in the VA hospital at Montrose, New York . . . into the alcohol rehabilitation program, run by the VA hospital. A twenty-eight day program, where we lived and ate there and received information about alcoholism. I was invited, in one of the sessions in which there were about six other fellows, to tell some of these war stories. What a job that was, trying to get it out. I mean, it was such a struggle . . . crying . . . such an emotional event. It had been buried away, all this plus all the other stories. I didn't know the repercussions throughout my life . . . . I never joined any of the veteran's organizations or talked to any veterans. I did subconsciously; I knew that I might break down. That I was hurting so bad that I didn't want to relate to it. Anyway, back to the story now.

After about seven hours or so . . . that's a guess . . . an amtrack, an armored vehicle, pulled up behind the hill and the driver got out and hailed us. [He] told us he was there to pick us up and take us back to the command post, and to take along some of the dead Marines. The amtrack consisted of a large opening in with a ramp that comes down, so that one whole side was open, in which they could put materials or troops into it and transport them. So, he drops this ramp and we proceeded to pick up about eighteen, twenty of the dead Marines and lie them down into this well. There was about three to six inches of water of this well, and as soon as the bodies started hitting that you could see some of the bleedings and liquids into the bodies, and the maggots started to come out into the water. I was never very quick to get ahead of anybody. I looked up and Lockwood, deLeeuw, and Grenade were up there with the driver in the seat, and there wasn't any room up there for me.

As the driver started to pull up the ramp, I immediately jumped into the well. The ramp closed, and I looked about and seen a small wire handle welded onto the side of the amtrack, and I grabbed hold of that. The amtrack was fairly level at that time, and he started to take off with this loud roar. It was deafening then, very hard to hear. As he progressed forward he started to go downhill, and the water started to deepen at the end of the amtrack away from me, and the fellows, the dead marines, started to slide forward. I looked in amazement at that, and then as he reached the bottom of that knoll and started up it started to reverse itself. The water started to come down towards me, and the fellows started to come down and slide towards me.

Well, I knew that I was in trouble. It wasn't . . . the first one wasn't that large a knoll to climb, and we started on the reverse side that was steeper, and now the fellows were tumbling forward and the water was splashing forward. He hit the bottom of that knoll and started up, and I started up, and I started to holler out for help. But the motor drowned out my voice, and now the fellows are all coming towards me. The water is around my neck, and the fellows are all bumping into me and starting to climb up on top of me. Now some of them, rolling . . . the guts stay like that . . . the heads start coming off, some of the arms start coming off, and now they are becoming a jumbled mess. Suddenly, you started the reverse again, and the hill, knolls are steeper, and as they are coming towards me they covered me, and the water covered me and I was drowning. And then the reverse happened. We were going forward, and as it gets to the steep end I was losing my footing, and on one of those rolls I lost my grip, and the forward movement went down on top of all those fellows. Then, when the reverse happened, I was on the bottom of all those guys. They all fell on top of me, and I was drowning and bringing into my system water, maggots, and bits of flesh, blood. Then I would be relieved when we were on the downside (Obviously very upset). One of my thoughts, believe it or not, was for them, those guys, that they were being so mutilated after their death. I was hollering out, or I felt I was hollering out, "Enough, enough, enough, enough" . . . and then I blacked out.

I came to when we were walking into the CP, into the command post . . . when the fellows who were seated around having their supper said, "Oh, wait a minute . . . God you guys stink and you look like death. Don't come near us." I didn't relate to that until many, many years. That was another form of rejection. They started to look around for some water for us to wash with. They found two and a half gallons in a five-gallon can . . . the four of us have taken off our clothes and are trying to scrape off the residue, blood, liquids, flesh, maggots . . . and with just cupfuls of water. We were completely naked and we could not put those clothes back on. So, they found remnants of something around, [with] which to clothe us. Some of the fellows went on a trek back to the rear to try to find uniforms for us, or some kind clothing. Then the fellows said, "You're in for a treat tonight because we have the Ten and One rations," which I imagine were stolen form the Army. So we had canned ham and canned sweet potatoes, a so-called wonderful meal, but when they opened the can of tomatoes, immediately I seen . . . I seen those seeds moving around like maggots. I couldn't eat. Later on, the other outfits came to us and clothed us, and I had a pair of brand new trousers that were way too big for me.

COMBAT FATIGUE

You know, if I did [have combat fatigue], it was so common that everybody had it.

—Bill Sams

Almost every veteran who spent any time in combat remembers a moment when a replacement came to them and called them "Sir," or deferred to them as if they were old men. Even years later, this event is related with a certain sense of befuddlement. "I was a kid myself," or "Old man? Hell, I had been only in combat for forty days." These Marines had crossed a line that they could not see, but that appeared clear to others. "Enroute to maturation, no station would be more significant, and battle would be the decisive rite of passage, entered upon as a boy, releasing one as a man."[67] Nor, continues Gerald Linderman in *The World Within War,* can one imagine the shock of how quickly the initial metamorphosis occurs during battle. Boys reach middle age in a matter of hours.[68] To survive in combat, individuals must repress their fears so they can function. "Repression of fear is achieved only at a great cost," writes Richard Holmes in *Acts of War,* "and the inner conflict it engenders may lead to psychiatric illness."[69]

Combat psychologically debilitates ninety-eight percent of all who participate in it for any length of time.[70] Those exposed to combat, especially for extended periods, pass beyond the physical manifestations of war to the psychological manifestations of war. Many observers of the phenomenon agree that, at some point, almost all combatants suffer from some degree of battle fatigue. The veterans of the Sixth agree.

"The psychiatric response to the stress of warfare has been recognized for centuries," and has been given many different names.[71] Marines in the Pacific had their own names for the common occurrence of combat or battle fatigue. They referred to it as the "thousand-mile stare," "going Asiatic," "shell-shock," or, more officially, "non-combat casualties." Yet knowing that combat fatigue existed did not eliminate reluctance to acknowledge it as a disorder. The concept of warriors as cowards has, for most, been too difficult to reconcile. Most veterans of war, however, will laugh at the supposition that combat fatigue has anything to do with cowardice.

Peter Watson, in *War on the Mind*, writes, "Combat psychiatry grew out of the need to care for individuals who, under the stresses of battle, suffered psychological disintegration."[72] The surgeon general of the Union Army acknowledged treatment of "nostalgia," as it was referred to in the Civil War.[73] However, it was not until World War I, which had large numbers of "shell shock" cases, that the medical world begin to see combat fatigue as the price of modern warfare. Interestingly enough, only in the twentieth century have combatants spent continuous months on the battlefield.[74] Before that, wars were long but time in battle was short and infrequent.[75]

Even in World War II, confusion in military circles regarding battle fatigue was highlighted when Gen. George C. Patton tried to slap a soldier back to his senses in a field hospital. At one point during World War II, the U.S. Army was discharging psychiatric casualties faster than new recruits were being drafted.[76] The dichotomy these examples represent is striking because it explains how unclear institutional perception still was in the 1940s. Roger Pitman, well known in the field of Post Traumatic Stress Disorder (PTSD), states that accurate observations were not often made, or retained when they were made, on those who were diagnosed with combat fatigue during World War II, therefore there are no studies regarding PTSD.[77] Information about what warfare does to the mind has only been gathered since World War II, and from recent combat situations.

Although "fatigue seems to be a natural effect of being under fire," many aspects other than the trauma of being on a killing field contribute to combat fatigue Physical exertion, lack of food, lack of sleep, and the impact of the elements are all factors that make a person vulnerable to combat fatigue.[78] These elements were all present in the Battle of Okinawa. Furthermore, many veterans commented that it was rarely green troops who "cracked up," but more often the battle-hardened veterans. They believe, and according to Pitman, some studies on Vietnam veterans support, that repeat campaigns make a person more susceptible to breakdown.[79] Most studies on combat agree that the most common element responsible for combat fatigue was prolonged exposure to battle. The policy during World War II of leaving troops exposed to combat for "eighty days at a stretch" exacerbated the number of combat fatigue cases.[80] Furthermore, the Marine Corps policy of no rotations contributed to combat fatigue because it led to hopelessness. Marines stayed and fought until they died, or were wounded so severely that they were evacuated. These factors predisposed the troops on Okinawa to retreat inward and seek escape from the environment that surrounded them.

Since World War II, students of combat have argued that there is a period of maximum efficiency for troops in combat. They become battle-wise around the tenth day of combat, and are most effective for ten to twenty days after that, and then rapidly decline to the point of combat exhaustion.[81] Combat exhaustion has many observable manifestations, and smart leaders, when able, sent troops showing these early symptoms to the rear. It often began with a simple slowing down, appearing less sharp, and losing memory and verbal ability. At this time, those affected often demonstrated the thousand-mile stare. There was a perceptible distancing, or tuning out. Eventually they either began to shake as they lost control or slipped into a vegetative state.[82] They neither fought nor ran away; they escaped into their minds, developed an outward tic, became deaf, paralyzed, or wept.[83] However, there are also incidents where troops simply "cracked", often when they had been isolated physically or mentally, even for short periods. Several veterans recounted stories about finding comrades in catatonic states who had spent a night without a foxhole buddy during an intense firefight .

In addition, those who had seemed invincible before suddenly lost their edge. Tom Jones relates this in *The View from My Foxhole*, about a hero, mentor, and guide to many—Lt. Richard "Heavy" Pfuhl:

> But the real damage of the bullet was not to his flesh. It was to his psyche. Finally, an enemy bullet had penetrated his invincible shield we were all relying on. It was the one that would somehow get us through those impossible desperate situations when everyone around us fell while we stood there unscathed.

But for Heavy and the rest of us who had already survived three years and three combat campaigns, the last nick in the shield at this point in the war was a sign that the gods had at last forsaken us. So as it happened to each of us, one by one, we felt like now we had been left to our own feeble resources. Such abandonment was intolerable to Heavy, so for the first time he began to take personal concern for his own safety. Sadly, it was noticed by the colonel and he was withdrawn from the front.[84]

On Okinawa, there were 26,211 non-combat casualties.[85] All the fighting units on Okinawa had high combat fatigue rates. The Sixth Marine Division accounted for 4,489 of them.[86] One set of statistics speaks for what the Sixth Marine Division experienced on Okinawa. In the battle for Sugar Loaf Hill alone, the Sixth suffered 2,662 killed or wounded, and there were 1,289 cases of combat fatigue. Those seven days in 1945 encapsulated all that was the worst of war. All the factors that make combat fatigue prevalent existed: rain, mud, flies, death, lack of food, fighting at night—all for days on end without relief. It became more than the mind could bear. Other places were equally bad. As Dick Whitaker points out, there were many places on Okinawa that could be a man's personal Sugar Loaf.

In *Acts of War*, Holmes contends that "every man has a breaking point but most never reach it." Perhaps this is the reason that so many of the Okinawan campaign survivors are so philosophical about combat fatigue; they realize how often they were close to that breaking point. Although a few veterans mentioned being resentful toward those who got out of doing their duty, most acknowledged that at least those who were removed due to the stress of combat had been there. They had tried. Few have any ill will toward the troops who went "Asiatic," as they refer to those who stepped out of the constraints of civilized behavior in war, or toward those who broke down completely. Each somehow seems to acknowledge that it took courage just to be there.

Since Okinawa, much research has been done regarding both the immediate effects and long-term impact of war on those who fight. Since Vietnam, recognition of PTSD has allowed all veterans to cope with the residual effects of war, including long-suffering World War II veterans.

Since World War II there has been a marked reduction in the number of troops that require removal from the field due to combat fatigue. In combat, they are no longer required to stay in forward positions for as long a period of time, not only because of improvements in equipment, but also because of the realization that the mind must also be protected. Troops are better informed about the battle they are fighting, compared to the infantrymen of World War II. Warfare today is seldom protracted. Tactics and strategies are less reliant on frontal assaults or employing troops as the only method of assault. Comfort in the field has rapidly improved; the food is better and military clothing is now more appropriate to climate. Most important, though, is the fact that our understanding of the mind has increased. Men and women in future wars will go off to test their courage, to prove their valor, while advances in battlefield medicine will improve the trend of fewer combat fatigue cases.

Whitaker

You know what it is . . . like to . . . let's say . . . have a bad night's sleep and how you feel the next day? Let's say that happens two days in a row. You know how you feel? Take eighty-two days of that. When you're in a foxhole that you've dug yourself, depending on another guy to stay awake while you sleep, living on the worst kind of food, drinking contaminated water, and having a touch of dysentery . . . being sick from time to time, being rained on, being shot at. What would be the natural effect? That's why I say . . . I think everyone had a touch of combat fatigue. What the hell is combat fatigue? If you're tired and you've been in combat, isn't that combat fatigue? We were goddamn tired and we were scared.

Joralemon

It didn't sound like . . . you almost have to blot that out of your mind I think. I mean you just can't sit and dwell on it. I think that's what, in battle or situations like that, I think you subconsciously blot that out, because if you don't you'll break down.

Jones

I'll tell you about that. I don't remember having any case of it prior to Okinawa in our battalion. We probably did, but not enough to notice. You have to realize there were several things working, especially with the guys who had been with us for a long time. You had no rotation plan. There was no hope. You were going to be there until you died or you had a leg blown off. There was no way to get out of it. The people . . . the people who did . . . many of us had been there three years by the time of Okinawa. We were already . . . without combat we could be a fatigue case just going through what we had been through for that length of time. The other thing is . . . it is never possible for the people at division headquarters and higher to really under- stand or feel what the front line troops go through. Even though they go make a visit . . . every . . . ya know, every general with his swagger stick likes to walk around and swagger around on the front line, and then get back. That doesn't give you a feel for what the troops are feeling. The people who didn't have combat fatigue were the guys who this was their first operation. It was our fourth . . . fourth landing and third major campaign . . . and four landings . . . anyone can go through one of these things . . . but you're not going to go through four successively without feeling it emotionally.

Fitzgerald

I think that was due to the length of the campaign, the mud and the diarrhea, the physical . . . physical chore of living day-by- day, fighting, and living in that rain and mud. Many of the guys still had dengue or malaria in their systems, and I'm sure we all suffered from malnutrition. It just broke you down and some guys just couldn't do it anymore. It was sad . . . big strong men.

Niland

We're assaulting the next hill at 0-seven-hundred. Well . . . pouring rain . . . we are at the side of the road. We had nothing to cover ourselves. We just slept in the mud, fended as well as we could. One of the guys during it started crying, I mean like a little girl or a little boy, cried like a little baby. "I can't go, I won't go," . . . fellow from my outfit, who I won't name . . . they called the Navy doctor, a Navy psychiatrist . . . they sent him back. We never saw him again until we get to China. I never spoke to him again because we all went back and he didn't go back.

So years later, after we got back, a bunch of us are down at the shore, down at the beach. Someone says, "Gee there's a party of nurses down the street, why don't we go down?" Fine, so we go down. I forgot to mention, on the way over this guy played the piano aboard ship, most popular guy in the outfit. We get to the party. I hear this piano playing, and I walk in the room. He took one look at me and left. He was ashamed. So, I held that feeling for years. Finally, Jim Scotia . . . he had a get-together for lunch and he brought this guy. Suddenly it disappeared. I said to myself, "Jesus, at least he went overseas. At least he didn't run to Canada or something. At least he put himself in harm's way." So, he was a great guy. He became a superintendent of school and really made a good life . . . he died a few years ago. We didn't have . . . . I saw them with funny looks in their eyes, but you just had to hang in. What could you do? If you did that on the line, someone would shoot you. I don't think company commanders . . . I never heard of a company commander ever sending someone in combat to a psychiatrist. You just stayed there. You just stayed there and did what you had to do. Maybe when you got back off the lines or something, but other than that, you stayed.

Pierce

We kind of felt sorry for the guy. We realized that he was breaking down, and we wondered what was wrong with them. Some guys would just sit there and start sobbing over nothing . . . just sit there with a terrible stare in his eyes. We would get a sergeant and he would come by, talk to the guy, and walk him around, maybe keep him around for a day or so, see if he would come out of it. Then they'd get him back, they'd tell someone to launch him back to the First Aid area. We'd never see the guy again. What was it . . . 2,600 guys went crazy or something like that? Yeah, we had one close guy who had a bag of gold teeth. We wouldn't go near him. No one would sleep with him. Gold teeth, the bag stunk, but that was his hobby, going and cutting the gold teeth out. I think it was quite common.

We also had the opposite of the guy cracking up. It would be the guy that was a little bit combat crazy. He would get a K-bar knife and say, "I'll see you, I'm going out on the lines." He'd go out at night. We wouldn't go out, but he'd go out there . . . many times in Naha and in little city areas he wouldn't even crawl, he'd walk, walk right toward the buildings in the city and patrol around and smell around all night. He'd come back in the morning and say, "I killed two." We didn't even know if he did. No one would go with him. Guys like that . . . we wouldn't go with them.

Moore

We had a first sergeant that was the poorest excuse for a Marine that any of us had ever seen. During training on the "Canal," he delighted in handing out punishments for lowly PFCs and privates. Everyone despised him except our colonel, whom he kept supplied with some bootleg liquor. The word got around to him that "if the Japs didn't get him, the Privates and PFCs would." During the last of our time in training, we noticed a change in his attitude. Still they hated him. We were in our seventh day on Okinawa and working our way up toward Motobu and, digging in for the night, the familiar sound of an M-1 rang out, and a bullet sailed over where our First Sergeant was digging in with the Battalion Chief. The chief, a big ol' China Marine, stood up and bellowed at the top of his voice, "Don't kill the son of a bitch tonight, I'm digging in with him. Get him tomorrow night." That was the final day on Okinawa for the infamous sergeant. He spent the rest of the war on Guam, feeding the wounded that couldn't feed themselves and assisting in the hospital ward.[87]

Drago

"Asiatic" attached to Marine had many connotations. In particular, he was in the Pacific too long . . . assault landings, wore an earring, walked with a swagger, custom made blues, etcetera. A Marine with the killer instinct to stay and not one to be trifled with.[88]

White, W.

On the 14th of May, I was crouched behind a stone wall next to "Babe" Ruth, executive for the company. He kept screaming at me to get across the field in front of us, which was being hammered by mortar rounds. I finally went, as much to get away from him as I didn't think I could make it. I wound up in a sixteen-inch shell hole with four other people. One of the four got up and ran toward the Jap lines, which I assume was his demise. I would credit this to combat fatigue.

The first day I was in the casualty company . . . after leaving Naval Hospital 111, an individual in the next tent slit his wrists. I could see the pool of blood on the floor in the tent when they carried him out.

The post office at this location was quite large. It had a window for each letter so you lined up on the letter of your last name. One day while waiting for my turn, a plane flew over and, for some reason, released a rocket. Everyone in all the lines hit the ground. We all got up and looked at each other somewhat sheepishly.[89]

Wilkins

I was wounded May 17, 1945, not real bad, but enough that I needed treatment. When I got to the hospital, they took good care of me and got me patched up. But there was nowhere . . . no beds . . . the hospital was overcrowded, and no place to sleep. This was just a makeshift field hospital. That first night I just rolled up on the ground and I was very, very miserable. The

next day I could get up and walk around. The only reason, really, that they were keeping me in the hospital is to make sure I
didn't get a bad infection. I found this compound with sandbags
. . . sandbags up, oh, about four or five feet. Then a tent
stretched over the top and wire all around it. It was closed in. I
could see that there were cots in there. There was a guard in
there, so I asked the guard, "What is this?" and he said, "This is
the psycho ward." He said, "These guys are all shell shocked
and shook up." I said, "How many cots are in there?" He said,
"There are twelve." I said, "And how many people are in
there?" He said, "Eleven," and I said, "Why can't I have that
other cot?" He said, "You can as far as I'm concerned." So he
opened up the wire a little bit and let me go in there.

It was very comfortable. I got, and I hoped to get good
night's sleep. Those guys . . . you couldn't sleep with those guys
carrying on, ranting and raving. Some of them were actually
shell-shocked. Some of them had run into a nambu and couldn't
move, bullets flying over their heads, and it finally got to them.
This one guy was really causing all the problems, just really
keeping everybody going. I finally got talking to him and he
finally confessed that he was really not shell-shocked. He was
not combat-fatigued. He had gotten a "Dear John" letter from
home. His girlfriend had married a 4-F from back home. [4-F
refers to someone not fit for military duty, or deferred because of
essential employment.]. Anyway, he had really gotten shook up.

I was a nineteen-year-old country boy, but I had always
been taught to go to Sunday school and church and try to help
people. So, I had to try to help this guy. I got to talking to him
and said, "You know what, you are really a lot better off. Glad
you found out about her now. You are too good for that gal." He
said, "What do you mean?" I said, "She ain't waiting for you
back home. Marrying that 4-F guy back there, when here you
are fighting for your country." He kind of thought about it a little bit. I said, "You know, I could be back there if I wanted to.
I'm a preacher, I didn't have to go in the military. I didn't want
to be back there with people like him, I wanted to be here with
people like you." I said, "I wanted to be with people like you,
fighting for your country." It hit him, really hit him right. He

said, "You know you're right!" He said, "Damn those people,
I'm a fighting Marine!" He said, "You're right." Some of the
guys were listening around. We were all jammed in. It was tight
in there. They heard the preacher thing. I think most of them
were happy. I kept trying to smooth everything down.

The next morning . . . this all happened during the night
. . . an orderly came around to give them medication and check
on them and everything. I said, "Do you have any cards, or
checker boards or anything?" They brought me a whole lot. We
had some checkerboards and pinochle deck. I got them . . . I
actually got the guys in a checker tournament. Who wins goes
on. The guys setting around, and we'd get to talking. Well, it
got back to the commander of the hospital. In fact, he was a
lieutenant commander in the Navy. It got back to him what I
had done. Three or four days, I guess four days, Sunday came
around. Father Gene Kelly was supposed to show up and hold
mass. He didn't show up. So the commander sent for me and
said, "Father Kelly is supposed to be here and hold mass. He
didn't show up. We would kind of like to have something, some
kind of religious service." He said, "I understand you're a
preacher." I didn't know what to say. Nineteen-year-old kid . . .
yeah . . . yeah, getting caught in this big lie. I thought, "What
the heck, I've been going to church and Sunday school all my
life." Under those conditions, five minutes was sufficient. I
studied about it and I went out and gave my little short sermon.

I went on back, and working with the guys. I stayed about
two more days. Of course, they were changing the dressing and
checking on me every day. After about three days the commander said, "It looks like every one of them is going to be able
to go back. Thank you for helping those people." He said, "We
can't find any reason to keep them anymore. They're even and
ready to go back." He said, "I want to get you transferred under
my command. I want to keep you here at the hospital." Of
course, I panicked then, "I'm going to be in the brig for lying."
(Laughs) I begged him to let me go back to my outfit because I
was afraid I was going to get caught in this big lie. I went down
to the staging area to be reassigned, waited awhile, and finally a
jeep showed up with a buck sergeant and he said, "I'm looking

for Claud, Claud up here?" I said, "That's me." He said what his name was, and he was from Third Battalion, Fifteenth Marines. He said, "I'm supposed to get you." I said, "You've made a mistake, I'm suppose to go to A Company, Twenty-ninth Marines." He said, "No, Colonel MaHaney, Colonel James MaHaney, told me to come pick you up." Anyway, I went on with him. He said, "You're supposed to go see the Colonel." So, I went in and told him who I was and he said, "Yes, you have been reassigned to my command." As it happened, the two first people I met in there, one of them was one that lived twenty miles from where I grew up and was raised on my mother's cousin's dairy. [He] knew all of my mother's relatives. The next guy I met was a guy who lived thirty, forty-five miles from me. We had played high school football, I guess.

Our outfit was mostly Yankees, and this outfit was about sixty percent Southern, so I found a home. Finally, I went on and told my lieutenant, Lieutenant Andrews, who was also from Memphis, Tennessee. I went and told him the story. He thought it was funny. Anyway, it got all the way back. Anyway, by the time we got to Guam it had gotten to General Shepherd. General Shepherd sent for me. Oh, my goodness, I was scared to death. I was scared bad! I told General Shepherd, "I am so ashamed of myself." I said, "I shouldn't have told all that big lie." He said, "All I have heard is what a great job you did." I said . . . I couldn't believe it! He said, "I think it's funny." He said, "You didn't do anything wrong. Everything you did was for the good." I said, "Thank you, sir. That relieves me." He said, "In fact I think you're so good, I think I'll appoint you bishop. Put you in charge of all the chaplains."

That was the end of it, until August . . . September of 1973, the third reunion of the Division, and General Shepherd showed up. I was setting down there and I told General Shepherd that I had had a talk with him one time, because I had told a bunch of lies. He looked back at me and said, "You're the bishop aren't you?"

Howell: F/2/29

[Pete Howell was from Ohio. Okinawa was his first campaign.]

My own experience with combat fatigue was not evident until I was aboard ship from Guam to San Diego, via Pearl Harbor. One day, outside Pearl a plane with tow target provided gunnery practice for the ship's crew, with no warning to those of us en route to the Naval Hospital in Diego. There was much trying to dig foxholes in the steel deck of the ship.[90]

THE ATTRACTIONS OF WAR

I don't attempt to deny that war is vastly exhilarating.

—Ernie Pyle

War does not consist entirely of intense battle or moments of hand-to-hand struggle. War often includes long periods of boredom and inactivity. Ironically, there are attractive aspects to war as well. Laughter and fellowship are common and, some might say, essential to those involved in combat. Friendly rivalries often develop to reinforce *esprit de corps* and to relieve boredom. Many times the stories most remembered by veterans involve different military branches, ranks, and specialties attempting to outfox one another.

Another reality of war is that men are often at their best during combat. They develop relationships with other males unlike any others they will have again in their lifetimes. Men dig within themselves and discover the ability to lead, when just a short time before they had doubted that they possessed any courage at all. It often appears that men have exhibited seemingly unbelievable leadership and heroism, according to after-action reports or citations. Other men have performed similar feats and have been unrecognized because no one around them lived to tell the tale.

War is a spectacle. Combat is so pivotal that most men believe it shapes their lives, and it becomes the event they refer to most in conversation. War is for fighting men, and "the experience of communal effort in battle . . . [it] has been the high point of their lives. Despite the horror, the weariness, the grime, and the hatred, participation with others in the chance of battle had its unforgettable side, which they would not have wanted to miss."[1]

COMRADES

> . . . *We band of brothers;*
> *For he to-day who shed his blood for me*
> *Shall be my brother.*
>
> —Shakespeare, *Henry V*

Since ancient times men have lauded the virtues of the warrior and the virtues of war. Perhaps what they are saluting is a moment in life when friendships take on an intensity that will likely never be experienced again. Samuel Hynes in *The Soldiers Tale* summarizes: "A soldier spends virtually all his time, awake and asleep, with his mates, he is with them even more continuously than most men are with their wives. And at critical moment his life may depend on their fidelity and courage. Most marriages don't come to that."[2] The value of combat friendships is multi-faceted. Comrades keep each other warm and safe; they nurse each other; above all, they keep each other alive—alive, in fact, in ways that veterans will admit they never were before and have never been since.

A deep-seated desire for belonging is fulfilled for most men in battle. Barbara Ehrenreich in *Blood Rites* explains: "The sociality of the primordial band is more likely rooted, after all, in the exigencies of defense against animal predators. We may enjoy the company of our fellows, but we thrill to the prospect of joining them in collective defenses against a common enemy."[3] War brings "fellows" together with a common goal and a common experience. Each of us has the desire to identify ourselves with something larger than ourselves,[4] and war affords men that opportunity. "Comrades in war are not chosen: they are simply the men picked to stand beside you."[5] J. Glenn Grey believes that camaraderie is one of war's appeals. "The communal experience we call comradeship, is thought . . . to be especially moral and the one genuine advantage of battle that peace can seldom offer."[6] Wartime friendships are so unique that they warrant their own description: Comrades-in-arms.

There are countless instances of men in battle risking their lives for other fighting men. The personal reward that came from protecting a comrade often overrode the fear of death for many men in combat. Combatants who are looking out for one another improve the chances that they will all stay alive. They also help each other to think outside of themselves, which, especially in prolonged combat, kept soldiers focused and able to continue witnessing death and killing. Most veterans firmly state that once they were in combat they no longer fought for flags or leaders. They fought for the men standing next to them.

As the battle intensified on Okinawa and the attrition rate became staggering, new men came in to replace those that were lost. The "old guys", boys who had faced their first landing just weeks before, remember that the replacements did not fit in and were dangerous to other men's survival. Yet, the veterans who were replacements themselves remember only how well they were treated, and how quickly they developed their own foxhole buddies, their own comrades-in-arms.

Honis

Anyway, I finally got to my company. There's three dead men covered up by ponchos. [I] checked in . . . I felt I was *home*. I've mentioned it to men and they'd say, "I know what you mean," and people would say that you're crazy. But it isn't any . . . oh boy . . . I'm gung ho. I just wanted to be back home . . . needed to be with the team. [With] your buddy . . . *your buddy*. Its something you can't explain, but it's there and it's still there.

McKnight: H/3/22

We were from different parts of the country . . . Mahoney with his Boston accent, McTureous with his southern drawl, me speaking what I thought was English. McDermott was just kind of, well, you know. We were at Lejeune and did all the training together, went on liberty together, did everything you can imagine together. Most of the time it was the three of us: McTureous, Mahoney, and myself, and McDermott was once in a while.

White, J.

We were in the same units in the replacement draft, and all went overseas together. I think they just took a list and said these would go into this company and these . . . down the list . . . will go into this company. Whitaker was in Fox Company, for example. And that comes just before "White" and there were a bunch of "Whites" in G Company. There were seven or eight. . . . Let's see, W. W. was in a foxhole [and] was hit by a mortar shell. John White lost either his left or right leg at the knee. R. S. White got shot through the biceps, triceps, and the pectoral muscle on his right arm. R. R. White was riding a truck and a 55-gallon drum bounced around, got him on the toe, and almost cut his toe off. Let's see, who else was there? W. F. White was in I Company and he got some mortar or grenade fragments in his legs. Who else was there? (Pause) That may have been all. We fared like everyone else did. Everyone in my company was wounded at least once. We had sixty-one killed.

Miller

I said, "Here's what we're going to do." I said, "We're going on top of the hill and we're not going to stop. We're going on the other side. We're going to get those Nips, and we'll get in and around them." I said, "Okay, you all got that?" "Yeah, yeah." "How 'bout you Cunningham?" He said, "I know." I said, "Okay Cunningham, go ahead." He said, "Fuck you, you're the squad leader, you go first." I couldn't help but bust out laughing . . . his eyes were this big (Indicates with hands the size of a saucer). I started laughing. The next thing you know the whole damn squad was laughing. What do you think those Japs were thinking about? "This is funny to them? It isn't funny to us!"

Loftis: C/1/22

[Garland Loftis had gone to Duke and was part of the V-12 program. Originally assigned to the Third Marines as a reserve replacement for the invasion of Iwo Jima, he was then transferred to the Sixth Marine Division]

> Seeing these young people coming into my outfit . . . I was just a young man of twenty-two, twenty-three years. They were about sixteen, seventeen, eighteen, and had been reading about Okinawa on April 1 when they were civilians. They gave them such fast training to get them over there. The ones that were coming in, you never really got to know them. They came in, the platoon sergeant or sergeant major would give you their names, you'd assign them to a squad, and that's it. There wasn't that closeness that you had with the others.

Leaders

> *[Leadership becomes] . . . I think it's called automatic response. You trained for it. So that you can do what needs to be done automatically.*
>
> —Henry Kemp

The Marine Corps maintains the philosophy that as long as there is two Marines together the senior Marine is always in charge. The Marines on Okinawa often tested this philosophy. Japanese snipers targeted anyone that even slightly showed a command posture. Lieutenants were taught to be out in front leading; therefore they were lost faster than they could be replaced. Because of this, leadership was often as much in evidence in PFCs as in officers. They took over, led men into battle, and continued even if a company was down to two men. Repeatedly, veterans explained that the true signs of leadership were a willingness to shoulder the pack and to do as much as the men below the men you lead.

Most men in frontline infantry units had only praise to offer for their officers and NCOs, because they were experiencing the same, or even worse, conditions as their men. In rear-echelon service units, or when men were in training for upcoming engagements, instances of leadership seem less apparent. There were, of course, exceptions, although those were infrequent and the Marine Corps usually removed such "leaders."

One such example of this kind of leader was Colonel Bleasdale. Every man interviewed who served in his regiment had bad things to say about him. After reading his official Marine Corps oral transcript, it became apparent that his problem was based on his misunderstanding of leadership. His mentor was Henry Larson, whom Bleasdale thought was "the best officer I encountered in the Marine Corps."[7] Larson was a disciplinarian. Bleasdale, a decorated hero of World War I, followed in his footsteps and perhaps took Larson's disciplinary style to an extreme. On Guadalcanal, according to men who served under him, Bleasdale worked the men twice as hard as those of any other unit. The Twenty-ninth, its veterans contend, may have been worn out by the time they hit the beaches of Okinawa.

Men also mention another type of poor leader: A Marine who asked of his troops something he would not do himself, such as bring back souvenirs or go into dangerous or unpleasant situations, while he stood back and watched. The insult to the troops was magnified when a higher-ranking Marine or soldier was rear-echelon and clean, a clear indicator that he had not earned a Marine's respect. Many times these men were ignored or told to "go to hell" in no uncertain terms. In combat, respect had to be earned.

In combat, true leaders did stand out and they were men that other men would willingly follow anywhere. Leadership was not necessarily about heroism. "Salty" troops learned to avoid leaders who were looking for recognition. Leaders respected their troops, looked after them, and bore their fair share of the burden. Jack Fitzgerald commented on the high quality of some of his leaders, many of whom had been in several campaigns by now. "We were blessed with some unusually gifted officers who were devoted, smart, courageous, and also with those who came along later." In this section, Gen. James Day, MOH, explains leadership at its most basic level. His explanation and obvious understanding of the burdens of leadership are a good indication of why this nineteen-year-old corporal on Okinawa rose to become Major General and the Commanding General of Marine Forces in Japan.

Sherer: F/2/29

[Robert Sherer already had a son and a job in the business world by the time he went to Okinawa. His wife literally took his job in the Marine Corps when he was reassigned to a combat unit. He describes why some officers were successful.]

> The officers in our company, for the most part, were a little older, and had a sense of "If we win support [we will be successful]." We [had to] win loyalty . . . so we worked with them on the basis of respect.

White, J.

In my platoon we had seven platoon leaders, that I know of, in the seventy days that I was there before. The seventh one was hit a few minutes after I was. He was a gunnery sergeant. We had some temporary platoon leaders. For example, Sergeant Mitchell, who took over after Lieutenant McNally was hit. Sergeant Mitchell was killed just a few minutes after he took over the platoon . . . it was because of the nature of the job. They were up and around more. They were usually up in the front when we were going . . . when we were going somewhere. I was behind three. I was the platoon runner. We would take a hill, we would kind of consolidate things, and then I'd head back to the company headquarters and make a report . . . maybe bring back a wireman carrying spools of commo [communication] wire, and maybe some chow and some ammo and some water. I would usually be behind the platoon leader. One was killed and two were wounded badly . . . I was right behind them. They were good folks. I don't know how they would be compared to a Prussian or even a Japanese. They weren't fearless, but they were . . . they wouldn't let their fear overcome them. They'd do the job.

Whitaker

[Only one Fox Company officer made it through the campaign; it was Robert Sherer. Whitaker recounts a more common occurrence for officers].

He lasted nine days. He was a replacement on Oroku. He got right off the ship from the States, came in, was assigned to Fox [Company], was there about a week, got hit, went on the hospital ship, and went home. I don't think he was overseas over a month.

McKinney

Colonel Shapley was a tall gentleman, about six foot two. He was a graduate of the Naval Academy, where he was a football hero. Years later he served as the commanding officer of the Marine detachment aboard the USS *Arizona* in Pearl Harbor on December 7. He was blowed off of the ship into the water by a bomb. His left cheekbone was blown out through the flesh, protruding. In the water he actually saved a sailor who was drowning. The sailor was screaming for help. The colonel, at that time he was a major, he saved that sailor. He kept him afloat until a boat passed by, and passed him up to the boat. Then he went to help other people.

He stayed in the Marine Corps. He was very much a Marine. He ended up as Commanding Officer of the Marine Raider Regiment that was later formed of all the four Raider Battalions. He trained. He made sure you knew what you were doing and why you were doing it. He was not the kind of man who would yell and scream and holler at people. He always had a kind word for you, and I appreciated him because when I first got to Guadalcanal and got to F Company, my company commander, Captain Homegrain, had the suspicion that I was extremely underage to be overseas . . . even to be in the Marine Corps. I was detailed to Colonel Shapley and General Shepherd as an orderly. I got to watch the Colonel very close, watch him work, listen to him talk to people. I knew this was the man that, I don't care where it was or what was happening, if he said, "Let's go," I would be on my feet and moving right along with him.

All the way through the campaign at Okinawa he was our leader. He always came up to the lines . . . many, many times I have seen him up on the lines where he did not belong. Fighting at Mount Yae-Dake, I had helped carry down some wounded.

Starting back up . . . it was a high place up there. Oh, I don't know . . . a good eight, nine hundred feet, but it was many, many hard footsteps going up that mountain. Every man that went carried water, rations, or something. After we brought the wounded down and started back up, I picked up a cloverleaf of 60-mortar ammunition. There was a staff sergeant there . . . I had never seen him before, but he was telling people, "Get this, get that . . . Come on let's get . . . Go up the hill." Well, he started up the hill but he wasn't carrying anything. Colonel Shapley said, "Sergeant, sergeant, you're carrying, too." He said, "No sir, I'm a staff sergeant." Shapley said, "I'm a colonel." Colonel Shapley picked up two five-gallon cans of water and started up that mountain. The staff sergeant picked up two cases of rations. People like that, those are real leaders. They are great people. They not only do what they tell you to do, they do it themselves. They do more than you do.

Fox

Ed Galuska . . . I had to find this guy again for being so helpful to me. He told me to dig a foxhole. I dug where he told me to dig. He told me to dig the thing two feet; I went three feet. . . . The camaraderie with the Marines . . . the Marines took care of each other, ya know. I landed on Okinawa . . . I didn't know anyone when we landed there. It was just the training we got. If this guy alongside of you . . . you put your life in his hands. I didn't know Ed Galuska from a hole in the wall. As long as I . . . he said do this, and do that, and I did. Whatever he told me to do, I did.

DeMeis

You had officers, and then you had *officers*. Like all things, some were better than others. The men got to really like them. They had class, as the saying goes in Brooklyn. Most were great. A few of the replacements were not so good. You'd get 'em in from the States. I used to call them Irish Setters. You ask why? Because they would point. He would say, "This is the objective today: We're going to take this hill." They would point, these guys. He would point. As soon as you would start the assault, major skirmishes, you'd turn around and the guy is still over there pointing, like he's after a bird. I gave him the nickname the Irish Setter. Then you had other guys. You did-n't have to look for these officers because they were always in front of you. We had this saying: There are officers and then there are *officers*. . . . On the other hand, we had many good officers, officers that you never had to turn around to find them for they were always right in front of you leading, as one should.

Day: Wpns/22

[James Day, from Saint Louis, Illinois, participated in combat in the Marshall Islands and on Guam. As a nineteen-year-old corporal on Okinawa, his actions resulted in his receiving the Medal of Honor.]

I have heard throughout my career, as a general officer in the Marine Corps, people come up to me and say, "Hey you have an awesome responsibility." When I commanded . . . as General of twenty-six thousand . . . when I commanded a division . . . the First Marine Division of twenty-six thousand people . . . people would often ask, "How do you do it? How do you take care of them? How do you take care of their medical needs, and their tactical needs, and their equipment needs, and their every being? 'Cause you're like a father image to them." They always said that was an awesome responsibility. Well, I always like to compare that general, who was a division commander, when you talk about awesome responsibility, to the Marine Corps fire team leader.

Now, that Marine Corps fire team leader is the leader of the smallest element in the Marine Corps. He leads only four peo-ple—himself and three others. It's called a fire team. His responsibility, I think, is almost beyond comprehension. If you take a look at the day in combat of that general officer who leads the twenty-six thousand men, and take a look at the young man, who is a corporal, [his] day in combat . . . I think you can see the correlation of the thing I'm talking about.

A general, when he gets up in the morning, in combat, he has had a good night's sleep. He usually gets up and has a nice cup of coffee and a nice breakfast, and he brings in his staff of at least eighteen people. They brief him on what they are going to do that day. He brings in an engineer officer, supply officer, a tactical officer, an air officer, a medical officer, and artillery officer. He brings them all in and they advise him about what's going to happen that day. He takes that advice, and that's the way he fights the battle that comes up that day. He might go forward to the front lines regiments, visit commanders, and says, "Hey, you're doing a fine job." Then he goes back to rear, debriefs again with these eighteen people, and then he prepares for bed at night. When he goes to bed at night he has a nice warm place to sleep in. He might not have sheets every night, but at least in a sleeping bag. He does not have to worry about being overrun by the enemy, or receiving a lot of incoming artillery, or air being used against him. He is in a pretty safe and pretty shallow place.

If you take that corporal who's a fire team leader and you look at him when . . . as he's waking up in the morning . . . you have to remember at most he's had two or two and a half hours sleep. Two men in a foxhole. There's usually eight hours of darkness, and because of the probes against the front lines, counter attacks, artillery fire that's coming in, mortar fire that's coming in, machine gun fire that's coming in, he doesn't get much sleep. So, when he gets up in the morning ready to move out, he's the man responsible to make sure that his men have had water and food, that they have rations, and that they're ready to move out. He has to take care of his casualties. He has dead. He has to see that guy is wrapped in a poncho and evacuated. If he has wounded, he has to see that their wounds are taken care of and they're evacuated. Then he jumps off the attack, and he doesn't have any respite from that attack. After he takes that hill, he takes another and another and another.

When his day comes to an end, he hasn't had anything to eat during the day. He hasn't had the advice of eighteen professionals to tell him what to do during the day. He does it on his own. When the night comes he digs in and prepares to do the same thing with a lack of sleep. So, when you talk about the awesome responsibility that the Marine general has, on one hand, as division command, it is awesome. Awesome enough to me because . . . simply because . . . it's very difficult to do, but often because of the amount of men.

Remember that Marine general has been in the Marine Corps probably about thirty-five years. He's been a platoon commander; he's been a company commander; he's been a battalion commander, and a regimental commander. He's been to seven or eight schools in the service, and he usually has a master's degree in civilian life. So, he's well prepared for that command.

When you take a look at that little corporal and what he's done . . . he's probably had one school in his entire life and that's the Marine Corps boot camp, which is the finest school in the finest organization or organizing force for Marines that I've ever seen, but that's all he has. So when you talk about awesome responsibility, I say to you, that corporal has more responsibility, tenfold, than the division commander.

Now, if you line these two men up side by side and you ask that general, "What would you like to see today in combat?" He'd probably like to see . . . "I'd like to see us accomplish our mission at a minimum loss of men." You put that corporal beside him and you ask that corporal, "Corporal, what would you like to see happen today . . . to happen in combat?" He'd say, "The thing I'd like to see is tomorrow. I'd like to see tomorrow." That's the kid that has responsibility. The general and everyone else involved has the responsibility to see that young man does see his tomorrows.

HEROES

Everybody couldn't get a medal for everything they did. Gosh, I don't know many guys who shouldn't have had some kind of medal.

—Claud Wilkins

What actions and characteristics do we use to measure heroism? Is it not heroic to have survived eighty-two days on Okinawa, or to have been wounded in that horrific campaign? In the military, statistics and medals often denote heroism. The Sixth Marine Division retained very few of the men from the rifle platoons who landed on Okinawa on L-Day by June 21, 1945. The Sixth sustained 8,227 killed or wounded men.[8] Five Medals of Honor were awarded, as well as twenty-nine Navy Crosses. The Sixth Marine Division received the Presidential Unit Citation, and very few men walked away without a Purple Heart. As well, the Sixth Marine Division captured the majority of the island, including the Yontan Airfield, Naha Airfield, and they broke the Shuri Line.

However, most veterans do not measure a hero by the medals on his chest, nor do they stand in awe of many. One veteran explained his feelings when he stated that there was a difference between being an icon and being a hero. Men like Dick Bush, MOH (The last surviving MOH recipient of the Sixth), James Day, MOH, and James Chaisson, NC, were heroes on Okinawa, but they also became icons. Anyone who knew them in later life understands this because the characteristics that made them heroes and icons continued throughout their lives. They continued to be natural leaders, and did so with great humor and modesty.

All of the veterans interviewed are in agreement that medical Corpsmen were unsung heroes. As Tom McKinney said, "When a guy was wounded, he wasn't yelling 'Marine.'" Corpsmen risked their lives constantly, These men were calm under fire, helped those around them, and risked their lives, often refusing to leave wounded men even when a retreat was necessary. They were usually physically strong, whether they were the smallest in the unit or the biggest, and survivors of Okinawa all feel they were the best that the United States had to offer. Many of them died, many of them never got a medal, but the veterans, the men they served with, have never forgotten.

Victor F. Bleasdale: Commanding Officer, Twenty-ninth Marines, 1944–April 1945

[Bleasdale was relieved on Okinawa because of his poor performance on the northern end. This World War I Navy Cross recipient, some argue, was just worn out, and perhaps suffering from battle fatigue. Others argue that he almost destroyed his regiment, especially its morale. He was replaced by Col. William J. Whaling.]

The question of outstanding heroism in battle and all that beautiful stuff requires a situation that permits the individual to do
something that's outstanding. Many a person said, "Well, how is
it that captain so-and-so, or major so-and-so, didn't do something spectacular and stand out?" Well, hell, he just never got
the opportunity, you see."[9]

Hoag: Sixth, Joint Assault Signal Company (JASCO)

[Jack Hoag was from California and worked for the phone company.
One of the early men to enlist during the furor after Pearl Harbor, he
left the States with the Third Division in December 1942.]

Now, my *heroes*. They were the Corpsmen. I can't remember
any of their names 'cause we always called them Doc. We had a
Doc in our outfit in the Third Division. On Bougainville he
cured my jungle-rot, and when we got back to the Canal, it was
the Doc who took care of my jock itch. When the Third Special
Weapons was broken up, and I became a part of Fourth
JASCO, I really had a hero. On Christmas Eve of 1944, I was
knocked down with dengue fever. I was so sick. Along about
midnight I crawled to the Doc's tent. He put me in his spare cot
and looked after me all night long. In the morning he helped
me to my tent and then the rest of the day, every hour on the
hour, he would check up on me. *And I don't even know his
name.*[10]

McKinney

[When people called us heroes] . . . We had to tell them that the
real heroes . . . are buried somewhere in the United States, and
those that aren't, somewhere on the stinking island in the
Pacific. We're not heroes, just people like them doing a job.

White, J.

You know, bravery is overcoming fear. You never know what to
expect. There's the fear of the unknown. I found out I was able
to overcome what fear I had. Fear on Okinawa was a cyclical

thing. There was always an underlying uneasiness while you're there. There are the spikes of pure terror . . . (Chuckles) . . . when a shell hit near you, or someone who was beside you took a sniper's bullet, or the burst from a nambu machine gun.

Whitaker

Anyway . . . it really doesn't matter. But you cannot be in a combat situation for eighty-two days and not have a chance to do something spectacular. I think everybody did spectacular things.

Niland

None of the people in my company got medals . . . not one single medal. They deserved hundreds of medals. Magliaro, particularly . . . he was really something. He died. I was with him when he died. We were cleaning out a cave. When you cleaned out a cave, you have people on one side, people on the other side, and people in the middle. The people on the right side make sure the Japs on the left side don't get you, and vice versa. Well, Magliaro was in the middle with a BAR [Browning Automatic Rifle], and someone on the left side let loose on a Jap and cut him right across the abdomen. We think the company captain choked. I can remember Pio Magliaro crawling fifty yards holding in his stomach, with his BAR in his other hand, cursing the captain and saying, "Where is he, I want to kill him." He died before we got him to the CP [Command Post]. His name is on the wall on Okinawa. I went to visit him and I cried when I was there. I miss him. He should have gotten the Congressional Medal of Honor in my opinion, and he never got anything.

Fitzgerald

Third Battalion was on our left. I think we had the ocean, and I think [Kiyamu] Ridge was the last firefight. Then we did some deep patrolling down towards the end. I don't know if you have

seen the big picture of Harry Kizirian? Well, Harry was with us.
He was in our second platoon. I wrote his Navy Cross citation.
Another guy and I pulled him out when he was wounded. Harry
came back to us, and so we went on a patrol, and we had a jeep
with us, and we went on this deep patrol. During this patrol
Harry started complaining about his leg. He had taken a bullet in
his thigh, I don't know. Anyway . . . I sent him back. I said, "Here
take my helmet and take my Tommy gun," and it's so damn hot
. . . and carrying all that stuff. Seemed like nothing was going to
happen on this patrol, kind of routine. Harry said okay. He carried my helmet and my Tommy gun, and he got back down
around our CP and somebody took his picture. That's the one
that got in the *New York Times*. (Chuckles) If you'll notice his helmet, it's not fully packed on his head. Kids in Heavy's [Pfuhl's]
platoon . . . Heavy used to put a ration can under his camouflage
to break the silhouette. . . . All those kids followed him, including
Harry. Harry joined us after Guam and the kids nicknamed him
"The Beast." He was kind of a homely kid out of Rhode Island.

Schlinder

Dick Bush is a Medal of Honor recipient . . . that on April 16,
he and his squad were up on Motobu . . . is that the name? He
got hit in the leg with machine gun fire. Four of his men threw
him on a poncho, grabbed a corner each, and ran to the back of
the hill. When they got down they stopped to take a rest. As
they stopped to take a rest, a Nip grenade came flying in. Dick
saw it, and if he wouldn't have grabbed it and pulled it in he
would have probably lost four of his buddies. I can see Dick
doing it because he's that type of man. He's a very unselfish
man, a brilliant man, a good man, and a brave man. One of the
best friends I've ever had. Nothing but good to say about him.
He got the Medal of Honor, and rightfully so.

McKnight

McTureous . . . great man, really. He played baseball . . . then he
went to junior college for a year because he couldn't get in the

services because he had a hernia. So he went back and told his brother Basil, and his brother Basil got him a job on a surveying crew. He went to the hospital to have his hernia fixed and the doctor says, "You have another one on the other side that has to be fixed too to go in the service." He said, "Oh, okay." The doctor said, "You want to go and serve our country, so the next operation is on me." I guess the only charges he had to pay were the hospital charges, not the surgeon's charges. Then he went to the recruiting surgeries and they disqualified him. Boy, he was down heart, really dejected. A lot of his friends were in the service and stuff. He waited a couple months and went back when they had a change in personnel and didn't mention anything about his hernias. A Marine sergeant came in to ask who wanted to go in the Marines. He was thinking about it. He put up his hand to scratch his head, and the Marine sergeant said, "Follow me . . ."

[McTureous received the Medal of Honor. The last time McKnight saw him alive was when they were separated on arrival at Okinawa as replacements at the height of Sugar Loaf.]

Pesley

Major Courtney is my hero there. He got us off there, in fact. When I told the battalion commander that we got to the top of the hill and that Major Courtney got us up there, he said, "That's no good." He [Courtney] was the executive of the battalion and had gotten wounded with [a walking wound], and the colonel said he wasn't supposed to be up there. He got us up there, and when I went back to get more ammunition on top of Sugar Loaf, I realized that Major Courtney did not even have a weapon. He asked to borrow my carbine, so I gave him my carbine. He used it while I was gone. Of course, when I came back I wanted my weapon. So, when I got back I asked for it and got my weapon. We made a sweep across that mountain and that's when he got killed.

Brining

Well, there were a lot of people who deserved the Medal of Honor, but there were no officers around to record it. My platoon leader, I would say, was one . . . he was a redheaded Irishman. He'd been in the old Marines . . . Phillip Farley . . . and he should have gotten the Medal of Honor. He pulled five of us out that day. He and our machine gunner. I talked to the machine gunner a few years ago on the phone. He said, "You probably don't remember me, but you was with me in the foxhole the night we stayed with the machine gunners." He said he had helped load five guys in the back of an amtrack and brought us out.

RIVALRIES

I knew he was an officer because he was cleaner than us.

—Stephen Kraus

Competition and rivalries are part of military life, in part because the structure is hierarchical. The drive to be the best is part of Marine Corps tradition and psyche. *Esprit de corps* requires Marines to believe that the other services are less qualified. Within the ranks, being the best is quickly noted and emulated, and poor performance is not accepted. Taking these factors into consideration, it becomes obvious why rivalries between the military branches are so commonplace. Rivalry, and perhaps resentment, also exists between officers and enlisted personnel. Although these sentiments are seldom observed during combat, at other times they are more apparent and simply a part of life in the military.

The Marines on Okinawa, who watched what the kamikazes did to vessels offshore, offer grudging respect for naval personnel, although they might not have admitted it at the time. The Seabees, a military service construction battalion, were also admired for several reasons: they were great go-betweens; they supplied good food from the Navy to the Marines in exchange for souvenirs; and they created an infrastructure on Okinawa, almost overnight. The First Division was the Sixth's interservice rival on the island, but "the Old Breed," as the First was called, just demanded respect because they had so much combat experience. The Army took the brunt of Marine antagonism, especially the Twenty-seventh Army Division, which had a poor reputation going into Okinawa—and lived up to it once they were there.

Marines called the soldiers many names, most often "doggies" or "dog-face." They resented the fact that they seemed to have better food and cleaner clothes, but most of all they resented having to finish the job when the Army was stalled at the Shuri Line. The Army and the Marines traded catcalls at each other as they passed along the roads of Okinawa. One veteran reflected that sometimes it was hard to remember that they were on the same side.

The Marines continually attempted to steal anything they could from the Army. As Bill Sams explained, "Hell, if they had size ten shoes, and none of our guys had anything but twelves, we still wanted them because the Army had them."[11] Tim Joyner retells a story by Sy Ivice, both of HQ/2/29 of one resourceful Marine in their unit who was known for his ability to "procure." He left the boys on the northern end and "found" a jeep for their captain, supplied inadvertently by the army. For the Marines, known for their ability to do more with less, procurement became the duty of choice.

The obvious friction that can arise when one person is appointed over another often surfaced between officers and enlisted. Officers, for example, were ordered to read and censor their troops' mail. Many veterans remember resenting their officers for having that access to their personal lives. When censorship was lifted, Bill Sams wrote home to his family, "Censorship has been lifted. For that, I am very glad as I am tired of people reading my letters . . . if anything was said against the officers it would come back real quick."[12] Behind the lines, officers had privileges that the troops didn't, and the troops resented that. Many veterans commented that when they returned to Guam, one of the first things to be built was the Officers Club—even before a chapel. Mostly the resentment of officers appeared more pronounced in rear units or rest camps. Still, the rivalry between the two groups usually remained healthy. Troops loved playing jokes on their officers. One story tells of how a group of Marines set the bathroom on fire when an officer was using the facility. The troops delighted in getting away with something that was prohibited, and most officers seemed to understand it as part of the game. Being young themselves, they often enjoyed the high jinx as much as the troops.

Over the years some resentment and rivalry has occurred between frontline Marines and support elements. Infantrymen perceived their expendability on the front lines in a way that no other group did, argued Gerald Lindermen in *The World Within War*. This forever set them apart from the tankers, artillerymen, pilots, and other rear echelon units.[13] Some veterans feel now that there is an inner sanctum of warriors, and it can even be seen in the Sixth Marine Division Association today. Combat veterans of the campaign sometimes hold themselves apart from engineers or artillerymen. Yet, as one member of the Fifteenth recalled, "They sure were screaming for us when they were in a fire fight and needed support!"

Although rivalry existed between officers and enlisted, there is still a brotherhood between them. Good leaders were most often the troops' heroes, and rank became a secondary importance. Especially in combat—the great leveler—mutual respect was far more apparent. The same can be said regarding frontline and support troops, then and now. As Dick Whitaker explained, if they had made it through Marine boot camp and been a Marine, they had passed the most essential test, the only test that mattered.

Joralemon

> Yeah, yeah . . . again, (Chuckles) as I say, I wasn't there. I wasn't in the club. There's a definite distinction. I . . . it's the old story. When it's all said and done, when you boil it all down, I think it's like one percent of the entire military during the war were on the frontline. You either were or you weren't. You were either exposed to it or you weren't. It's just like day and night, and those that were there form a brotherhood that's in its own club. You were either in the club or you weren't. That's why I say they do it, many of them, I'm sure, very subconsciously. They don't say, "Hey he didn't" . . . it's just that that's their club. That's about as simple as I can put it. That's why I say I go to reunions, and I'm sure I'm accepted as one of the guys, but I don't feel . . . I feel like . . . "You shouldn't really be in this club." That's all. It's hard to explain.

Whitaker

I don't think there was ever any resentment. In my life after the Marine Corps I never made any distinction between people who were in combat or not in combat, or went overseas or didn't go overseas. I fully realize that this is the luck of the draw . . . how sometimes it was alphabetical, so whether that has ever meant a thing to me. . . . If a guy was in an artillery outfit, I don't care; he was there. He was in the Marine Corps. He's a Marine. If he went through boot camp, that's enough for me. I don't need to know any more about him. You know, if he was in combat and happened to be in my platoon, then we can drink a beer together and tell about the day we blew up the mess hall or something.

Joralemon

Oh yeah . . . extremely prevalent, extremely prevalent. The Marines have a long history of pride and tradition and so forth. The one thing they stress all the time, starting with boot camp, is: "You're the best; you're the elite. No one else can do anything like Marines can do, and have done in the past, and you can do." It's a built-in *esprit de corps*. The way to satisfy all that, too, is to downgrade or make fun or whatever of the other forces, particularly the Army. I mean, that's to the extreme. I can think of some of the things that went on. You look at it now and say, "My God, the names we called them." That was particularly prevalent when we were in the north and we were assigned to go south, and the Twenty-seventh was relieved on the southern line because they couldn't do anything. They came up, and they were coming up as we were going back down. We were up there. We had already secured the north. Here we are heading south. They are going up there as if they expected to fight the enemy. They are out in the fields, cautiously looking around with their rifles at the ready, and all that stuff. We were just howling and, my God, calling them all kinds of things. Most polite was probably "dogface." That was one of the favorite things that you would yell at an Army . . . at soldiers. "All doggies eat shit out of rusty mess gear and bark at the moon." That's what I remember.

Sams

The only relationship I had with the Army is, down at Guadalcanal they had a pretty good supply depot, and we'd steal anything we could from it. If you can call that a relationship. Steal anything from the Army. The Army was open territory.

I stole a whole truckload at Guam. Two hundred and twenty-eight cases. [I] put it on the ship. We put it on the LST going to China. We drank beer, and until it ran out, sat up at night and played pinochle, drinking beer. We set every one of the bottles back in that box, in that case, and threw that thing over the side. An officer, when he came to our reunion in Washington or Atlanta, one or the other, he said, "Sams, I want you to tell me something. What was it that you all were drinking off that LST?" He said, "We tried to catch you all, whatever you were doing, and we could not." I said we were just drinking a little beer.

First got to steal it down off Guadalcanal. We would be out on the firing range, on maneuvers, working our behinds off all day, and come in late that afternoon. The Sergeant Major called and said, "Go get Sams and two or three more sergeants. They've got working detail. Got to go down to the dock and unload ships for the Army." Oh Lord, we'd be mad, naturally. So Foster, Paul Foster, and I worked up this little deal. Sometimes I would have to go and take a working party to unload the ships, and he wouldn't have to go . . . or vice versa, he'd have to go and I wouldn't have to go. We got us a hundred feet of telephone wire.

How we would have to unload the ship . . . an NCO would ride this DWUK out to the ship. The ship was out there a quarter of a mile, out there in the bay where they were off the shore. They let this net down over the side of the ship and unload. This cargo net . . . and put the whole thing in this DWUK. They would go back to the beach. At the beach, there would be floodlights and everything Army. They'd jump on there with their guns, all ready to shoot you. They'd take the beer off to their warehouses or wherever they took it. We didn't get any. What we would do is take this piece of telephone wire, about a hundred feet long. Just with that DWUK, on the way in from out there in the dark, we would tie wire around two cases of the beer. Just before we got up to the shore, in those spotlights, throw that beer over the side and hold on to that wire. When the DWUK got up there on that dirt, throw that wire off on the side there. Whoever the other one . . . if it was me throwing it off or Paul . . . he'd be out there, he'd be watching. He'd walked by and we had a loop in there in that wire. Walk by and hook your foot in the end of that loop and walk on down there, out of the light, and reel those two cases of beer in. We'd have a truck stashed up there, and we could get a pretty good haul in a night. We could get fifteen, twenty cases on a night that way. Anything you could steal from the Army that was fair game.

When the war was over we were on Guam, as everybody knows. Shepherd made that famous speech about "I'll see you and China." We got our guns cleaned up and loaded . . . we did-n't load them . . . hooked from our trucks on the proper day. Go down to the loading place on the beach down there. Got our trucks in there. All stashed down and dogged down chains and everything. Got assigned our quarters . . . we were assigned our quarters. Then two more sergeants got assigned to the chiefs' quarters of the LST. . . . The chiefs' quarters were the forward compartment quarters. It had six bunks in it, maybe eight. There were, say, four chiefs in there. They put us in there to fill up those other bunks. We hadn't got China-bound good, that night it got dark. Break out the working parties. We had to get down in that hold and unload your truck and unhook your gun. At night in the hold of that damn ship, you understand me . . . mad! Got to go unload beer for the Army on Guam . . .

In the process, we hauled beer until about midnight to the Army depot. I found out what their pattern was and asked a few questions. They took the serial number of my truck every time it left the dock down there where they loaded it with beer. They put 229 cases, my men stacking 'em, and we'd go to the Army depot and unload it. They take the serial number of my

truck down when we left the dock, they read the serial number
down when we got to the depot. I found out that they tallied . . .
the next day at twelve o'clock they tallied how many times it left
the dock and how many times it got to the depot. I knew the
next day at twelve o'clock we were supposed to be on the high
sea.

So we got a load, and I told Shalier, "Head to the ship."
"What!?" "I told you, head for the ship." "Man, I don't know
what you're going to do Sergeant, but you're going to get us all
in the jailhouse . . . the brig!" I said, "Head to the ship." We
went up the ramp and down in the hold of that ship there . . .
artillery down there, light scattered around. I went up the ladder . . . it's called a ladder on a ship.

I had met this chief bosuns mate on the ship, named
Pearson. He had been in the Navy a long time. He had been
busted up and down the ladder, no telling how many times. He
was lying in the bunk in there, in the same quarters I was
assigned. I shook him, woke him up . . . I said, "Pearson," I met
him when I got in there, "I got some beer out here, where can
we stash it?" He said, "Just slide it under your bunk." He said,
"Just slide it under your bunk; it will be all right under there
tonight." I said, "Pearson, I have 228 cases." He said, "God
Almighty!" He came up out of there. We went . . . right in forward of that there were ammunition locker, twenty-millimeter
ammunition locker . . . had the rounds for the guns . . . twenty-
millimeter shells in that thing. We carried them things up and
threw them over the side, to make room for the beer. We put
those 228 cases of beer in that forward ammunition locker on
that thing, threw that ammunition over side. We weren't going
to need it; the war was over. What we need all that ammunition
for? Threw it over the side. He had a big old lock, that big,
(Indicates something about the size of a softball) locked on the
door there. He was the only one I ever knew had a key
to it.

The chief steward was in the same place. In the afternoon
we'd get enough of that beer . . . we'd stack a garbage, a clean
GI garbage can, and fill it full of beer and put it in the cooler
back in the galley, and get it cool. At night, everybody secured,

we were up there playing poker, I mean playing pinochle, drinking beer. We'd throw all the empties over the side . . . don't never leave none around. We would be about used up in that chow line. Captain Abney and them never could figure it out. We drank that beer going to China.

One Saturday morning . . . you know the Navy is going to have an inspection every Saturday. They had an inspection coming up. We all got up too. Pearson had been drinking on the beer with us quite often, real regular. He was in on the pinochle playing and the beer drinking and what have you. The inspection party came through . . . see your passageway wasn't as big as nothing, and there was an inspection party. I guess the Captain . . . I don't know who it was; there would be two or three more and then Pearson. He was the chief bosuns mate. I thought that morning, "God Dang, we're in trouble now." They was looking all everywhere, under this and that, opening up doors and what have you. They got to that ammunition locker . . . see he had one bulk, one door, between them and the beer. It was just like that. Got there and there was that big old lock on that door. That captain of the ship, or the exec or somebody, the head man anyway, said, "Bosuns Mate, come unlock the lock here." Here comes Pearson back down the line. There were four or five between him and Pearson. He comes 'round . . . he had a wad of keys on his belt, that big around. (Indicates the size of a fist.) He tried this key; he'd try that key; he knew which key it was all the time. (Laughs) He never could find the right key. Pearson knew exactly where the key was. He wasn't going to try that one, every one but that one. Sure did . . . Captain Abney wasn't believing that when I told him how we did that. You had to do something. Good God. You had to do something; you'd go wacky.

Robert Luckey: Commanding Officer, Fifteenth Marines

[Luckey had been involved on Guadalcanal and in operations on Cape Glouster. He served as director of the artillery school at Quantico. Ordered back overseas in 1944, he assisted in preparing the Fifteenth for Okinawa. Luckey describes how professional fraternity can cross military branches and negate military rivalries. The Twenty-seventh, a division that all others hold in contempt, had a good relationship with the Fifteenth.]

> Those guys [the Twenty-seventh] left their artillery down south, and when the Sixth Division [got] down there [they] wanted my operational control. They [the Army] were commanded by a brigadier general. The Army division artillery officer was a brigadier general. And this guy moved into my CP [command post] and couldn't have been nicer than anybody I ever knew. He said, "I'm not here to bother you. You just take my artillery and shoot it the way you want." . . . We all spoke the same language.[14]

Chaisson

> The Tenth Army was made up of us, and we seemed to be the dominant group because there may have been more of us as a unit than, say, the Ninety-sixth Army or the Seventy-seventh or the Seventh . . . but they were great units, great army units. The only unit that was a failure on Okinawa was the Twenty-seventh Division. They were a division out of . . . New York. Politicians, ya know, and what do you call the local military . . . National Guard? They were National Guard. All their officers were politicians and they got the hell knocked out of them everywhere they went. They finally ended up as our occupying group in the north end of the island . . . where the war ended. That's where they were. But they took some pretty bad hits as they moved south with the Army and the Marines, and they got caught over on the . . . west side of the island. They got just beat to hell. The Japs were there for them. We didn't think very much of the Twenty-seventh Army Division, and neither did the Twenty-seventh Army Division think very much of themselves.

Miller

> I thought they [Army] were shitty, and they did exactly what we expected of them. There was an outfit called the Twenty-

seventh Army Division. They were worthless, less than worth-less. No, they were [catcalling at] us. They were doing stuff like this, (Mimicks using a movie camera) doing stuff like this, tak-ing our picture . . . one guy offered to shoot a couple.

THE BOMB

I just knew we were scheduled to hit the main island of Honshu in
January of 1946. So, I knew the date of my death.

—James White

The Sixth Marine Division's G-3 Periodic Report, prepared by Lieutenant Colonel Victor H. Krulak on June 21, 1945, stated, "After 82 days on the island, the Division is fatigued and depleted in Pers.[personnel] . . . its offensive capabilities are estimated as follows: 4th Mar (Reinf.), 29th Mar (Reinf.), and Sixth Engr Bn, 60%. The 22nd, 61%, the Sixth Tank Bn. 66%, and the remainder of the Division were at 71%." Krulak also reported that morale was high and that "Opns [Operations] for the day resulted in destruction of the last organized resistance in the Sixth Div. Z [zone] of action."[1] The campaign was over. The Sixth had been mauled and depleted, and Operation Iceberg was far more costly in time and life than anyone had imagined. The Tenth Army continued mopping up on the island and regained their strength. Units participated in periodic firefights and the capture of Japanese infiltrators until they boarded ships the first week in July. Many veterans mentioned that the rough seas on the weeklong trip made them as fearful as any artillery barrage.[2] As the exhausted Division arrived on Guam and bivouacked in a partially prepared camp, rumors were rampant regarding where the Sixth would go next.

Most veterans remember being exhausted, sick, and skinny, and that a bed seemed almost too much to expect. They remember moments of intense relief as buddies whom they had carried off on ponchos in April, May, and

June rejoined them in their camps. They rested and recovered, played ball, and read mail. Eventually they began to realize that their job was not finished. The next landing was even more costly, and even more horrific than Okinawa or Iwo Jima. For some, this realization began when they were put on details burning the sea bags of their fallen comrades from Okinawa. For others, it was the sight of so many wounded troops. Those who two or three years earlier would have returned home after injuries were now merely patched up. For some there was a sense of doom, for others numbness and a fatalistic live-for-the-day attitude. Whatever their personal feelings, they began loading ships and cleaning their equipment. They were veterans now. They understood what was to come.

Pacific strategy had been set for two years. The objective was clearly stated in a memorandum by the Joint Chiefs of Staff in May 1943. It called for unconditional surrender and stated, "This objective may require the invasion of Japan."[3] Okinawa had been the first strike in this strategy. On L+2, Gen. Douglas MacArthur began detailed planning for the invasion of Kyushu, as directed by the Joint Chiefs of Staff.[4] The final reconsideration of the plan occurred in conferences at the White House in June 1945. Okinawa was winding down; Sugar Loaf was in the past and was merely a set of statistics to the men in Washington.[5] On June 18, the day of General Buckner's death on Okinawa, President Truman gave his final approval for Operation Olympic—the invasion of southern Japan. The invasion began on November 1, 1945, in an area known as Kyushu.[6] Operation Coronet, the invasion of Honshu, followed Olympic in March 1946. Operation Downfall eventually defeated Japan, and on July 26, 1945, the Potsdam Proclamation was issued. It called for Japan to "surrender unconditionally or face total destruction."[7]

In May 1945, General Douglas MacArthur formulated his plan, and subordinate commanders filled in the details and arrived at staggering projections. MacArthur's staff's statistics were progressively modified, always upward, and he did not assume that this two-phase operation would necessarily lead to the complete capitulation of Japan.[8] The Third and Fifth Fleet supported Olympic. The ground element was the Sixth Army, consisting of four corps controlling three divisions each. Two more divisions followed and three were held in reserve. The projected operation commitments were 766,700 troops, 134,000 vehicles, and 1,470,930 tons of materiel for the initial invasions. CINCPAC (commander in chief, Pacific Operations Area) also projected that 1,315 major amphibious vehicles would be needed, and that once a base could be established it would number forty air groups and approximately 2,794 aircraft.[9] The majority of the fighting force was U.S. units; however, the British Commonwealth contributed British, Canadian, and Australian Divisions, as well as the British Pacific Fleet and air squadrons.[10] Operation Olympic was the opening act; Operation Coronet would dwarf it in comparison.

Operation Olympic allowed the Allies to establish airfields and bases, and to give the troops who had fought in Europe time to be transferred to the Pacific. Then Operation Coronet began in March 1946.[11] The assault forces were the Eighth and Tenth Armies comprising fourteen divisions, three of which were Marine divisions. The First Army, made up of ten more divisions, would follow. The commitments projected for Operation Coronet were 1,026,000 personnel, 190,000 vehicles, 2,640,000 tons of materiel, and fifty air groups totaling 3,328 planes. Seven of the divisions that partook in the invasion of Japan had fought on Okinawa.[12]

If the logistics and personnel seem staggering for the invasion of Japan, the projected loss of life is numbing. With a projected invasion force of 766,000 for Olympic and 1,026,000 for Coronet, the statistics were planned around ninety-day campaigns. MacArthur's command staff projected calamitous battle casualties, minus the Navy, but including some air and ground elements: At fifteen days into the campaign, 9,727; thirty days in, 22,576; sixty days, 55,906; and 124,935 at the ninety-day mark.[13] MacArthur had been extremely accurate at projecting casualties in previous campaigns. He made dire predictions in the spring of 1945 when he estimated that in the invasions of Kyushu and Honshu alone there would be more than one million Allied casualties.[14] The final victory, the success of Operation Downfall, might surpass all past U.S. casualties in both theaters of the war to date. Military planners believed that to force a Japanese surrender by land-combat attrition would require a full year.[15] For the Marine Corps, the future was appalling: "The estimate for U.S. Marine casualties in the attack force was nearly one hundred percent."[16] Veterans recall hearing after the war that, in many of the war plans, the Marine Corps eventually stopped being mentioned. The Marine Corps, according to the estimations, would have ceased to exist as it had previously been known. It was believed that "fifteen percent of all able bodied men alive [at the time] would have been killed or wounded invading Japan."[17]

The Japanese were also planning and calculating. Although some argued that the Japanese calculations were too low, even the Japanese officers thought it was "not unreasonable to expect to be able to destroy thirty to fifty percent of the invasion forces."[18] With Ketsu-Go, their defense plan, in place, the Japanese were in position to suffer and inflict tremendous casualties.

On June 28, 1945, Tokyo radio discussed the loss of Okinawa: "The U.S. Army is sure to attack and indeed has the power to do so. The sooner the enemy comes the better for us, for our battle array is complete."[19] The Japanese had been preparing for quite some time, although this was cloaked in propaganda. Troops were called home from Manchuria, the kamikaze pilots continued to ready themselves, frogmen prepared underwater mines for Japanese harbors, and others prepared themselves to become human bombs who would deliver explosives to the U.S. fleet.

In March 1945, Japan began genuine preparations. Public Law Number 30 was enacted. It mobilized all civilians in the coastal areas. School was suspended and children were mobilized for production and other tasks. The Cabinet ordered the formation of the Patriotic Citizens Fighting Corp to protect Japan.[20] "Tokyo police referred to this as the final people's movement."[21] By July, the Japanese propaganda machine was broadcasting declarations of total mobilization. "There are no civilians in Japan."[22] Twenty-eight million Japanese became part of the fighting force. They were trained in beach defense and guerrilla warfare. Civilians were armed with conventional modern weapons as well as swords, long bows, and bamboo spears.[23] Since most of the men were gone, "busily killing women and children in other countries, including 100,000 civilians in Manila," argues W. Pat Hitchcock, a former POW in his book *Forty Months of Hell,*[24] the final defense would, to a great degree, fall to women and children. It was next to impossible for U.S. troops to distinguish between civilians and military personnel because that line had been erased. Had the invasion been necessary, military planners estimated that twenty million Japanese would have died.[25]

In projecting casualty rates, citizens and prisoners of war need to be considered as well. It was already, at least in part, understood how Japanese treated civilians. Asians—the Korean "comfort women" (who were forced into prostitution by and for the Japanese military) and the Chinese, in particular—had suffered horribly from Japanese aggression. Furthermore, bacterial warfare and poison gas were already used and available in the Japanese arsenal. It is estimated that the Japanese held 350,000 POWs by the end of the war, 102,000 of which were Allies.[26] These prisoners continued to die and suffer until they could be liberated. Nearly to a man, Allied POWs believed they would be killed if the Japanese homeland were invaded. The United States already had evidence that this would be the case.[27] After the fall of Okinawa, Field Marshall Count Hisaichi Terauchi issued an order that the moment the enemy invaded his Southeast Asia Theater, prison camp officials were to execute all captives.

In projecting the loss of life that Downfall would cause, the U.S. military had many assets and factors to assess. The Americans had broken the Japanese code with a project known as Magic. This gave planners not only access to information regarding the Japanese order of battle, but also insight into the Japanese military mindset. Another factor that had to be considered was that the Soviets had promised to enter the war. Whether this would have exacerbated the heavy casualties or whether their entry could have forced the Japanese capitulation sooner is unclear, but it would have added another element to the situation.[28] The planners of Operation Downfall also had the example of Okinawa to help inform them. The ratio of Japanese combat deaths to American was more than ten to one on Okinawa.[29] The estimated 150,000 Okinawans who died during the campaign were proof of how the Japanese would sacrifice civilians. It showed how thoroughly convincing Japanese propaganda had been, and its message was even more strident

to the populace of the mainland. The number of Japanese citizen suicides was staggering. As well, the terrain on Okinawa was, up to that
point, the most similar to the mainland of Japan in the island hopping
campaign. Places such as Yae-Dake and Sugar Loaf had proved how
costly that similarity could be. General Buckner referred to the fighting
on Okinawa as "Prairie Dog Warfare." It was a battle fought yards and
inches at a time.[30] Okinawa had also proved the Japanese military's
determination to fight to the last soldier, and their code of Bushido
encouraged them to take as many of their enemy with them as they
could. This is the information that President Harry Truman had available to him in the spring of 1945. Gen. George C. Marshall explained
later that when they made the decision to drop the bomb, "We had just
been through the bitter experience of Okinawa."[31]

Operation Downfall never began. An alternative was available and
President Truman chose to use it. On August 6, 1945, at 8:16 a.m., the
first atomic bomb was dropped on Hiroshima. Truman, who was
aboard the USS *Augusta* recalled, "I was greatly moved . . . and then said
to a group of sailors around me, 'This is the greatest thing in history. It's
time for us to get home.'"[32] On August 9, 1945 the second bomb was
dropped on Nagasaki. The war was over shortly after. Later, Truman
often recalled that after making the decision he went to bed and slept
soundly. He also wrote at the time, "It seems to be the most terrible thing
ever discovered, but it can be useful."[33] He continued to feel that way.
Harry Truman wrote in a letter to James Cates in January of 1953,
"Dropping the bombs ended the war, it saved lives."[34] Five days after
Nagasaki the emperor, despite the objections of military leaders and
advisors, decided to surrender.

Critics of Truman's use of the bombs attribute his decision to many
things, including U.S. fear of the Soviets and racism. These fears, so
prevalent at the time, cannot be discounted, but allowing them full credit would be an oversimplification. The argument that casualty projections were grossly skewed seems to be used by those on both sides of the
issue. Civilian casualties are often mentioned in discussions about
whether the bomb should have been used or not. The incendiary bombs
that were dropped on Tokyo or Dresden are seldom mentioned with the

same degree of horror—nor is Nanking mentioned often enough in this context. The Japanese citizens, as their preparations in the spring of 1945 reflect, had stopped perceiving themselves as civilians. The Allies dropped 720,000 leaflets warning the Japanese to evacuate before the bomb was dropped on Hiroshima. Few did.[35] The Chinese citizens in Japanese research facilities, who were used in experiments, had no such option. The most common argument is that the Allies only needed to drop one bomb to effectively end the war. This is despite the fact that between the first bomb on Hiroshima and the second on Nagasaki, the Japanese sank ships and submarines and continued to execute prisoners of war.[36]

Paul Fussell argues in *Thank God for the Bomb and Other Essays* that, "Understanding the past requires pretending that you don't know the present. It requires feeling its own pressure on your pulses without any *ex post facto* illumination."[37] Jim White in *Point of the Spear* concurs: "With the wisdom of hindsight those people say that Japan was already suing for peace. The recollection of history of these revisionists is convenient for supporting their contention."[38] Perhaps to understand the decision one had to have survived Normandy or Iwo Jima or Okinawa. Some argue, "The Japanese themselves have called the ending of the war a form of merciful euthanasia."[39]

The troops who served on the front lines in World War II have few questions regarding the use of the atomic bombs on Japan: They believe the bombs saved their lives. As summarized in *The Soldiers Tale,* "The immediate effect of the bomb on the story of the Pacific war was obvious and apparent. Suddenly and unexpectedly the war was simply called off. There would be no invasion of Japan, no great conclusive battle, no victory won by hard fighting."[40] Perhaps, then, the conclusive battle was Okinawa.

The Marines of the Sixth, like other World War II veterans, feel very strongly about the decision to drop the atomic bomb. It ended the war and lessened casualties. They feel just as strongly about postwar attempts to vilify that decision. Nothing brought their concerns more in focus than the controversy over displaying the Enola Gay at the Air and Space Museum, which resulted in its eventual removal from the institution. John McCormick, author and veteran of the Fourth Marine Regiment, wrote a letter to the Smithsonian in March 1995, expressing his frustration. He reminded modern historians how thankful he and his contemporaries were for the bomb, how thankful that they were not forced to kill millions of Japanese civilians and that by ending the war, countless Japanese citizens had the "doors to freedom opened."[41] He reminded these guardians of history that a high cost was paid for their right to retrospectively criticize. "When you agonize over the consequences [of the bomb] talk to some veterans who are horribly mangled." McCormick concludes, "You need not strain your pretty principles to render me euphoric. For fifty years, I have felt just fine about the way America won the war in the Pacific. I feel proud to have been a Marine armed with a Browning automatic rifle and in the front ranks of a great crusade. Because of the atomic bomb, I was given a chance to see my children and grandchildren grow and prosper."[42]

The Sixth Division Marines on Guam knew nothing about the life altering events on mainland Japan. They were still hoping for "the Golden Gate in '48," if they weren't killed or badly wounded before then. They were preparing for the fight of their lives. When the first word reached them of this strange new bomb, it was simply beyond comprehension. The announcement of the Japanese surrender came over the radio at about 10 p.m., and many of the Marines had already gone to bed.[43] When they heard the news they celebrated with a degree of incredulity. Even after the surrender, Bill Sams wrote home warning his family not to put much store in the Japanese giving up.[44] The Fourth Marine Regiment was whisked from Guam to be involved in the surrender in Tokyo Bay on September 2, 1945 aboard the USS *Missouri*. In General MacArthur's speech of that day, he talked about young men who were on their way home to "take up the challenges of the future."[45]

This did not happen immediately for the Marines of the Sixth. Several weeks after the surrender, as men adjusted to life without evening blackouts and with evening alcohol, they began to adjust to the idea that they would be going home. They began to plan again for a future. Much to their dismay, and in some cases anger, instead they were ordered to China to repatriate the Japanese and fight the Chinese communists. On the way they endured a typhoon that destroyed more boats than the kamikazes had off of Okinawa. They learned to act like young men again and slowly they began to go home. On April 1, 1946, a year after the invasion of Okinawa, the Sixth Marine Division was redesignated as the Third Marine Corps. General MacArthur concluded his speech on the USS *Missouri* by giving this guidance to his audience and the world: "Their spiritual strength and power has brought us through to victory. They are homeward bound. Take care of them."[46]

Buchter

We were in preparation for the invasion of Japan. We were resting up, getting refitted, getting new clothes, getting new gear, all the way through. There were entertainers there. The food was getting better, [we were] putting on weight . . . nice bases. We knew it wouldn't be too long until we probably would invade Japan. Of course, we realized . . . I guess most of us realized . . . that that would probably be our last ride. They weren't going to make it very easy for us. So dropping the bomb . . . we felt better about that, and of course, in a few days, the surrender came, and then a little later the formal surrender.

Pierce

I did have an incident which I may have mentioned. They told us to bring trucks to the Quonset hut one day. We loaded all the sea bags onto the truck. We thought we were going down to the pier with these sea bags. Instead, we went up into the Guam hills and threw them into the fire. I would say we made two trips that day. On each truck . . . on my truck would be hundreds of sea bags, and on the next truck the same. After we stopped for lunch we cut them open with K-bar knives, and we'd grab a pair of shoes or whatever we'd want. There were a lot of personal things in there . . . photos and blankets, envelopes. The Marine Corps burned them all. They were all dead men's sea bags. The Marine Corps couldn't afford to go through them. The cheapest way is to burn them . . . so they did.

White, J.

I remember being on Guam and being in a shower and we were all naked, of course. So this old boy, one I remember he was very muscular, and he had prominent back muscles. A bullet had gone through his right back muscle and his left back muscle and he had four holes. All the scars were pink and ridged, and all the people with all kinds of scars.

DeMeis

Then the word came that we had to go down to a work party. We went down to the piers and we start loading these two ships. I think one was the *Ozark* and the other was the *Pope*. Those were the ships that we'd wind up sailing on in Task Force Thirty-One to Japan.

[DeMeis tells about the repatriation of Japan and accepting surrenders. The Marines found cases of Axis carbines on the mainland, and they uncovered caves and suicide boats. They were all too aware that these would have been used against the Allies had a landing been necessary.]

This one officer came up, and he had riding shoes. He was all squared away with his white collar turned down, had a nice leather belt, and he was carrying a saber. He put down the pistol and he was ready to turn around to walk away. Stormy said, "The saber." He stopped; he was ready to turn. I pointed to the, ya know, one of those samurai jobs. I said, "The Captain said your saber." He gave us both a dirty look. He didn't even go for his buckle, to unbuckle it." I had a carbine; I just jammed the bolt back and put a round in the chamber. Stormy told me, "We will have none of that." I don't know if he understood or not, but next thing he unbuckled his belt and just made it fall off his hip. He didn't bow; he backed away, then he turned and walked away. Defiant to the end. I would have cracked him in the mouth if I could.

Rittenbury

I think anyone who's ever been in combat and faced the conditions we did loses a little bit of his humanity. We actually get to the place that we are reacting instinctively without thinking, doing things that we never thought of doing as a civilian. Anything less than that I don't suppose would have been sufficient to secure the island.

The Japanese would have fought to the last man. We found that out at Okinawa, and I've always believed the Okinawan campaign was what influenced Harry Truman to drop the two atomic bombs. The Japanese fought with such tenacity and fierceness at Okinawa that the President was convinced that should we invade Japan, which was scheduled for November of 1945, that every man woman and child would be armed with a spear or with something. The Japanese were sworn to fight to the death, and the end result would have been that the war could have lasted fifteen more years and fifteen million more deaths.

Whitaker

You asked about heroes. Harry Truman is my hero. As big as anyone else . . . he had a lot of guts, and he pulled it off, and he did the right thing. If it had to be done over again, I would only wish that this country was being led by a man like Truman.

McKinney

It was announced we had dropped an atomic bomb on Hiroshima and everybody was trying to figure how big was that damn bomb? To kill all that number of people. For the next two days, rumors really flew. Most of us said, "I'd like to see that damn airplane."

Honis

The day before we were emptying all the sea bags of all the casualties, mainly the ones that were killed. Then the next day we heard about the bomb. It's funny . . . we knew . . . we concluded it was an atom smasher. It's funny we had heard that term before. We knew anything that powerful could not be a . . . it had to be something really sophisticated.

Niland

Happiest day of my life. I was at the outdoor movie watching *Meet Me in Saint Louis* with Judy Garland, and we were drinking 3.2 beer. We were all feeling pretty good. The word came that some kind of strange bomb had been dropped on Hiroshima and Nagasaki. I was so happy then. I knew I was a dead man. I knew we were invading Japan. They had released me from the hospital. They released people with holes in their heads, holes in the bellies, their chest. Ordinarily they would have been sent home, but they didn't have enough to do this, so they sent us all back to our units. It must be like being a prisoner on death row. I knew I was dead, because there was no way. All we were thinking was, "By God, before they get us we're going to get plenty of them." That's just how we were thinking. It was desperate time. When they dropped the bomb, it was like getting a new life. I couldn't believe it. Every day I have said a prayer for Harry Truman.

Wanamaker

We were actually loading our ships for our attack. We had them pretty well loaded. When the bomb dropped, we were pretty well sure that we were going to have to go to Japan but when they surrendered, they sent us to China.

Sams

That was one of the days when the war was over. How many days later . . . when they signed the thing [the surrender] in Tokyo Bay. You know what yours truly was doing? He was sergeant of the guard, division sergeant of the guard. Signed in that day. Wasn't much to sergeant of the guard. Our procedures weren't the greatest in the world. I had a tent. When you were sergeant of the guard, you were there for twenty-four hours. Corporal of the guard was over here, a guard there, and what have you. About three o'clock in the afternoon . . . the chaplain's tent was right there next door, I believe. I didn't know he was. He walked into my tent and said, "Sergeant, do you take a drink?" I said, "I have been known to, but I haven't had one in quite a while." He said, "I brought [this] with me from San Francisco for just this occasion. Will you join me?" I said, "I'd be delighted." So the chaplain and I drank vodka. It was about 117 degrees on Guam, so half a bottle (Indicates a bottle size), no chaser, no nothing in the middle of the afternoon. I had to retrieve the colors. I did get me some men. The flagpole was out in front. I got out and gave enough commands to bring it down. They got it down and I could not remember the command to proceed from there. I told 'em, "Take care of it boys," and they folded the flag. (Goes through the motions of folding a flag.) So, I was sergeant of the guard, division sergeant of the guard.

McConville

Believe it or not, we went into Naha Harbor. We were on a LST heading for China, Tsingtao. We were supposed to stay there three days, but there was a typhoon heading up through the Formosa Straits. We were advised to weigh anchor and get the hell out, so we rode that thing out. We lost three destroyers in the Formosa Straits; it was so severe. We were aboard the LSTs and it's a flat bottom boat, right. We'd ride these big waves, and it would come up out of the water and whack. You would feel the whole thing shudder.

McKnight

[Many men talk about this typhoon, during which they would have invaded Japan had the war not ended.]

As far as the bomb, an announcement came over the PA [public announcement] at the movie as part of the news broadcast that a

special destructive bomb was dropped. Nothing else. We specu-
lated, but no more announcements. Later we were loading the
ships for the invasion of Japan when all the ships in the harbor
blew their horns and tooted. Then the PA announced that the
war was over. All Marines were given a case of beer at the "Slop
Chute" tent. Jim Reeder (wounded at Mount Yae-Dake) and I,
not being drinkers, decided to drink our case of warm beer.
After about fourteen beers, he said, "McKnight, you knuckle-
head, get up off your butt out of that puddle and drink your
beer." It seems the regular afternoon rainstorm caused some
water to run into the tent and produced a puddle. I looked down
and sure enough, I was setting in it. I said, "I think I have had it;
let's go back to our tent." He agreed and we staggered back and
flopped down on our bunks and passed out.

Next morning I heard him groan. I looked over and saw
that he didn't get under his mosquito netting. His face was
puffed up like a pumpkin, and his hands were swollen like boxing gloves. I started to laugh, but it hurt. I was the same way. We
both staggered to the showers and sat under the water, clothes
and all. Took two days to feel good again. After we went to
China, we had a report from the Marines who went to Japan that
we would have had massive losses trying to invade. Hooray for
Paul Tibbets. He saved our lives, and many of the Japanese civilians. I got to meet Paul Tibbets several years ago. He only lives
several blocks from us here in Columbus. He is gone a lot on
speaking tours. He autographed my copy of *Enola Gay*. I personally thanked him for ending the war, since the invasion was
scheduled for November. He told us another couple talked to
him in Indianapolis and the wife personally thanked him, as her
husband was a prisoner of war. He and a group were digging
their own graves when the war ended. Paul Tibbets is still in
good physical shape.[47]

Long

Our LST [landing ship, transport] was about halfway between
Guam and Pearl Harbor when a sailor came over to me while I
was sitting on deck, and in great excitement he asked, "Hey

CAST OF CHARACTERS

Nils Andersen (H&S/29) was from Brooklyn. He enlisted in 1943, right before his seventeenth birthday. Okinawa was his only military engagement. He became an artist in New York. A tortured soul, he-suffered from Post Traumatic Stress Disorder, and was tragically mugged and killed in New York City soon after completing the tape used in this work.

Tom Baird (B/1/22) was from Jellico, Tennessee. He enlisted in 1942 at the age of seventeen. He resides in Tennessee.

Donald Brining (H/3/29 [6th Med.]) was drafted in 1943. He was from Bradford, Ohio. He was selected to be a Corpsman and went to Great Lakes for naval boot camp, and then to Balboa hospital for medical training. He became a farmer after the war.

Norris Buchter (H&S/29) had been delivering ice and working on fishing boats when he enlisted. Okinawa was his first landing. He worked for the phone company and now resides in Florida, where he is the Marine Corps League President for his chapter.

Richard Bush received the Medal of Honor for his actions on Mt. Yae-Dake. He was the last surviving MOH of the Sixth Marine Division: he died in 2005.

George Carne (6th Tank Bn.-CC) was born in Nebraska. He had completed four years of college and was twenty-two when he enlisted in 1943. He now resides in Reno.

James Chaisson (G/2/22), who was born in Canada, was married and a thirty-four-year-old PFC when he landed on Okinawa. He had already proved he was above the ordinary. He organized boxing aboard ship and ran the ship's newspaper en route to Guadalcanal. He was then chosen to be part of the Underwater Demolition Team that would be an advance party prior to the invasion. He received the Navy Cross and Bronze Star for his actions during Operation Iceberg. He founded his own company after the war and was very successful, eventually settling in Georgia. He died in 2001.

James Day (Wpns/22) was from Saint Louis, Illinois. He had participated in combat in the Marshall Islands and on Guam. As a nineteen-year-old corporal on Okinawa his actions would result in his receiving the Medal of Honor. The corporal would attain the rank of Major General. He died in 1999.

Paolo (Paulie) DeMeis (K/3/4/&22) was from Brooklyn, New York. He was given the choice of a state juvenile facility or joining the military. Recruiters often waited in the back of courtrooms in those days. He joined the Marines at fifteen and spent forty-one months overseas. He returned at nineteen and had been part of three major campaigns with the Fourth Marines. He was known as the "Bazooka Kid." Now lives in California where he often speaks at schools and to marines about his World War II experiences.

John (Jack) Dornan (F/Wpns/2/4), one of my many e-mail contacts, remained in the service and served in Korea. He now lives in Texas.

Joe Drago (I/3/22), one of my e-mail contacts, was from Boston. Okinawa was his only campaign. He was wounded on Sugar Loaf.

Bob Everett (A/3/22), one of my e-mail and snail mail contacts, served and was wounded on Saipan and received the Bronze Star for action on Okinawa. He now lives in Indiana.

John (Jack) Fitzgerald (E/2/22), a lieutenant, joined the Twenty-second on Guam. By Okinawa, he was considered "an old salt." He had been an athlete in college. He would be a teacher and administer. He now divides his time between Chicago and Arizona.

Edward (Buzzy) Fox (G/2/29) was a self-professed "jock" and had played sports for the marines. He was one of the many who were transferred to the front in 1944–1945. He was a replacement on Okinawa. He was instrumental in the completion of the monument on Okinawa honoring Japanese, Okinawans, and Americans.

Ray Gillespie (K/3/22) spent much of his last year trying to find a little girl who haunted him. He contacted Japanese, Okinawans, and Americans but died unrewarded. His wounds would take years to heal and would always bother him. He was a teacher and author. He died in 1999.

Jack Hoag (6th JASCO) was from California and worked for the phone company. One of the early men to enlisted during the furor after Pearl Harbor; he left the States with the Third Division in December 1942. He would return home in November 1945 and return to the phone company. Until recently, he was the Sixth Marine Association's Historian.

Don Honis (I/3/29) had two older brothers—one who landed at Normandy, one on Iwo Jima. As the youngest child, his parents had not wanted him to join the Marine Corps. He was short and so thin that he could not pass the physical. The recruiter had him go across the street and eat as many bananas as he could hold, a common practice. When he returned, he weighed enough. He now lives in New York.

Pete Howell (F/2/29) was from Ohio. Okinawa was his first campaign. He returned to Ohio and attended Kent State. He is a past president of the Sixth Marine Division Association.

Jack Jackson (Wpns/7/1)

Thomas Jones (HQ/2/22) had joined the Marine Corps in 1942. Love Day would be his fourth landing. By this time he was one of the most senior lieutenants and was the battalion liaison officer. He rose to the rank of colonel. On his eightieth birthday in 2000, he ran eighty miles in consecutive days to commemorate the event.

DeWitt Joralemon (H&S/3/15) came from the Bronx. He had graduated from high school early and had spent some time in college. He had already served in the Merchant Marines by the time he enlisted. He was the chairman of the Sixth Quantico Memorial Project. He has held various other positions including editor of the Association newsletter and resides in Rhode Island and Florida.

Tim Joyner (HQ/2/29) is one of my e-mail sources and is an author and professor.

Navy Cross recipient Harry Karizan and this photograph are mentioned in one of the stories by Jack Fitzgerald. The unusual angle of his helmet was a badge of honor, a sign of "saltiness," and a form adopted by G-22 Marines. This style was started by "Heavy" Pfuhl. Placing a can under the helmet distorted a man's silhouette and gave some protection against sniper's head shots.

Henry Kemp (E&F/2/29) was from South Carolina. He had just turned twenty-two at the time of the invasion and was a first lieutenant. He became an accountant and market analyst and resides in South Carolina.

Stephen Kraus (E Bty/2/15) was from Brooklyn, New York, and enlisted at eighteen. Okinawa was his only battle. He was a printing pressman for the *New York Times*. He still resides in New York.

Garland Loftis (C/1/22) had gone to Duke University and was part of the V-12 program. Originally assigned to the Third Marines as a reserve replacement for the invasion of Iwo Jima, he was then transferred to the Sixth Marines. He now resides in Atlanta.

Ken Long (I/3/29) enlisted at seventeen in 1943. He was from Minnesota. He used the GI Bill and became a teacher and coach. He has worked hard to collect memoirs of members of the Sixth.

Alan Manell (6th Combat Photographer) had taught himself photography. He was picked and was the only "amateur" who was retained. He was already combat-hardened by Okinawa. He reminds you that as a photographer "being put in reserves" never happened. He became a police officer and his recollections have been featured on the History Channel.

Joseph McConville (L/4/15) was born in County Down, Ireland, and came to the United States as a boy. He had been on Guam and had been augmented into the Fifteenth when it was formed. The piper for the Sixth Marine Division Association, he travels all over the country playing the bagpipes.

Thomas McKinney looked so young that on Guadalcanal they separated him and made him an aide because they though he was too young to be overseas. He was almost eighteen. Okinawa was his first invasion. He rose to the rank of first sergeant serving in Chosin, Inchon and three tours in Vietnam. A past president of the Sixth Association, he now lives in North Carolina.

Harry McKnight (H/3/29) would land with a replacement group during the peak of fighting on Sugar Loaf. He would use the GI Bill. He served in Korea and became an officer in the Air National Guard and a teacher. He recently returned to visit Okinawa.

Charles Miller (I/3/29) is now hospitalized in Texas near his son.
Ralph Miller (B/1/29 [Med. Bn.])

Glen Moore (HQ/2/29) is from New Jersey. He tried to enlist in 1942 but was told all enlistments were frozen. Late, he went directly to the draft board and requested to be drafted. At twenty-one he would have been "an old man" going into Okinawa. He became a teacher and a coach and currently resides in New Jersey.

George Niland (L/3/22) is from Boston. His father was a fireman. Operation Iceberg was his first landing. He went on to graduate from Boston University, raise eleven children, and now delights in twenty-five grandchildren.

Ed Pesley (F/2/29) was a pre–Pearl Harbor marine who was selected out of the ranks on Samoa and commissioned. By Okinawa he had spent three years in the Pacific. He now resides in California.

William Pierce (Wpns/29) made his first landing at Okinawa; however, he had served stateside prior to joining the Sixth overseas. He used the GI Bill and became a vice president for a firm in New York. Now retired, he lives in South Carolina and is the Association's public relations person.

Charlie Rittenbury (H Bty/3/15) was from rural North Carolina. Okinawa was his first landing. He had a "girl back home" and the thought of getting home to her is what kept him going. He and the girl, now married, still are by each other's side in a nursing home in North Carolina.

Bill Sams (I Bty/3/15), from Georgia, had been an orphan since he was twelve and was raised by his half sister. He worked at a clerical position at Parris Island after boot camp. But seeing "the writing on the wall" that he would be replaced as a typist when women joined the Marine Corps, he worked at getting himself assigned to artillery. By the time of the landing on Okinawa, he was a sergeant. He used the GI Bill to attend the University of Georgia and still lives in Georgia. He organizes reunions of the Fifteenth Marines biyearly.

Ray Schlinder (K/3/22) is from Illinois. He enlisted in 1943 at the age of twenty. Ray was near death when he was pulled off Sugar Loaf. He now says he is the "luckiest man on earth." He divides his time between Florida and Wisconsin.

Tom Schicker (1st Mar Div.)

Robert Sherer (F/2/29) already had a son and had been in the business world when he left for Okinawa. His wife literally took his job in the Marine Corps when he was reassigned to a combat unit. He attained the rank of major. He worked for the airlines after the war and is greatly admired by "his men."

Jack Stephenson (F/2/29) joined as a replacement. After the war, he went to college and also served in Korea. He now divides his time between Minnesota and North Carolina.

Harold Stephens (F/2/29) is from Pennsylvania. He joined the Marine Corps at seventeen. He used the GI Bill, became an author, and now lives in Bangkok, Thailand. His most recent book, *Take China*, was released in 2002.

Edward Sukowatey (C/1/29) is from El Paso, Wisconsin. He enlisted in the Marine Corps in 1942 and stayed on for thirty-nine months. His wounds from Okinawa bother him to this day.

Charles Taylor (6th Recon) was born in Topeka, Kansas. He had almost completely finished officer training when he decided to enlist at age seventeen. Not knowing what he was doing, he "volunteered" for a reconnaissance unit. He currently resides in Tennessee.

Howard Terry (F/2/29) is from Nashville, Tennessee. He ran away and joined the Marine Corps in 1942 at the age of fifteen. He says he had some trouble readjusting after combat, but with the GI Bill he went to watchmakers' school. He has been a watchmaker ever since.

Okinawa was George Tremblay's (1st Armored Amphb. Bn.) third Pacific landing. A hardened veteran of nineteen, he was called back to service during Korea. He now lives in Ohio.

Ike Wanamaker (F/2/29) enlisted in the Marine Corps immediately after his junior year in high school in 1942. He was from Toledo, Ohio. He also served in Korea. He died in June of 2002.

Richard Whitaker (F/2/29) turned nineteen en route to Okinawa, his first landing. He is from Saugerties, New York. He used the GI Bill to attend college, and afterward, he worked for private schools and colleges. He now resides in South Carolina.

James White (G/2/29) had graduated high school at sixteen and had two semesters of college when he enlisted at seventeen in Nebraska. He was wounded on Okinawa, his only invasion. He attended college and became an engineer. He lives in Oklahoma where he keeps many amused with his commentary on life via e-mail from the "White House."

William "Red" White (G/2/29) is from Pennsylvania. By the time he had finished high school, young men could no longer enlist. They were being drafted. Red made arrangements to join the Marine Corps. He was wounded and evacuated form Okinawa. He now resides in New York.

Annie Wilkins, wife of Claude Wilkins

Claud Wilkins (A/1/29 and H&S/3/15) is from Henderson, Tennessee. He graduated from high school and was then drafted. He continues to live in Tennessee and, true to his early days, has remained the Sixth Division Association Chaplin.

Marine have you heard the latest?" I said that I hadn't, and he continued, "We dropped a bomb on Japan that blew up a whole city!" Knowing the poor reputation the Navy had for telling the truth, I was just a little skeptical until I did some further checking and found out it was true. IT WAS A HAPPY DAY, and the other eleven Marines aboard the ship felt the same way. We were all thankful that our president, Harry Truman, had the courage to "pull the big trigger." A group of us from the Sixth Division, twelve to be exact, had the opportunity to return to the United States and attend Villanova as part of the V-12 Program, but before we shoved off we had heard that the next battle was going to be Japan, so our training would be conducted with that objective in mind. It wasn't until after the war that I learned of the elaborate defenses the Japanese had set up to greet the guys making the landing, and casualties were estimated about a million or more with at least that many for the Japanese. I feel that dropping the bomb actually saved lives, both the Japanese and ours. It sounds calloused but I feel it's true. There is no doubt in my mind that things would be a lot different if the bomb had *not* been dropped. One thing for sure is that fewer names would be present on our e-mail mailing list.[48]

Annie Wilkins: [Wife of Claud Wilkins]

They had been given some very dire info re: the percentage of casualties expected. I think if they were polled, probably all of them would say that they did not expect to survive that landing. Naturally, they were elated when they learned of the "big one" being used. Truman had his faults, but he always got Claud's vote for that and the firing of MacArthur . . . I don't think anyone in our generation will ever regret the use of the bomb, just the necessity of having to use it, and having to fight World War II in the first place. Similarly, I think all of us hope and pray that it will never be necessary again.[49]

McKinney

[The Fourth Marines were given the honor of being in Tokyo Bay at the surrender. Then they landed and began the occupation.]

The peninsula like that sticks out in Tokyo Bay. On that island were great twelve, fourteen-inch guns that would have really raised Cain with our ships if we had ever tried to come in. We found trenches. Their trenches were concrete-lined where they didn't have to keep shoveling them out. They had pillboxes. They had machine guns that they took the fifty caliber and the twenty millimeter which they had taken out of the American planes that were shot down. They were in those positions that they were going to use against us. The ammunition had been laid up on the bank behind them. The guns . . . the breeches were open and the barrels were pointed towards the sky. We worked just about all day clearing that island, and we must have taken four or five hundred Jap prisoners. They were all Navy; they weren't Army. They took them. I don't know, they put them on some Mike boats and I don't know where they took them. Late that afternoon they mustered up and we went across the bay to Yokosuka Naval Shipyard. We spread out in the naval shipyard. The Japanese were still there. They had stacked their weapons in there and, my God, there was enough there for two divisions. . . .

Oh, Lord. That stuff that was on there. The Japanese had trenches and pillboxes all over those beaches. They had a pole we called a "yeah hoe pole" . . . a pole maybe six, eight feet long, maybe two feet in diameter. . . . They're sharpened and then . . . and then they're embedded into the sand in irregular patterns so that you could not run through them. They had concertina wire, they even had what we call . . . we still use, I assume . . . what we call tangle foot, which was barbed wire on the ground about eight to twelve inches up off the ground, in no given pattern, so that you cannot step through it, maybe fifteen twenty yards deep. To get through it you have to either blow it up or using landing mats or something to get across it. At one time they had had an awful lot of mines buried in the beaches. They had had to go and take those up. But you could see where they had taken them up. You knew where they had been. The guys looked at that and said, "My God!"

The thing that really scared us . . . when we moved in the barracks . . . we were in the barracks. If I recall, they were two stories tall and a half a block long each. They were the barracks for the Japanese . . . we'd call them frogmen. Their sole job was to walk on the bottom of Tokyo Bay. Walk on it, [and] they each and every one had a pole that had fifty-pound charge on it. They didn't have flippers like we do now, but they had something on their feet that was made out of wood. They would walk under the water and as our boats passed over them [they had planned] they would reach up and slam that weight along the bottom of our boats and blow us out of the water. Consequently, they would kill themselves undoubtedly because the blast would kill them.

HOMECOMING

*Like I said, it was six months before I got back. The bloom was off
the rose; it was all over. All the heroes had long returned before I got
there.*

—Ike Wanamaker

Much attention, especially in movies, has been paid to Vietnam veterans' dif-
ficulties in adjusting to life after war. Many Vietnam veterans resent this por-
trayal. The problems of adaptation back into civilian life can be attributed to
the following factors: (1) How young the men were, (2) The fact that they
had no ticker tape parades at their homecoming, (3) "Their war" was fought
in places the average American could not understand, (4) The proximity of
civilians to combatants, and (5) The brutality they witnessed. The majority
of Vietnam veterans though, like their World War II predecessors, did
adjust and returned to live productive lives. The Pacific World War II veterans encountered much of the same adversity that their future comrades in
arms faced. Still, there are significant differences between the two groups.

The troops who fought in the Pacific came home slowly. Their return to
the United States was based on a point system, and the Marines who had
been in several campaigns left China quickly. Others did not return stateside
until late in the summer of 1946. Others remained in the Marine Corps and,
after stateside leaves or training, returned to China or mainland Japan.

Whenever the Pacific veterans returned to the United States, except for
those who had been wounded, it was long after the war was over. Very few
of them, except for those who had been seriously wounded, returned by air.
Rather, they traveled by troop transport. On these return voyages they were

surrounded by other veterans. They played cards, drank, shared dreams or aspirations, and mentally prepared themselves for the world they would reenter. They returned with at least one ethic that was still the same—they firmly believed they had just been doing a job, a job in which sixteen million like them had also been engaged. The trip and this attitude, in part, account for some of the differences between World War II veterans and the subsequent Vietnam veterans. World War II veterans had decompression time surrounded by those who had similar experiences of war. They also returned to the United States with the knowledge that most of those in their age group had also served in the military in some capacity.

The World War II veteran returned, like the Vietnam veteran, to a war weary nation. Although few World War II veterans experienced overt hostility upon their return, neither did they receive a hero's welcome. Instead, they encountered indifference. Family gatherings and parental and spousal joy were common, but too few young men had returned for the survivors and their loved ones to be too demonstrative. They quietly tried to assimilate back into their former lives. For many of the Pacific veterans this was difficult. The majority of the returning European veterans had beaten them home. Jobs would be scarce in some areas, especially for those who had known no other job in life but combat.

One avenue available to the veterans of the Sixth was the Servicemen's Readjustment Act, better know as the GI Bill. This bill provided educational and home loan benefits for returning sailors, soldiers, and Marines.[1] Many veterans came to believe that education was the road to take. They did not have to return to farms, factories, or mines. The GI Bill allowed unprecedented numbers of Americans to receive a free college education. Some chose technical schools and learned trades or honed skills they had acquired in the Marine Corps. Others planned to attend colleges or universities. Often for these potential students who had not been previously enrolled, there was a year or longer wait to get into college.

During this stressful and potentially non-productive period, there was another coping mechanism available to these young men. As they readjusted and waited for jobs or school, there was a stopgap measure known as the 52/20 Club. The 52/20 was a provision of the Servicemen's Readjustment Act, and was an unemployment benefit that every serviceman was entitled to upon separation from the military. Servicemen received twenty dollars a week for up to fifty-two weeks.[2] This allowed those returning from war the income and time needed to readjust. Several veterans recalled taking trips, seeing the country, visiting family, or just sitting around local taverns with other former servicemen. This may have been a crucial decompression period for the veterans.

Whatever the differences between Vietnam and World War II veterans may have been, veterans of World War II suffered their share of bad dreams, experienced problems with alcohol, and showed residual effects of the combat they experienced. In a time when Post Traumatic Stress Disorder was not yet acknowledged, most felt they had no choice but to just to go on. Most locked their memories away, often never even sharing them with loved ones. Not until their children were grown and they had begun to think of retiring did most of them begin to seek out their old foxhole companions. Only now, in their twilight years, when they understand the importance of the stories being told for themselves and for those who never came home, do they revisit those times and places. Almost all of the veterans speak with some level of resentment about the lack of attention that was given their homecoming. They quickly remind anyone who will listen that at least they had a homecoming. They are keenly aware that millions of young men—millions of families—never got to experience such reunions. They are, above all, grateful.

Joralemon

> You see pictures of V-J day or whatever with the sailors kissing the girls in the square . . . that probably lasted, ya know, a couple of days, and then as the guys first came home they were probably greeted with all kinds of enthusiasm. But by the time Bill Pierce or Jim White or myself got home it was like ho-hum. It wasn't antagonistic like Vietnam, although the indifference was almost the same.

Buchter

When I got home it was nothing 'cause everyone had given welcome homes for those who came home right after the war. We were forgotten people. So I get home. I call my mother from the station. Mom says, "That's great, I'll be here for ya." So I get to the railroad station with my sea bag. Got a troll . . . got a taxi home to come, brought me to the house, walked up to the door, opened, it was locked, dropped my sea bag . . . boy some nice welcome. So, it really wasn't a hero's welcome.

Chaisson

While I was in OCS [Officer Candidate School] the war ended, and we . . . they . . . then they came to us and said anyone twenty-six years or older is out of the Marine Corps. Anyone twenty-six years or younger can take one higher rate and stay in the Marine Corps. But I was an old man. I was so glad.

Sams

There was no homecoming. I got home in March. That was it. It was six months after the war. "Who are you? Where you been the last few years?" I am being serious. I rode the bus from Atlanta to Albany and I had on my uniform, 'cause that's all I had. I had been discharged and that's all I had. I had my uniform (Indicates right sleeve), I had medals (Indicates his left pocket) . . . sharpshooter medal and other decorations. People were looking at me like I was some kind of freak! That was my homecoming.

Niland

I came home in April. Oh, my homecoming was joyous with my family. Everyone was wonderful. I saw a lot of the guys I hung with before I went in the service. We went out drinking, which is normal. The second night I came in about one in the morning and my father was waiting there. He was a fireman in Boston, wonderful man, very pragmatic and practical. He looked at me and said, "Listen you bum, you either go to work or go to college but you're not going to continue coming in here."

DeMeis

[DeMeis came home in the middle of a snowstorm. Snow and trash were piled so high along the streets that he momentarily felt lost and couldn't recognize his old neighborhood.]

He was the organ grinder. He talked to me in Italian. He recognized me. He said, "No, this way, your house is over there." I thanked him, and I started to walk down, and I started to visualize the houses and remembered. I noticed the bungalow where we lived near my grandmother. The girl next door saw me, and she came out and she was kissing me. Then my sister came out and then my aunt came out, and I was getting kissed from all over. I was overseas forty-one and a half months. I was nineteen.

Jones

You come back to a new culture. After three years it was like visiting a new planet. I mentioned that I go up to the Top of the Mark, the Mark Hopkins, and I see these soft looking civilians. We're still in our jungle greens; we're in combat boots, and we're crude people. It must have been like when the Goths or the Huns or whoever they were went into ancient Rome. Here are the civilized Romans and these Mongols. That's how we felt coming back to civilization . . .

[In an article in the *Daily Breeze*, Jones elaborated]

"In the world of soldiers, there are no hard feelings. They know they may be trying to kill each other, but it's not personal," Jones said. After the war, he would have preferred to sit down with a Japanese solider for a drink than with an American who didn't fight. "We'd have something to talk about."[3]

Honis

I remember I took a train from Great Lakes. A lot of the guys were already out. Of course, we never locked our door, so I took a cab home and my parents were still around, and my two brothers were home. So it was a great day. There wasn't any big, big party or anything, more a silent gratitude that all three of us were alive. Again, my oldest brother was at Normandy, my other brother was at Iwo Jima, and I was at Okinawa. . . . It was kind of rejoicing, but subdued because we had lost . . . maybe five were killed from my block.

McKnight

The 52/20 Club was for returning veterans who could not find a job right away. It was limited to one year, fifty-two weeks at twenty dollars a week. Each week they would report to the VA office and report their progress finding a job. They would then be given a check and instructed to return if they did not find a job. Most jobs were filled by veterans who had enough points to be discharged early after the war. Points were based on months of service, foreign service, Purple Hearts rated five extra points, and decorations like a bronze star, and so forth.[4]

Joralemon

I didn't get home until late August 1946, and fortunately I was able to enroll at NYU as a former student. I started school right away, getting my monthly payments under the GI Bill; hence, I didn't join the 52/20 Club. A bunch of my buddies were in the "club," and most of them got their "ruptured ducks" (A pin with a symbol of a ruptured duck, indicating one was an honorably discharged veteran) months before I got home. Many of them had either gone to work after looking for it (Winks) for several months, or were coming to the end of their search (Winks).

Frankly, I thought it was a great idea. It took the pressure off the veterans, many of whom had been away for three or four years, to immediately change back to being civilians. In many neighborhoods, such as mine in The Bronx or Dick Whitaker's in Saugerties, many of the "Club Members" hung out in the local bar (Now a more dignified "pub"), and it gave them a much-deserved "last liberty" before settling down to the business of getting on with their lives. If I hadn't gone right back to school, I'm sure I would have been an active member of the "Club."[5]

Howell

Ah, yes, the old 52/20 Club. Routine: Each Monday, hitch a ride to the UI (Unemployment Insurance) Office to sign up for the $20.00, confer with Veterans' Counselor regarding plans for employment or schooling. Most prevalent in southeast Ohio was the coal mines. My Dad—a miner since the age of nine as a mule driver, rose to level of Fire Boss and then Check Weighmen—had passed on when I was fourteen. His admonition to my brother and me was, "Never go to work in the mines. If you do and I am alive, I will kick your butt. If I am not here, I will haunt you."[6]

Stephens: F/2/29

[Harold Stephens was from Pennsylvania. He joined the Marine Corps at the age of seventeen.]

After Okinawa and China duty I went back to the States, completed my college education, and decided I wanted to continue traveling and become a writer. As a result I have spent most of my life since then overseas, mostly in the Pacific and Asia. Aboard my own boat. I had a great opportunity to revisit many World War II battle sites—New Hebrides, Solomons, Rabaul,

Guadalcanal, Bataan and Corregidor. What was so disturbing was that these sites, as battlefields, exist only in the memories of those men who had fought there. In most places there is not even a plaque or a sign.

I lost contact with fellow Marines and knew nothing about Sixth Marine Division and China Marine reunions, until a few years ago when Eddie Tomalio read something I wrote and wrote to me. After that I made it to one reunion and hope to do more in the future. I never thought much about meeting old buddies, but now I am learning the meaning of old friendships.[7]

Moore

I would make one more comment about the GI Bill of Rights. Many of the millions of veterans who took advantage of it received a good education. They got degrees, paid their taxes, and the government got an excellent return on the amount of money they invested in us. Businesses were started, the standard of living was raised, unemployment was down, and all of this came from the U.S. government's investment in us.[8]

Stephenson: F/2/29
[Jack Stephenson joined as a replacement on Okinawa.]

The 52/20 Club formed by the government in an honest attempt to help out dischargees in getting started. I reenlisted in the reserves on being discharged and was headed for college on the GI Bill, so I didn't need any help, but I was standing next to a guy in line to be processed at Great Lakes. He was telling me he had a great future in the 52/20 and I should seriously consider applying.[9]

McKnight

Some afterthoughts: In 1944 and '45, while our gang was at Camp Pendleton, we would get a weekend pass and had no trouble getting a ride to L.A. The three of us would go out to the main highway and stick our thumbs up, and if not the first car but soon after a car would stop and tell us to hop in. The same when coming back to camp. Sometimes the driver would take us out of his way by several miles to get us where we were going. We were told to go in groups of three because the "Zoot Suiters" would pick a fight with single Marines. We took a bar of soap in a sock for protection. Made a good black jack. After the war it was quite different. We could stand for hours thumbing, and only when a former GI or Marine came by we would get a ride. We began riding the train. How soon they forgot! The used car salesmen were out to get our mustering out pay. Cars were scarce and they would fix up old junk and sell us a bill of goods on what they were doing for our guys in giving us such a good deal. Mine had a cracked block that had to be replaced and when I slid on a patch of ice into another car's bumper, not hard enough to do any damage to him, all the fender putty fell off revealing where the fenders had been welded together.[10]

Pierce

I bought a motorcycle, took the twenty dollars a week and rode all over the East Coast with some other motor nuts for about a year. Of course my parents did not like this, as I was really to them a "bum of the year". No job, education . . . but I did go on to college after the year, on the GI Bill. Another horrible experience to a combat Marine, sitting there learning English, poetry, business, arithmetic . . . drove me batty![11]

WAR'S WISDOM

We became very combat savvy.

—Bill Pierce

From their first day at boot camp Marines acquired bits of wisdom about their new military life, and how to survive it. When they crossed the equator and survived the hazing of the Shell Back ceremony they learned that military life was often brutal. They learned that writing "FREE" on a letter meant that their mail did not cost them anything but time, and so they spent the six cents to get it home faster, in hopes that they would receive one just as quickly. They discovered that their mothers' Sunday dinner, mailed to them in cans, tasted almost as good a month or so later on an island in the Pacific. They learned how much they could drink and what not to drink. They passed information along about who the good leaders were, and survived tongue-lashings. They grew lean and prepared for combat.

As the Marines approached battle their education began in earnest. The veterans of other campaigns gathered the green troops to them and distributed ammunition, grenades, and advice. Don't bunch up. Take a grenade apart, cut the fuse in half, and the Japs can't throw it back at you. Kill anything—even if it is speaking English—if it doesn't know the password. They became aware that lighting a cigarette could be a risky proposition, or it could save your life. A day came when they learned the lesson of loss; of losing a friend and advancing on with no time to grieve or make sure he was cared for properly. They learned to keep from volunteering, to keep their heads down, to share mail with their foxhole buddies, and to pray.

Veterans from Okinawa know those eighty-two days, or however long they participated, changed them forever. They became wise quickly; it was the only way to survive. Yet, they have very little advice to offer if they could transport themselves back in time and stand next to some green Marine on L-Day of 1945, except to "Listen to what you're told," and "Stay off the skyline."

Pierce

The average Marine, when the bullets would fly or something, he would be down so low you couldn't imagine. Your face would get in the mud, or you would try to crawl somewhere but just can't move because you are covered so viciously with fire that it would be almost impossible to move. We became very combat savvy. We would take a hand grenade, for example, and screw the top off . . . the fuse stuck out maybe two inches, laid it on a rock, cut the fuse in half with a K-bar knife, and then screw it back on. That made the five-second fuses two seconds. So that went off almost . . . so you knew the guy couldn't throw it back at you. Stuff like that. You carried your clips . . . I asked Tom Terpinas, "How come you never got hit with the Corpsman's pack?" He said, "I never carried one. I kept all the syringes and bandages and everything in my pockets," because anyone that was dressed different was shot by the Japanese riflemen. They would zero in on an officer with a strap that went across his top, or anything that looked different would be the man that they would try to kill. That, and automatic weapons, anybody who had a machine gun, or a BAR, [Browning Automatic Rifle] or something that fired automatic. Sometime word was passed not to put your BAR on automatics single shot only, 'cause you fired it automatic you might draw border fire.

McConville

There was no joy. . . . It's something you never get over. I think
of the war every day of my life. Every day of my life. I think part
. . . something that happened to me while I was overseas. There
are some happy moments I have, too.

Rittenbury

Let me tell you about my son-in-law who went to Vietnam as an
Army colonel. He had never been in combat before. He came to
see me, and he asked me, "In commanding my troops, do you
have any advice that you could give me?" I said, "Listen to your
sergeant. He has been through hell, and if you want someone to
help you get through, you listen to him. He is an old, wise sergeant, a veteran, and he'll pull you through" When my son-in-
law came back from his tour in Vietnam, he thanked me. He
said, "I listened to my sergeant. You were right."

Not only a sergeant, but anyone at Parris Island that's
placed over you. You acted, you didn't ask why or where or
when. You jumped. That is where discipline comes in again.
We were trained at Parris Island to kill or be killed. That was
drilled into us again at Lejeune and Pendleton and
Guadalcanal. They wanted to impress upon us that if we hesitated one minute to kill, we'd be the one that would be that
casualty. I would tell any young Marine going in that he's going
into the most elite of all military organizations to obey orders
. . . call it blind faith, or whatever you want, but don't ask any
questions. Ellie and I went back to Parris Island a few years ago
so I could show her where I went to boot camp. Believe it or not,
they appointed a general to escort us over the base. The general's calling me Charlie . . . I said, "Sir, I was only a corporal. By
the way, you didn't treat me like this the first time I came down
here." He said, "Charlie, you know that was necessary to teach
you discipline." I said, "Yes sir, it was, and I thank you for it

now." At one time I had made up my mind that if I ever got my drill instructor in my sights before the Japanese, he was going to get it first. After it was all over I could go over and shake that man's hand and thank him for what he instilled in me because it's been valuable for the rest of my life.

Honis

I think [I would say] keep your head down. Raise it when you have to, but don't go skylarking, looking around when you don't have to. A fair number—I never went through the roster—but there were a lot a bullet wounds to the head, a large part of our casualties. So, keep your head down, don't expose yourself needlessly unless you have to. Again, whatever the job called for. Obviously, if you're in a firefight, to be able to do your job, you have to be firing so . . . what you're firing at can also be firing at you. That part you know. I don't mean there'll be a time when you've got to risk it all, and, of course, what happens in combat to me is you kill your spirit. You have to ratchet yourself into the mentality of . . . not that you feel you're going to die but that you've got a job to do. Okay, now in doing that you're going to have to expose yourself to danger. You have to put that aside, your fear, once you do that. Once you ratchet yourself through that, you can function. If you're going to be preoccupied with your fear, you won't get to do your job and that means you're going to let your buddies down. I think that is the biggest thing that a guy has to keep in mind. You have to balance it. In fact, I'm reading a book about Tarawa right now where guys will leap up and not that this . . . it had to be done, where you stuck a grenade in a pill box or a demolition charge and then go to the next one, but that is part of it. But again, it's not being careless. There again, there's going to be a lot you have no control over when a guy's dropping a mortar round down the tube, or a lanyard over an artillery piece. You have no control over that. But you do your job professionally. . . . I was one of sixteen million. I don't have any illusions about [it]. I am similar to other vets. We don't like to talk about it. Again, some talk quite blatant about their experiences. I know in the case of some, they never heard a shot fired but they try to portray themselves as doing more than they did. Me, I just thought that I was one of sixteen million. I'm grateful that I survived and my country owes me nothing, absolutely nothing. I married, I had five kids, and there's my reward. I don't need more than that. I know some who feel that the country owes them, and they spend a lot of time getting what they can.

Whitaker

You know what Marines tell each other in similar situations? "Keep a tight ass." I don't think you can tell anybody anything if you haven't learned it in boot camp. If you haven't learned it in infantry training and you don't know it. It's a matter of being fully aware of everything that is going on about you. Things you hear, see, and smell. . . . It's a matter of your self-preservation. . . . Stay off the skyline. It says, "Don't take unnecessary chances. Don't expose yourself. Take advantage of concealment and cover because there is always someone out there to shoot you"— if you forget that for an instant . . . you'll get shot. I had something in my scrapbook that says, "Anything you do can get you killed, including absolutely nothing."

Jones

The first thing I would tell anybody going into combat [would be], don't go in there with the idea of winning medals. If you're going to go in to win medals you may win it, but you'll probably get it posthumously. That's the first thing you don't do. The second thing you don't do is hunt souvenirs. More people get killed hunting souvenirs than just doing their job. The third thing is, your job is to do your job. You don't have to volunteer to do more, but you don't do less. You do your assignment. That's all the Marine Corps really wants out of the individual Marine. You got to do your mission.

Loftis

I want people to really know what really took place in World War II, how these young men sacrificed their lives and went there to fight. There is very little knowledge of World War II. It's not even taught in the schools. If anything, I would want people to recall and remember that these men fought to save the U.S.A. and the world.

Taylor

We were doing what we were told to do, and I don't think it was in vain. We had to take the island to make Japan surrender, which they did. I just don't want people to forget that men went over there. Whether they were killed or survived, they still sacrificed their lives and it's important. Everybody made a sacrifice to some degree. It's something that we shouldn't forget. I want my grand-kids to realize, and really know what we went through, and appreciate what we did.

DeMeis

I go to schools and preach about war and what freedom is . . . that it isn't free. The price we had to pay for it. . . . These guys who all gave up all their tomorrows so that we, the people living today, could enjoy this freedom. They don't even remember. These kids in school, they don't even know the name Okinawa, Iwo, Peleliu. They don't know none of that, they don't know them.

Niland

I'd tell him to stay off the skyline and keep five paces between himself and fellow Marines. There's really not much else you can tell him. . . . They used to say, "Get close to the old salts." That was the worst thing you could do because they were the first to get killed, ironically. I don't know why, but they did. So

I don't know what you'd tell someone. To survive you certainly can't hesitate. If you run into a Jap and he's got a weapon, you've got a weapon. You'd better kill him first because he'll sure kill you. I'd tell 'em that—to do whatever he has to do to survive. To be proud that he is a Marine.

Wanamaker

Lacey: It's April 1, 1945, and you have a boot recruit standing next to you. You have all the knowledge you have today. What one piece of advice would you give him to survive Okinawa?

"Stay off the skyline. . . ."

SEA STORIES

"Sea stories" is a term that Marines have given their tales of adventure. They start with the phrases, "No shit," or "Remember that day . . . " They are often stories that recount a moment when the average "Mac's" path crossed with an event of true historical significance, whether they knew it at the time or not. James Chaisson believed that a book should be written about all of the funny things that happened preparing for and being in combat. It was, for many, a grand adventure and a time when they were unfettered and wonderfully uncivilized. At reunions these are the stories the men love to share—the good times—almost all involving buddies, and many of those buddies now long gone. It is a testament to remember those young Marines, as they pulled pranks, broke bread, and sang songs, rather than as heaps of flesh or as bent, old men.

What these veterans want to ensure is that humanity is not lost in telling the stories of war with emphasis on defensive lines and grand strategies. Battles are about young men far away from home fighting other young men. The men who fought in World War II had the experience etched onto their souls. They, like men before and since, would not do it again for anything, but would not have missed it either. Sea stories are often the stories that best explain the allure of war. They are the laughter, the men's brushes with greatness, the moment that they witnessed the best in themselves and others.

Fitzgerald

The story is indirectly about Jim Day. On our approach to Okinawa, we went ashore on an island named Mog-Mog, a navy recreation island. The guys from our Battalion 222 went ashore. We got on the wrong island . . . it was a British controlled island. We had a little difficulty with them, trying to buy a drink. Anyway, that was all resolved. There also in their club was Jack Dempsey, former heavyweight champion of the world, who was with the Coast Guard and landing with, I guess, the First Marine Division. Also [there] was Ernie Pyle, the famous war correspondent. Ernie ended up with Dick Pfuhl and me and a couple other guys and Jim Day's lieutenant, a guy by the name of Kev Tashjian . . . he was killed later on. Anyway, Ernie Pyle was wearing a gung ho cap with a Seabee emblem on it. Kev was wearing his soft cover cap and he took the emblem off. He said, "Mr. Pyle you're landing with the Marines, would you wear my Marine emblem." Ernie said, "I'd be proud to." He put it on his gung ho cap. Ernie was killed and Tashjian was killed.

Stephenson, J.

But I sure remember the guitar. I bought it for twenty-five dollars, while on liberty in Los Angeles, and it was one of my better investments because I had such fun with it. By the time I got to Okinawa the strings were just about shot, rusted, and broken. Someone I met there suggested that communication wire would work, so I got some and peeled the insulation off, cut it up to the proper length, and tuned it up. The wire sounded terrible but it worked. When we were getting ready to move south, one of the cooks asked if he could have it while we were gone, so I left it with him, and he promised he would give it back when we got back. We left all of our extra gear in a pile for Fox Company, and when we got back to the area after the island was secured I found that the cook had been transferred back to the States. But there, on the very top of the pile, was my precious guitar waiting for me to come and get it. I remember sitting with a bunch of guys and playing it until my fingers got all bloody. We sang all night long.

By the time we were on the APA [landing ship] headed for Guam the guitar was so warped, I couldn't play it anymore. I remember one night, after taps, I decided I should give it a proper funeral in respect for the wonderful time it had given me. So Hal Stephens and I went up the ladders to the upper deck and outside to the rail. There was quite a wind and it was pitch dark. We could look down at the ship's wake roaring along the side of the ship, with all the sparkles that show in the water. We held the guitar over the side and said a silent prayer, and I let it go. We watched for a long time as it hit the water and then floated farther astern, bouncing on the waves until the guitar disappeared out of sight in the darkness. My, that was sad.[1]

Chaisson

So then . . . then came the episode of the organ. We were waiting, waiting forever, and we had secured the north end of the island. We had done our patrol, patrolled the area, and we had come back, and we are waiting to be reassigned, which meant going all the way south where the heavy fighting was. 'Cause we had secured all of the north end, two-thirds of the island, and most of the fighting was going on south in the bad fighting. I had been on patrol to a little village called Ada. When I was on patrol we went into this little town, shot to bits, and went to the school, and I saw . . . got some pictures and souvenirs. We were looking for souvenirs 'cause we were just on patrol where there weren't supposed to be any Japs anyway. I found in the school a little portable organ. You could play it, you could pick it up and carry it, but it was pretty heavy. It was in the school and I said, "Oh, dang, its too big to carry." So we left it there.

When we got back, there was a little school that the officers had as their headquarters, at Hedo Point. I was telling one of my buddies. I said, "You know, I got some souvenirs and some of these pictures." I had some pictures and I had some other stuff, and whatever, just junk. I said, "The thing I would have really liked to have taken was that organ." I said, "I wanted to bring it to Father Kelly so he could have it for mass." It was Saturday, I guess, and Sunday was mass. Old Courtney, Major Courtney, was listening, and he was a good Catholic. He said, "Hey, Chaisson, do you remember where that thing was? Do you think you could go back and get it?" I said, "Oh God, it's back at Ada, and I . . .how the hell . . .we couldn't go back there again." I'm thinking going on the ground. He said, "Well, what about if I get a DWUK?" (Land/Sea vehicle) "I ask Captain Long if he'll give us a DWUK and get that damn organ. We'd like to have that for mass on Sunday." I said, "I'll go back and take a couple of men and I call and get that organ." "I'll call Captain Long to assign you a DWUK, and you go down and get that durned organ for me. I want to give it at . . . I want to have it tomorrow for Sunday for music." This is quite a thing. We got in the DWUK, we had a driver, and we went down to Ada, and went ashore again, went into the school. I got the organ and got up . . . gathered up some souvenirs and junk and put it in the DWUK and sailed it back, and ran out of gas . . . God dang. The winds are pretty high in the China Sea. I guess they would be coming all the way from China and Japan.

So, here we were, out of gas and trying to keep ourselves off the coral. And out of the estuary comes another patrol. They were in some kind of vehicle, maybe another DWUK, I forgot. Anyway, they throw us a rope. They had a load of natives that they had pulled out of a cave on their patrol. They had about four or five, maybe six, women and a little old man and they were "howing" and bowing all the time. We got towed and got the vehicle ashore. I think we left it on the embankment, on the shore, and we went back with the fellas that had rescued us. It started to pour down rain, and I remember the old man. He was sitting there all curled up and cold. I put my poncho . . . pulled it over him, and I didn't mind. We could see that he hadn't heard about us being good to 'em. . . . Then, when the women were ashore, they all had to go to the bathroom when we got landed. When we were back to where we were dug in, all the women ran up the beach or so and bared their butts and let it fly. That was quite a sight itself.

So . . . I think it was . . . it may have been a morning or two later, we went to mass, and at the mass the priest was on one side and the reverend, Reverend Price, was on . . . the Protestant minister . . . on the other side of the chapel. We're all in church together, and old Major Courtney talks about what I had brought them, and they brought it up to the Catholic side, our church. When we got halfway through the service Colonel . . . Father Kelly says, "We got an organ now fellas. Who's the organ player?" Nobody, not one Catholic person knew how to play a damn organ. So Kelly offered it to the Protestants and the Reverend said, "Send it over to this side; I've got an organ player." So, we had to send it over to the Protestant side. The other side of the school, which we were headquartered in . . . so, that was the end of that. The Protestants had the organ and they had the flair. Poor Major Courtney had to deal with not having his Catholic service get their music or an organ player. That was just one thing, of course. Then we got orders to move south.

Taylor

[George Taylor's reconnaissance unit went into Naha two or three days in advance of the frontline troops.]

In Naha, when we went into the city . . . I may get in trouble . . . we saw this bank and we blew the safe. Oh, we got money out of it too. I have no idea where these folks came from. They must have stayed there, because no one was in back of us. This guy says, "If you give me some money, I'll put your name in the paper." I said, "Sir, we just got word that we weren't supposed to touch anything. This bank was wide open." So, he talked to me and I have the article. So we blew that bank and we were some of the first people in Naha.

Moore

One other point of interest was that Guam was the crossroads of the Pacific, and every branch of the service was represented there. We found that many were stationed in the area from our old high school. A reunion was planned at the Marine Air Wing, and we had twenty-three service men that went to Boonton High School. The Air Wing fed us well and gave us all the ice cream we could eat. One of those attending was Al Marrone, who became the welterweight champ of the Pacific. When he won that title General Geiger was so thrilled that he had him transferred to a private tent in his Corps Headquarters, and his assignment was to train, train, train for the defense of that title. Good duty—fight those other services and you don't have to fight them Japs![2]

Whitaker

Oh, that happened like in 1949. First of all, when we went to Tsingtao, Sherer was only there a couple weeks, and he went home and that was the last I ever saw of him. Then in 1949 or so I was sitting at a subway stop, in my car, in Long Island City, waiting for a girl I knew to get off the subway from work. And I was reading a *Saturday Evening Post* or something, and a guy walked by my car. There were thousands of people coming out of this subway stop. As he went by I looked at the back of him. There was something about him that was compelling, and I just I couldn't take my eyes off him. I watched him walk, and I finally got out of the car and started following him. We walked about a block, and it dawned on me who it had to be, and his code name was "Scissors." I just yelled "Scissors" and . . . that was it . . . Well, I followed him halfway over that stupid island.

Sams

Well, I can do that too. We moved in this certain position in Naha. We were in a relatively clear area. No protection, no walls, or anything. Unfortunately, a day or so before, Laura, several of the people or men developed dysentery. I'm going to tell it like it is. We got a latrine built (Gestures off to the side), well, portable. We had to set it up. Late in the afternoon, or mid afternoon or so, there were some men in dire need of the latrine, and all of a sudden machine gun fire erupted from somewhere, and across the road they came with their britches at their knees and what have you. Finally, someone saw a flash from a chimney of the sugar refinery. At least one or two snipers up in the chimney. When they, our commander, Captain Abney, at that time, called down for all the guns, as to who could get what they called the line bore, they call that. The line bore is when you depress your tube to your gun and have a direct site to it rather than an arch. That was a line bore. Direct fire. Due to the rubble, walls, and what in the area, my gun was the only that could get a good line bore at the base of the stack. So, I was given the order to bring it down. Called the fire direction to me. To the best of my memory, they called for a white phosphorous, which gave you when it exploded, . . . it showed you whether you hit or missed or what have you. (Making motion with hand to right and left) I fired, to the best of my memory, I fired one, missed it on one side; I fired, missed it on the other side. Then I fired it with a high explosive, with a delayed fuse. Turned the fuse to delay (Making turning motion with hands), which meant it would go through the first, whatever, and on the next impact. When I fired, we got good results out of it. In the movies, the documentaries, you can see a Jap falling out of there.

McKinney

My big moment came when we landed down on Oroku Peninsula. Oroku Peninsula had the big Japanese naval airbase, and the big radio station had a tower that went up, I imagine, oh, a thousand feet, real easy. It was also on the Oroku Peninsula that we ran into the bakka bombs. [Means "stupid" in Japanese] The one-man, jet-propelled human bomb. We found some of those. Along about the fourth or fifth of June, we were up—the whole team—we were up on a ridge where we could look to our left and we could see the entire harbor at Naha, and to the right we were looking down, which turned out later on to be Mezado Ridge. Yeah, we were sitting . . . we were laying up there, you never sit because then you were a target. We were laying up there and we were sucking on D. Bars. A D. Bar is a chocolate bar; they called it a tropical bar; it was made by

Hershey. It was real good chocolate but it was extremely hard. It was best if you just took your bayonet and chopped you a piece off and put it in your mouth and sucked on it until it finally dissolved. I happened to look off to the right and there was a small bush about two, two and a half feet high. The first time I looked over at that little bush, it was standing still. Then I looked over just a few minutes later and that bush was moving. I told Corporal Doris, "There's something wrong with that bush." He looked over at it and it quit moving. He said, "What you talking about?" I said, "It was moving." He said, "What kind of chocolate bar have you got?" About that time, that bush started moving again. I told him, "Look!" and he said, "I'll be damned."

I crawled over to it, looked around, and lo and behold right alongside that bush was a vent pipe coming up. The pipe was made out of wood, a wooden pipe that came up. It was only about two inches above the surface of the ground. Keep in mind that this ridge is mostly coral. I told Doris, "There's a pipe sticking up here." He looked at it and said, "Yep, there sure as hell is." He said, "Let's pull it out and see what comes up." We pulled it, and we pulled about six or eight feet of it out. It came out and left a much bigger hole and he said, "Chick, do you think you can get down through there?" I said, "Well, I can give it a damn good try." So we put the harness on and I took the pistol and the flashlight and I went in head first going down. They held me by the rope and I kept whispering, as loud as you can (chuckles) with a whisper, "Little further, little further," and I went on down. The all of a sudden my head and shoulders came out into a large opening. I told them, "Let me down." When they did, I had the flashlight on and I was standing in the end of a passageway of some kind. Right across from me was an opening, well, let me digress; the floor was snow-white sand, the walls, some of them had paneling on them. There was posts, big heavy timbers here and there along the walls. Directly across from me was an opening, like a door: a doorway without a door. There was a blanket hanging down on that door. I whispered back up the pipe to him and told him, "There is a door down here that has a blanket on it, and I am going to pull it down and

see what's in here." I did, and there was a complete room, beau-
tifully paneled, the ceiling, the walls, everything. Against the far
wall, this room wasn't maybe six or eight feet long maybe six or
eight feet wide. Against the far wall was a bunk, a built in bunk.
On that bunk laid a complete naval officer's uniform. On the
bed was the dress shoes, a sword, a ceremonial sword, a little
one, and the hat, that had a set of white gloves laying on it. On
the coat, when I got to it, was a set of ribbons. I gave that room
a real good search and there was a set . . . a large set of binoculars hanging off the foot of the bed. When I come out of there,
I called back up the pipe and I told Doris, "Send somebody else
down." So another guy, Chick Lindsky, out of Pittsburgh,
Pennsylvania, he came down. He came down feet first, and
after he got down, he said, "I wish to hell I can come down
headfirst like you did." We got in there, and he and I started
walking, covering each other as we went.

There were rooms . . . we found out later the area we was
in was mostly officers' . . . officers' places. Then the smell started getting bad; I unbuckled the harness to get out of it, so did
Chick Lindsky, and we stared walking very carefully and
checking the different rooms. It was a radio room. There were
two, the remains of two, Japanese sailors, still in their blue uniforms sitting at a table with their heads down; the radios had all
been turned off, they were not operating. But both operators, I
assume they were operators, were lying with heads down on the
tables. We left them and went on, and that's when we noticed
the stink was getting real bad, and we turned the corner and
looked down this one tunnel [and] there was nothing but dead
Japanese sailors and soldiers stacked along both walls. The little
white, wiggly worms were creeping and crawling all over the
floor. Chick Lindsky says, "We're not going down there." I
think that was the infirmary. We went just a little further, and
here is this room. It was carved out of coral and here laid a big
platform, tatami mats on it, [and] laid on it was five officers.
The one in the center, according to our pictures, said this was a
rear admiral. The two on each side were Navy captains. They
were in full uniform, except they did not have shoes on. They
had the white, split toed, [socks] . . . Each one of them had a cer-

emonial hari kari knife an inch or so below their belt buckle.
The blade was buried all the way into their abdomens. Each one
of them had been shot in the temple. From my estimates, they
were all shot from the left side. The bullet went in on the left
side, because it left powdered burns, and where it exited on the
right there were no powder burns. We knew what we had
found. We hunted around in there and found machine shops
and armory where weapons were in different states of being
repaired. We found different rooms where there were kitchens,
where different people could eat. There was rice in there, but a
lot of that rice was already rotted from being in there and being
wet. We finally discovered that there was a draft blowing
through that entire area. We found the major opening for it.
Sky said, "Let's go up and take a look."

   We came out to where we were looking towards Mazado
Ridge and down towards the valley where there was a huge
field. I don't think it was sugar cane. I think it was the Kunai
grass that grew out there. We hollered up there and Corporal
Doris and the other men came down; they brought our weapons
and all with them. They said, "What did you find." I said, "We
found Admiral Ota's cave, and Admiral Ota is inside waiting
for you." He said, "What do you mean, waiting for me?" I said,
"He wants to shake your hand for being so diligent and sending
us two guys in there while you stay out here where it's safe."
After we told him what we had seen and all, he sent Chick
Lindsky and the other man, Morris. He said, "Get back to battalion and tell Major Carney what we found." We went back.
We told Major Carney, and Major Carney said, "Are you sure?"
I showed him the pictures that I had, that were given to us that
showed different rank structure. I said, "This is the rank that's
on the those five people lying on that table." I said, "Those
sailors laying in that radio room, this is what they had on their
sleeve." He said, "You must have found it. You stay here, we
will notify regiment, and we will get somebody up here to get
in there and take care of it."

   Three days later, I know that Doris was getting kind of
antsy—what the hell happened to McKinney and Chick
Lindsky?—here came six damn jeeps. Made me angry because
everybody in those jeeps were clean. They were nice and clean.

They had maps, and they all had nice Thompson machine guns, and all this good stuff. This officer got out, and he was wearing a lieutenant colonel's leaf and I thought to myself, "This guy's stupid. He's up here. There's Japs all around here, and he's wearing a lieutenant colonel's leaf." He had a briefcase. There was a captain with him. The captain was wearing a briefcase also. The colonel said, "I understand that you found something important." I said, "Yes sir, we found Admiral Ota." He said, "Is he alive?" I said, "No sir, he's been dead awhile." He said, "All right, let's go." So we took 'em down, took them to the cave, and they took one group up and showed them where I had found the opening, and come to find out later there were four other openings on that hill besides the one that I found. We took them in. They weren't going to go; we had to go in first. We took them in and showed them where the kitchens were, the kitchens were up more or less closer to the big entrance. We took 'em into where the armory was, where the weapons they had and then next we found . . . we took them to where Admiral Ota and his people were, his officers. The captain took out his brief case, took out a bunch of 8 x 1 glossies, and started looking, and he named each one of those officers. They knew who they were. They had the picture of them. I never did ask where they got them, or how they got them, but they had them. We took them, we took their people on through and showed them where the radio room was. There was a generator in there for power for those radios. We took them and showed them where the officers' quarters were. Finally, the colonel said, "Well, you men did real fine. You are really outstanding. Go on back out and join your unit and we'll take it from here." So we did. We got out and after we got back down to where the battalion was, Major Carney asked us, "What kind of souvenirs did you guys get?" Old Doris turned around, patted his butt, and said, "This." We didn't take any souvenirs out of there. Later on in the Division History Book you will find a Lieutenant Colonel Williams. He gave credit to the Division intelligence people. He did not say that it came out of the Second Battalion, Fourth Marines. Later on, he did claim that he was the man who discovered it. I have some of the writings that he made. He didn't even get into it until three days after we found it. We counted dead Japanese soldiers and sailors in that cave. We counted 167, but in the officers' rooms we never found one. Not a one, but along the walls, where the hospital and the dispensary was, we counted 167. That included the Admiral and his five people, four people. There was no foodstuffs in there that I would have even considered eating. The rice had molded. They had sacks of onions that had rotted, and we didn't bother with anything. All we wanted to do was take a look, get in and get out. That's exactly what we did.

We went back and joined the battalion and told them what we had found and everything. F Company had gone up and over that very hill. Nobody had found anything. We were following in trace [behind] of Easy and Fox Company. That's when John McCormick and his people had gone out of that one little cement building. They were told to go up and over to support another unit up there that was taking fire; that's where they got hit. John McCormick, out of his five men, McCormick was the only one who survived.

OBJECTIVE ACHIEVED—REMEMBER US

Comparisons have often been made between the Vietnam veteran and the World War II veteran. The experiences of the men of the Sixth Marine Division is, in some ways, remarkably similar to the experiences of the men who fought in Vietnam. Each group fought in the jungles of Asia on a foe's territory, and each returned home to a country weary of war and unable to understand the experience. The fathers who saw their sons go off to Vietnam were men who had experienced it first hand in World War II. Although they were unable to understand "draft dodgers," few told their sons to volunteer for the Vietnam War. The biggest difference between the men who participated in the two conflicts is the unification of the United States in support of the task that needed to be accomplished in World War II, and the sense of life and death, good and evil, that the people of World War II were participating in. To the World War II generation the threat was imminent. In addition, with

Vietnam there was no bomb or overwhelming victory. The atomic bomb and the surrender of the Axis will always overshadow the men of the Sixth Marine Division. Veterans of World War II worry today that the contribution they made will not be remembered, that their generation will only be remembered for the bomb. The irony is not lost on them that the event that saved their lives also relegated them to a back seat in history. They have gladly made the trade but still insist their story be remembered correctly.

They laugh at the concept of theirs as a "good war". There was very little good on Okinawa, except what they found in each other or in the smile of an Okinawan child to whom they offered a piece of candy. However, they are very proud of the contribution they made to the world's salvation, and firmly believe they were fighting an evil force. They believe that Harry Truman had great fortitude and made the right decision. To them, this decision saved not only their lives but also the lives of countless Japanese, and brought an end to the war as quickly as possible. They understand they have a special place in history, and yet they feel they are owed nothing except respect. They believe that those to whom the country is indebted are the ones who never came home. That is what they want future generations to remember. They were a tough generation, raised to do a tough task. They went to do a job; they did it; they came home.

They returned to families and wives and began living normally again. Many used the GI Bill to attain an education, an opportunity that would change the United States forever. Having been exposed to the world, many did not go back to boroughs, farms, or ranches, but instead headed to school and suburbia. They raised the Woodstock Generation who would fight another Asian war. They lived their lives to the fullest extent possible, partially in remembrance of those who would remain seventeen or eighteen forever. Most suffered their memories in silence, often not even sharing the terror with their wives who watched them thrash in the grips of nightmares too difficult to imagine in the dead of night. The Sixth Marine Division Association formed as the men began to slow down, after they had established their families and jobs, or retired. For the first time, in many cases, loved ones learned that their husband or father was a leader of men, a hero, or a practical joker. They

gathered; they shared; they healed. For a generation that had no understanding of Post Traumatic Stress Disorder, these reunions were often
an analyst's couch. Now they share their memories with outsiders in the
hope that future generations will understand their war.

There are those who never attended a reunion or mentioned their
time in service, men who were so emotionally battered by war that they
never recovered, or just felt it better to forget. They sometimes saw the
war as something to be ashamed of, and there are men in veterans' hospitals who never spoke again. However, for the vast majority of the sixteen million who fought in World War II, it is service they are proud of
and, surprisingly, grateful for having participated in. It is something
they neither want to repeat, nor particularly want their sons to endure,
but they are proud. Marines are proud of their time in service, whether
they served for a year or made it a career, and members of the Sixth are
typical in that respect. It is always touching to watch this group when the
Marine Corps Hymn is played. Then they are no longer seventy or
eighty. Their backs become ramrod straight as they stand at attention
and, for just an instant, one captures the essence of who these men are,
and the war that created them.

This work has been about perspective. Undoubtedly, perspective is
shaped by one's own interest. But there is a great deal to be learned about
a group of individuals, as well as the individuals themselves, in exploring their perspective. History is, after all, how and what we choose to
remember. The Sixth Marine Division only hopes they will be remembered as small but integral witnesses and players in the biggest event of
the twentieth century.

In September of 2002, the Sixth Marine Division held a reunion.
They are very aware that there will not be many more. Five more is
what most of them predict, five at the most. In the 1990s, those present
at reunions numbered close to one thousand—the most recent had three
hundred members present. Perhaps their shining moment occurred in
April of 2000, when they gathered to dedicate the Sixth Marine Division
Monument at Quantico. That final task complete, many felt relieved
that they had lived long enough to see their comrades so honored. Their
average age now is close to eighty. At each reunion, they toll a bell for
those who passed that year. The bell tolled one hundred and forty times

in 2002. In this study, more than forty men were interviewed. Eight have since died, and four are in hospitals or nursing homes. As DeWitt Joralemon explains, "We are falling out fast and there are no replacements." How right he is. It will be hard to replace this special group who, even now, want nothing more than to "stay off the skyline."

NOTES

CHAPTER 1

1. Samuel Hynes, *The Soldiers Tale: Bearing Witness to Modern War* (New York: Penguin Books, 1997), 159.
2. George Feifer, *Tennozan: The Battle of Okinawa and the Atomic Bomb* (Boston: Houghton Mifflin Company, 1992), 578.
3. Roy E. Appleman and others, *The War in the Pacific Okinawa: The Last Battle* (Washington, DC: Historical Division, Department of the Army, U.S. Government Printing Office, 1948), 468.
4. Ibid., 488.
5. Robert Leckie, *Okinawa: The Last Battle of WWII* (New York: Penguin Books, 1995), 202.
6. Feifer, 509.
7. Leckie, 202
8. Appleman, 473.
9. Ibid.
10. Appleman, 415.
11. Joseph Alexander, "The Final Campaign: Marines in the Victory on Okinawa," In *Marines in World War II Commemorative Series* (Washington, DC: Navy Yard Publishing, 1996), 48.

12. J. Robert Moskin, *The U.S. Marine Corps History* (New York: McGraw Hill, 1987), 396.

13. Feifer, 69–71.

14. Appleman, 474.

15. William Tyree, "Okinawa to be a Springboard," *United Press*, 25 June 1945.

16. "WWII" *Marine Link*,http://www.usmc.../77f992b2qcb682eb852564 d70059c642?OpenDocument&ExpandSection Accessed 28 Jan 2002, 1.

17. Applemen, 492.

18. CINCPOA Communiqué, No.313, 29 March 1945, http:// www.ibiblio.org/pha/comms/1945-03.html.

19. Appleman, 68.

20. D-Day Museum, New Orleans, LA. Pacific side.

21. CINCPOA Communiqué, No.285, 2 March 1945, http://www. ibiblio.org/pha/comms/1945-03.html.

22. Feifer, 595.

23. C.L. Sulberger, ed., *The American Heritage, WWII* (New York: American Heritage Publishing Company, 1966), 589.

24. David Nichols, *Ernie's War* (New York: Random House, 1996), 407.

25. Feifer, 596.

26. Sid Moody, "The Last Battle," *Arizona Daily Star*, 1 April 1995, 1A.

27. Richard B. Frank, *Downfall: The End of the Imperial Japanese Empire* (New York: Random House, 1999), 264.

28. Ibid, 285.

29. Stanley Weintraub, *The Late Great Victory: The End of World War II, July/August 1945* (Old Saybrook, CT: Konecky and Konecky, 1995), 665.

30. Sid Moody. *Arizona Daily Star*, 1A.

31. John Whitclay Chambers and G. Kurt Piehler, *Major Problems in American Military History* (New York: Houghton Mifflin Company, 1999), 310.

32. Bevan Cass, ed., *History of the Sixth Marine Division* (Nashville: Battery Press, 1987), 1.

33. Cass, 11.

34. Edwin H. Simmons and J. Robert Moskin, eds., The *Marines* (Quantico, VA: Marine Corps Heritage, Hugh Lauter Levin Associates, Inc., 1998), 73.

35. John T. Hoffman, "The Lore of the Corps. Okinawa; 6th Marine Division, Only One Formed, Fought and Disbanded Entirely Overseas," *Navy Times* (August 1999).

36. Jack Jackson, inscription to Laura Lacey in the *Old Breed.*

37. Cass, 1.

38. Wilbur D. Jones, *Gyrene: The World War II United States Marine* (Shippensburg, PA: White Mane Books, 1998), 250.

39. Edward E. Ellis, *A Nation in Torment: The Great American Depression 1920–1939* (New York: Capricorn Books, 1970), 533.

40. Gerald Linderman *The World Within War* (New York: Free Press, 1997), 48.

41. Ellis, 231.

42. Micheal Kammen, *A Season of Youth: The American Revolution and the Historical Imagination* (Ithaca, NY: Cornell University Press, 1978), 13.

43. Ibid., 66.

44. Ernie Pyle, *The Last Chapter* (New York: Henry Holt Company, 1946), 138.

45. Ibid., 140.

46. Lawrence H. Suid, *Guts and Glory: Great American War Movies* (Reading, MA: Addison-Wesley Publishing, 1978), 92.

47. Suid. 91.

48. Ibid., 25.

49. Ibid.

50. Simmons, 303.

51. Suid, 25.

52. Simmons, 304.

53. Suid, 40.

54. Ian Gow, *Okinawa, 1945: Gateway to the Pacific* (London: Golden House, 1985), 30.

55. Hiromichi Yahara, *The Battle For Okinawa* (New York: John Wiley and Sons, 1995), 3.

56. Ibid., 3–26.

57. Ibid., 32.

58. Ibid., 35.

59. Gow, 89.

60. *Special Action Report On Okinawa Operation*, Phase 1 and 2, Vol. 1. Quantico Archives Sixth Marine Special Collection, Box 7, Folder 1.
61. Gow, 80.
62. Gow, 40–41.
63. Applemen, 2.
64. Ibid., 6.
65. Ibid., 3.
66. Applemen, 3.
67. James Hallas, *Killing Ground on Okinawa: The Battle for Sugar Loaf Hill* (Westport, CT: Praeger Publishers, 1996).

CHAPTER 2

1. Kammen, 19.
2. Samuael Hynes, 2.
3. Ibid., 8.
4. Ibid., 4.
5. John Hersey, *Into the Valley: A Skirmish of the Marines* (New York: Schocken Books, 1942; reprint, New York: Schocken Books, 1987), ix (page citations are to the reprint edition).
6. Ibid., 12.
7. S.L.A.Marshall, *Island Victory* (Washington: Infantry Journal, 1945), 1.
8. James MacGregor Burns, "The Naked Truth of Battle," *Military Affairs 11*, Issue 4 (Winter 1947): 223.
9. Paul Thompson, *The Voice of the Past: Oral History*, 3d ed. (New York: Oxford Press, 2000), 81.
10. Roger Horwitz, "Oral History and the Story of America and World War II," *The Journal of American History* (Sept. 1995): 617.
11. Burns, 223.
12. Ibid.
13. Ibid.
14. Gerald Linderman, *Embattled Courage: The Experience of Combat in the American Civil War* (New York: Free Press, 1987), 267.
15. Kammen, 19.
16. Thompson, 163.

17. Valerie Raleigh Yow, *Recording Oral History: A Practical Guide for Social Scientists* (Thousand Oaks, CA: Sage Publications, 1994), 7.
18. Ibid.
19. Ibid., 14.
20. W. Fitzhugh Brundage, "No Deed But Memory," in *Where the Memories Grow: History, Memory, and Southern Identity* (Chapel Hill, NC: University of North Carolina Press, 2000), 23.
21. Ibid., 4.
22. Yow, 19.
23. Thompson, 130–131.
24. Yow, 19.
25. McGaugh for PBS, *Scientific American,* 1:13:10.
26. Ibid., 1:14: 45.
27. Ibid., 1:20: 25.

CHAPTER 3

1. Caroline Allison, "V-12: The Navy College Training Program," http://homepages. Rootsweb.com/-uscnrotc/v-12-v12-his.htm.
2. Paul Fussell, *Wartime* (New York: Oxford University Press, 1989), 153.
3. Gilbert P Bailey, *Boot* (New York: Macmillan Company, 1943), 27.
4. Richard Holmes, *Acts of War: The Behavior of Men in Battle* (New York: Free Press, 1989), 44.
5. Burns.
6. Henry Kemp Interview, September, 2001.
7. Conversation with Charlie Rittenbury, Dunn, North Carolina, May 2002.
8. Bruce Manell, *When I Went to War* (New York: Readers Digest Association, Inc., 2002), 0019.
9. James Chaisson scrapbook, Battle of Okinawa Museum, Okinawa, Japan.

CHAPTER 4

1. Grant Dunnagan, *Grinnin, Dusty, Fighting Men* (Raleigh, NC: Shelly Books, 1955), 37.

2. Special Action Report on Okinawa Campaign, Phase I and II, vol, 1 Quantico Archives, Special collection, Box 7, folder 2.

3. Ibid.

4. Moody, 8-A.

5. Doug Struck, "Elegy in Okinawa: After 55 years of Peace, Survivors Revisit the Battlefield Memories," *Washington Post*, 20 July 2000, page#.

6. "Cincopoa Communique" no. 308 24 March 1945, http://www.ibiblio.org/pha/comms/1945-03.html.

7. James Chaisson interview, date.

8. Thomas E. Donnelly, "Lieutenant General Alan Shapley. Oral History Transcript," History and Museums Division, headquarters U.S. Marine Corps, Washington, DC, 1976, 91.

9. Moody, page#.

10. Cass, 40.

11. Gow, 100.

12. Cass, 76.

13. Thomas E. Donnelly, "Lieutenant General Alan Shapley. Oral History Transcript," History and Museums Division, Headquarters U.S. Marine Corps, Washington, DC, 1976, 84.

14. Ibid., 91.

15. Tom Jones, *The View from My Foxhole* (Rolling Hills Estates, CA: Jones, Maher, Roberts, Inc., 2001), 157.

16. William White, e-mail, 34 March 2002.

17. Glen Moore, e-mail, 24 March 2002.

CHAPTER 5

1. Hynes, xiii.

2. James White, "Point of the Spear," *Sixth Marine Division Newsletter* 1–4 (2000): 20.

3. J. Glen Gray, *The Warriors: Reflections of Men in Battle* (New York: Harper Row, 1967), 173.

4. Dick Whitaker, e-mail, 2002.

5. Admiral Minoru Ota's Telegram, Naval Underground Museum, Okinawa, Japan.

6. E. R. Mosman, Lt. Commander, "War Diary of Military Government Detachment," B-5, 23.

7. Admiral Minoru Ota's Telegram, Naval Underground Museum, Okinawa, Japan.

8. Author, 19–20.

9. Haruku Taya Cook and Theodore Cook, *Japan at War* (New York: New Press, 1992), 355.

10. Cook, 355.

11. Seizan Nakasone, *Himeyuri,* (Okianwa, Japan 1989), 32.

12. Ibid., 36.

13. Admiral Minoru Ota's Telegram, Naval Underground Museum, Okinawa, Japan.

14. Ernie Pyle, *Last Chapter* (New York: Henry Holt and Company, 1945), 125.

15. Ibid., 109.

16. Ray Gillespie, e-mail, 23 September 1997.

17. Joe Drago, e-mail, 14 February 2002.

18. Fussell, 137.

19. John Gregory Dunne, "The Hardest War," *The New York Review* (20 December 2001): 51.

20. Hynes, 163.

21. Tom Schicker, e-mail, August 2002.

22. Pyle, 26.

23. Linderman, 167.

24. Barbara Ehrenreich, *Blood Rites: Origins and History of the Passions of War* (New York: Henry Holt and Company, 1997), 206.

25. Ibid., 215.

26. Linderman, 144.

27. Ibid., 147.

28. Akira Iriye, *Across the Pacific* (New York: Harcourt Brace Jovanovich, 1967), 226.

29. Fussell, 116.

30. Iriye, 143.

31. Ibid., 149.

32. Linderman, 157.

33. Pyle, 5.

34. Hynes, p. 163
35. Fussell, 116.
36. Linderman, 163.
37. Merrill Goozer, "Japan sacrificed everything for defense of Okinawa," *Post and Courier*, 23 June 1995, 10-A.
38. Linderman, 183
39. Ibid., 153.
40. Frank Benis. General Lemuel C. Shepherd, Jr. Oral Transcript, Historical Division, Headquarters, U.S. Marine Corps. Washington, DC.
41. Benis Frank, "Lemuel C Shepherd, Jr. Oral History Transcript," Historical Division, Headquarters U.S. Marine Corps, Washington, DC, 225.
42. Gray.
43. Don Honis, interview.
44. William Manchester, *Goodbye Darkness* (Boston: Little Brown and Company, 1979), 437.
45. Linderman, 17.
46. Howard Terry, e-mail, February 2002.
47. Manchester, 439, 979.
48. Taylor interview.
49. Hynes, 163.
50. Ehrenreich, 207.
51. Holmes, 50.
52. Lenly Cotton, *The Brig Rat* (Burbank, CA: Little Prince Productions, 1992), 212.
53. Bill Sams letters, April 1945.
54. Oral History of Okinawa.
55. White.
56. Conversation James Chaisson, Gainesville GA, 2000.
57. Tomiko Higa, *The Girl With the White Flag* (Tokyo: Kodansha International, 1991).
58. Phone conversation Bill Sams, 2002.
59. Glen Moore, e-mail, 19 February 2002.
60. Ken Long, e-mail, 19 February 2002.
61. Dick Whitaker, e-mail 21 February 2002.

62. Holmes, 191.
63. Hynes, 20.
64. Linderman, 58.
65. Hynes, 21.
66. White, 42.
67. Linderman, *World Within War*, 26.
68. Ibid., 26–27.
69. Holmes, 207.
70. Dave Grossman, *On Killing: The Psychological Cost of Learning to Kill in War and Society* (Boston: Little Brown and Company, 1995), 50.
71. Lawrence Hertz and others, "Psychophysiological Assessment of Posttraumatic Stress Disorder Imagery in World War II and Korean Veterans," *Journal of Abnormal Psychology 102*, no. 1, (1993): 152.
72. Peter Watson, *War on the Mind* (New York: Basic Books Inc., 1978, 233.
73. Ibid.
74. Grossman, 44.
75. Holmes, 216.
76. Ibid., 1.
77. Dr. Roger Pitman, telephone interview, April 2002.
78. Grossman, 68–73.
79. Dr. Roger Pitman, telephone interview, April 2002.
80. Grossman, 44.
81. Holmes, 214.
82. Ibid., 218.
83. Hynes, 62.
84. Jones, 228.
85. Applemen, 490.
86. Ibid.
87. Glenn Moore, e-mail, March 2002.
88. Joe Drago, e-mail, March 2002.
89. William White, e-mail, February 2002.
90. Pete Howell, e-mail, March 2002.

CHAPTER 6

1. Gray, 44.
2. Hynes, 9.
3. Ehrenreigh, 224.
4. Lawrence Leshan, *The Psychology of War* (Chicago: Noble Press, Inc., 1992), 24.
5. Hynes, 9.
6. Gray, 39.
7. Benis M Frank, Brigadier General Victor F. Bleasdale. Oral History Transcript. History and Museums Division, Headquarters, U.S. Marine Corps. Washington, DC, 267.
8. Cass, 177.
9. Benis M Frank, Brigadier General Victor F. Bleasdale. Oral History Transcript. History and Museums Division, Headquarters, U.S. Marine Corps. Washington, DC, 269–270.
10. Jack Hoag, e-mail, April 2002.
11. Bill Sams, phone conversation, February 2002.
12. Bill Sams, letter to Mrs. C.H. Mullins 9 Sept. 1945.
13. Linderman, *World Within War*, 32.
14. Benis M. Frank. Robert B. Luckey. Oral History Transcript. Historical Division, headquarters, U.S. Marine Corps, Washington, DC, 167.

CHAPTER 7

1. "G-3 Periodic Reports. No. 82" *Sixth Marine Division Collection*, Quantico Va. Box 10, 38–93. June 21, 1945.
2. Feifer, 567.
3. K. Jack Bauer and Alan Cox, "Olympic vs. Ketsu-Go" *Marine Corps Gazette 49*, no. 8, (August 1965): 1.
4. Feifer, 568.
5. Bauer, 2.
6. Feifer, 568.
7. James Martin Davis, "The Story of the Invasion of Japan." COM-PHIBPAC Operations Plan A11-45, Serial no.0013.

8. Frank, 117–118.
9. Frank, 118.
10. Bauer, 2.
11. Ibid., 3.
12. Feifer, 572.
13. Frank, 137.
14. Fifer, 572.
15. Fussell, 15.
16. Bruce Lee, *Marching Orders: The Untold Story of WWII* (New York: Crown Publishing Inc., 1995), 323.
17. Ibid.
18. Bauer, 14.
19. Feifer, 556.
20. Frank, 189
21. Feifer, 570.
22. Frank.
23. Davis, 10.
24. W. Pat Hitchcock, *Forty Months in Hell.* (Jackson, TN: Page Publishing, 1996), 167.
25. Ibid., 584.
26. Hitchcock., 166.
27. Frank., 161.
28. Frank, 356.
29. Feifer, 572.
30. Davis, 10.
31. David McCullough, *Truman* (New York: Simon and Schuster, 1992), 441.
32. Weintraub, 420.
33. McCullough, 444.
34. George Easily Papers, Truman Library, Document 18F.
35. Fussell, 31.
36. Ibid., 18.
37. Ibid., 24.
38. White, 59.
39. Bauer, 21

40. Hynes, 175.
41. Mccormick, 1.
42. Ibid., 2.
43. Cass, 195.
44. Bill Sams, letters, date.
45. Andrew Carroll and Robert Torricelli, eds., *In Our Word* (New York: Washington Square Press), 149.
46. Ibid., 151.
47. Harry McKnight, e-mail, 10 April 2002.
48. Ken Long, e-mail, 11 April 2002.
49. Annie Wilkins, e-mail, 11 April 2002.

CHAPTER 8

1. E.Chasen, e-mail from Veterans' Administration, 29 January 29 2001.
2. Ibid.
3. Josh Grossberg, "Veteran Relives Horrors, Returns Cherished Letter," *Daily Breeze*. Torrance California, 27 August 2001, A1.
4. Harry McKnight, e-mail, January 2002.
5. Dewitt Joralemon, e-mail, January 2002.
6. Pete Howell, e-mail, January 2002.
7. Harold Stephens, e-mail, January 2002.
8. Glen Moore, e-mail, January 2002.
9. Jack Stephenson, e-mail, January 2002.
10. Harry McKnight, e-mail, January 2002.
11. Bill Pierce, e-mail, January 2002.

CHAPTER 10

1. Jack Stephenson, e-mail, March 2002.
2. Glenn Moore, e-mail, date.

SELECTED BIBLIOGRAPHY

BOOKS

Alexander, Joseph. "The Final Campaign: Marines in the Victory on Okinawa," in *Marines in World War II Commemorative Series*. Washington, DC: Navy Yard Publishing, 1996.

Appleman, Roy E., James M. Burns, Russell A Gugeler, and John Stevens. *The War in the Pacific: Okinawa: The Last Campaign*. Washington, DC: Historical Division, Department of the Army, U.S. Government Printing Office, 1948.

Aquilina, Robert V. "World War II Chronology: April–June 1945." *Fortune: Marine Corps Historical Bulletin* 24 (Summer 1994): 20–23.

Bailey, Gilbert. *Boot*. New York: Macmillan Company, 1944.

Baker, Dale L., ed. *Hitting the Beaches: The First Armored Amphibian Battalion in World War II*. Atlanta: First Armored Amphibian Battalion, 1996.

Bauer, K. Jack. "Olympic vs. Ketsu-Go." *Marine Corps Gazette* 49, no. 8 (August 1965): 1–22.

Beau, Jerome J.C. *The U.S. Marine Raiders of WWII: Those Who Served*. Richmond, VA: American Historical Foundation, 1996.

Bergerud, Eric. *Touched with Fire: The Land War in the South Pacific*. New York: Penguin Books, 1996.

Boatner III, Mark M. *The Biographical Dictionary of World War II*. Novato, CA: Presidio Press, 1996.

Brokaw, Tom. *The Greatest Generation*. New York: Random House, 1998.

Brundage, W. Fitzhugh. "No Deed But Memory," in *Where Memories Grow: History, Memory, and Southern Identity*. Chapel Hill: University Of North Carolina Press, 2000.

Burns, James MacGregor. "The Naked Truth of Battle." *Military Affairs 11*, no. 4 (Winter 1947): 223–228.

Carrol, Andrew and Robert Torricelli, eds. *In Our Word*. New York: Washington Square Press, 1999.

Cass, Bevan G., ed. *History of the Sixth Marine Division*. Nashville: Battery Press, 1987.

Chambers, John Whitclay and G. Kurt Piehler. *Major Problems in American Military History*. New York: Houghton Mifflin Company, 1999.

Cook, Haruku Taya and Theodore Cook. *Japan At War*. New York: New Press, 1992.

Cotton, Lenly M. *The Brig Rat*. Burbank, CA: Little Prince Productions, Inc., 1992.

Dower, John W. *War Without Mercy: Race and Power in the Pacific War*. New York: Random House, 1986.

Dunnagen, Grant. *Grinnin', Dusty, Fightin' Men*. Raleigh, NC: Shelly Books, 1985.

Dunne. John Gregory. "The Hardest War," *The New York Review*, 20 December 2001, 50–56.

Ehrenreich, Barbara. *Blood Rites: Origins and History of the Passions of War*. New York: Henry Holt and Company, Inc., 1997.

Ellis, Edward Robb. *A Nation in Torment: The Great Depression 1929–1939*. New York: Capricorn Books, 1970.

Feifer, George. *Tennozan: The Battle of Okinawa and the Atom Bomb*. Boston: Houghton Mifflin Company, 1992.

Frank, Benis M. *Okinawa: Touchstone to Victory*. New York: Ballentine Books, Inc., 1969.

Frank, Benis M and Henry Shaw. *Victory and Occupation*: Vol. 5, *History of the U.S. Marine Corps Operations in World War II*, by The

Historical Branch, G-3 Division, Headquarters Marine Corps. Washington, DC: Battery Press, 1968. Reprint, Washington, DC: Battery Press, 1994.

Frank, Richard. *Downfall: The End of the Imperial Japanese Army*. New York: Random House, 1999.

Fussell, Paul. *Wartime*. New York: Oxford University Press, 1989.

Gow, Ian. *Okinawa 1945: Gateway to Japan*. London: Golden House, 1986.

Gray, J. Glenn. *The Warriors: Reflections on Men in Battle*. New York: Harper and Row, 1959.

Grossman, Dave. *On Killing: The Psychological Cost of Learning to Kill in War and Society*. Boston: Little Brown and Company, 1995.

Hall, Tony, ed. *War in the Pacific: Pearl Harbor to Tokyo*. New York: Smithmark, 1991.

Hallas, James H. *Killing Ground on Okinawa: The Battle for Sugar Loaf Hill*. Westport, CT: Praeger Publishers, 1996.

Hersey, John. *Into the Valley: A Skirmish of the Marines*. New York: Schocken Books, 1942. Reprint, New York: Schocken Books, 1987.

Hertz, Lawrence, Natasha Lasko, Scott Orr, and Roger Pitman. "Psychophysiological Assessment of Posttraumatic Stress Disorder Imagery in World War II and Korean Veterans." *Journal of Abnormal Psychology* 102, no. 1, (1993): 152.

Higa, Tomiko. *The Girl with the White Flag*. Tokyo: Kodansha International, 1991.

Hitchcock, W. Pat. *Forty Months in Hell*. Jackson, TN: Page Publishing, 1996.

Holmes, Richard. *Acts of War: The Behavior of Men in Battle*. New York: Free Press, 1989.

Horowitz, Roger. "Oral History and the Story of America and World War II". *Journal of American History* (September 1995): 617–624.

Hynes, Samuel. *The Soldiers Tale: Bearing Witness to Modern War*. New York: Penguin Books, 1997.

Iriye, Akira. *Across the Pacific*. New York: Harcourt, Brace, Jovanovich, 1967.

Jones, Tom. *The View from My Foxhole*. Rolling Hills Estates, CA: Jones, Maher, Roberts, Inc., 2001.

Jones, Wilbur, D. *Gyrene: The World War II United States Marine.* Shippensburg, PA: White Mane Books, 1998.

Kammen, Michael. *A Season of Youth: The American Revolution and the Historical Imagination.* Ithaca: Cornell University Press, 1978.

Leckie, Robert. *Okinawa: The Last Battle of World War II.* New York: Penguin Books, 1995.

Lee, Bruce. *Marching Orders: The Untold Story of WWII.* New York: Crown Publishing, 1995.

LeShan, Lawrence. *The Psychology of War: Comprehending its Mystique and its Madness.* Chicago: The Noble Press, Inc., 1992.

Linderman, Gerald. *Embattled Courage: The Experience of Combat in the American Civil War.* New York: Free Press, 1987.

————. *The World Within War.* New York: Free Press, 1997.

Lyons, Michael J. *World War II: A Short History.* New Jersey: Prentice Hall, 1989.

Manchester, William. *Goodbye Darkness: A Memoir of the Pacific War.* Boston: Little Brown and Co., 1979.

Marshall, S.L.A. *Island Victory.* Washington, DC: Infantry Journal, 1945.

McCormick, John. *The Right Kind of War.* 2d ed. New York: Penguin Books, 1992.

McCullough, David. *Truman.* New York: Simon and Schuster, 1992.

McMillan, George. *The Old Breed: A History of the First Marine Division in World War II.* Washington, DC: Infantry Journal Press, 1949. Reprint, Nashville: Battery Press, 2001.

Millet, Allen R. *Semper Fidelis: The History of the United States Marine Corps.* New York: Macmillan Company, 1980.

Moskin, J. Robert. *The U.S. Marine Corps History.* 4th ed. New York: McGraw Hill, 1987.

Nichols, David. *Ernie's War.* New York: Random House, 1986.

Okinawa Prefecture, Department of Welfare. "An Oral History of the Battle of Okinawa." Okinawa, Japan: Bunshin Printing Company, 1985.

Peatross, Oscar F. *Bless 'em All: The Raider Marines of World War II.* Irvine, CA: Review Publications, 1995. Reprint, Irvine, CA: Review Publications, 1996.

Pyle, Ernie. *Last Chapter.* New York: Henry Holt and Company, 1945.

Sherrod, Robert L. "On to Okinawa," *Marine Corps Gazette* 70, no. 4 (April 1995): 72.

Simmons, Edwin H. and J. Robert Moskin, eds. *The Marines*. Quantico, VA: Marine Corps Heritage Foundation, Hugh Lauter Levin Associates, 1998.

Sledge, E.B. *With the Old Breed*. New York: Oxford University Press, 1981.

Suid, Lawrence H. *Guts and Glory: Great American War Movies*. Reading, MA: Addison-Wesley Publishing Company, 1978.

Sulberger, C.L., ed. *The American Heritage, WWII*. New York: American Heritage Publishing Company, 1966.

Thompson, Paul. *The Voice of the Past: Oral History*. 3rd ed. New York: Oxford Press, 2000.

Watson, Peter, *War on the Mind*. New York: Basic Books, 1978.

Weintraub, Stanley. *The Last Great Victory: The End of World War II, July/August 1945*. Old Saybrook, CT: Konecky and Konecky, 1995.

Wheeler, Richard. *A Special Valor: The Marines and the Pacific War*. New York: Harper and Row, 1983.

White, James. "Point of the Spear." Sixth Marine Division Newsletter 1–4 (2000): 20.

Yahara, Hiromichi. *The Battle of Okinawa*. New York: John Wiley and Sons, Inc., 1995.

Yow, Valerie Raleigh. *Recording Oral History: A Practical Guide for Social Scientists*. Thousand Oaks, CA: Sage Publications Inc., 1994.

Young, Charles. *Luck of the Draw*. Edmonton, Alberta, Canada: Commonwealth Publications, 1994.

SPECIAL COLLECTIONS

Donnelly, Thomas E. "Lieutenant General Shapley, Oral History Transcript." History and Museums Division, Headquarters U.S. Marine Corps. Washington, DC, 1976

Frank, Benis M. "Brigadier General Victor F. Bleasdale. Oral History Transcript." History and Museums Division, Headquarters U.S. Marine Corps. Washington, DC, 1967.

———. "General Lemuel C. Shepherd. Oral History Transcript."

History and Museums Division, Headquarters U.S. Marine Corps. Washington, DC, 1967.

———. "Lieutenant General Robert B Luckey. Oral History Transcript." History and Museums Division, Headquarters U.S. Marine Corps. Washington, DC, 1967.

G-3 Periodic Reports. No 82. Gray Research Center. Special Collections, Sixth Marine Division Collection. Box 10, 38–93. June 21, 1945.

George Easily Papers, Truman Library, Document 18F.

Mosman, E. R. Commanding Officer. War Diary, Military Government Detachment. B-5 Western Historical Manuscript Collection. University of Missouri. Collection Number: C-445. Folders 1–4.

Special Action Report on Okinawa Operation, Phase 1 and 2, vol. 1. Quantico, VA: Gray Research Center. Special Collections, Sixth Marine Division Collection. Box 7, Folder 1.

OTHER MATERIALS

Chaisson, James. Scrapbook. Battle of Okinawa Museum, Okinawa, Japan.

CD-FMFRP-12-34 History of US Marine Corps Operations in World War II, Marine Corps Doctrine Division, Quantico, VA. 2000.

Davis, James Martin. "The Story of the Invasion of Japan." COMPHIB-PAC Operations Plan A11-45, Serial no. 0013.

Gilbert, Cliff. Scrapbook. In possession of widow.

Admiral Minoru Ota's Telegram. Naval Underground Museum, Okinawa, Japan.

Nakasone, Seizan. "Himeyuri." Himeyuri Peace Museum, 1990.

Sams, Bill. Personal Letters to Mrs. C.H. Mullins, 1943–1946. Bill Sams Collection.

Special Publications Branch. "Nansei Shoto Ryuku Islands-Loochoo Islands: A Pocket Guide," reproduced by 30th Eng. Base Top Bn. Usafcpbc No. 5356.

ORAL HISTORY—INTERVIEWS

All interviews conducted by the author, unless otherwise noted.

Anderson, Nils, monologue on tape, 1996.

Baird, Tom, 6th Marine Division convention, St. Louis, September 8, 2001.

Brining, Donald, 6th Marine Division convention, St. Louis, September 8, 2001.

Buchter, Norris, 6th Marine Division convention, St. Louis, September 7, 2001.

Carne, George, 6th Marine Division convention, St. Louis, September 8, 2001.

Chaisson, James, taped interview by George Moning, Gainesville, 1996.

Day, James, interviewed by Jim Scotia, Scottsdale, Arizona, 1994.

DeMeis, Paolo "Paulie", via telephone and e-mail, March 5, 2002.

Dornan, John "Jack", via emails.

Drago, Joe, via emails.

Duke, James, Covington, Louisiana, April 2002.

Everett, Robert, via emails.

Fitzgerald, John "Jack", via telephone, April 2002.

Foley, John, via e-mails.

Fox, Edward "Buzzy," interview, Covington, Louisiana, April 2002.

Gillespie, Ray, via e-mails.

Hoag, Jack, via e-mails.

Honis, Don, via telephone, May 2002.

Jones, Tom, via telephone, March 2002.

Joralemon, Dewit, via telephone, April 2002.

Joyner, Tim, via e-mails.

Kemp, Henry, 6th Marine Division convention, St. Louis, September 7, 2001.

Kraus, Stephen, 6th Marine Division convention, St. Louis, September 7, 2001.

LePore, Augie, interview, Covington, Louisiana, April 2002.

Long, Kenneth J., via e-mails.

McConville, Joseph, interview, Covington, Louisiana, April 2002.

McKnight, Harry, via telephone, March 5, 2002.

Miller, Charles, 6th Marine Division convention, St. Louis, September 8, 2001.

Miller, Ralph, 6th Marine Division convention, St. Louis, September 8, 2001.

Moore, Glenn, via e-mails and newsletter, March 5, 2002.

Niland, George, 6th Marine Division convention, St. Louis, September 7, 2001.

Peasley, Edward, via telephone, April 2002.

Pierce, Bill, via telephone, March 5, 2002.

Rittenbury, Charles, Lillington, North Carolina, May 2002.

Sams, William, 6th Marine Division convention, St. Louis, September 8, 2001; Sylvester, Georgia, August 2002; 40 personal letters from 1944–1946.

Schlinder, Ray, 6th Marine Division convention, St. Louis, September 8, 2001.

Sherer, Robert, 6th Marine Division convention, St. Louis, September 8, 2001.

Stephenson, Jack, via e-mails.

Stephens, Harold, via e-mails.

Sukawatey, Edward, 6th Marine Division convention, St. Louis, September 8, 2001.

Taylor, George, 6th Marine Division convention, St. Louis, September 8, 2001.

Terry, Howard, via e-mails, April 2005.

Tremblay, George, 6th Marine Division convention, St. Louis, September 7, 2001.

Wanamaker, Warren, 6th Marine Division convention, St. Louis, 9/7/2001.

Whitaker, Dick, via telephone, March 5, 2002.

White, George, via e-mails, March 5, 2002.

White, James, via telephone, May 1, 2002.

Wilkins, Claud, 6th Marine Division convention, St. Louis, September 8, 2001.

INDEX

air assets, 10
Air Wing, 208
aircraft, 44, 169
aircraft carriers, 51
airfields, 9–11, 45– 46, 55, 59, 169
airplanes, 2, 177
amphibious, 6, 10, 12, 14, 169; landing, 14
amtrack, 117–118, 123, 156
Andersen, Nils, 95, 119
antiaircraft, 50
April 1, 3, 11, 23, 46, 47, 52, 96, 143, 175, 201
Army, 2, 4, 6, 9, 11–12, 16, 26, 30–31, 40, 45–46,
   48, 54–55, 61, 63, 117, 124, 126, 156–157,
   159–161, 164, 170, 182, 197; Sixth, 168; Tenth ,
   2–3, 6, 11, 13, 45, 106, 164, 166, 169
Army Corps, Twenty-fourth, 3, 54
Army Divisions: Eighty-first, 6; First, 169;
   Ninety-sixth, 3, 61, 64; Seventh, 6; Seventy-
   seventh, 3, 6, 45, 164; Twenty-seventh, 3, 6 12,
   156, 164
artillery, 6, 10, 14, 23, 36, 45, 88, 93, 118–119, 149,
   158–159, 162–164, 167, 199
artillerymen, 18, 158
Asa-Kawa, 12
asiatic, 125, 129, 133
Atomic Bomb, 4, 5, 172–174, 177, 215; first tested, 4

Bailey, Gilbert, 21–22
Baird, Tom, 70, 97
Bataan, 78, 81, 83, 192
Bleasdale, Victor, 144, 151
boot camp, 7, 22–23, 26, 29, 32, 34, 36, 59, 81, 91,
   150, 158–159, 195, 197, 199
Brining, Donald, 59, 84, 155
British Pacific Fleet, 169
British Task Force, 3
Bronze Star, 34, 100, 190
Browning automatic rifle (BAR), 153, 196
Buchter, Norris, 64, 66, 84, 175, 188
Buckner, Simon B., 2–3, 12, 14, 168, 172
Bush, Richard, 82, 151, 154
bushido, 71, 79, 86–87, 172

camps: Camp Butler, 36; Cape Glouster, 163;
   Camp LeJeune, 23– 24, 36: Camp Pendelton,
   24, 192; Camp Perry, 26; Camp Schwab, 54

Carne, George, 87
casualties, 2, 14, 26, 33, 46, 59, 84, 87, 97, 100,
   110, 113, 125–126, 128, 149, 169–173, 77
   181, 198
caves, 9, 53, 61–63, 72, 76, 78, 86, 95, 99, 100, 176
Chaisson, James, 34, 44, 46, 53, 69, 107, 151, 164,
   203, 205–206
Charlie Hill, 95–96
China, 5, 10, 82, 83, 85, 131 160, 163, 174, 178,
   179, 180, 185, 191, 192, 206
China Marine, 132, 192
China Sea, 133, 206
Chinese people and culture, 171, 173–174
Cho, Isamu, 71, 86
CINCPAC, 169
civilians, 1, 2, 8, 14, 45, 58, 61–64, 68–70, 72–75,
   82, 84, 88, 111, 143, 170–171, 173–174, 180,
   185, 189, 191; Civilian Conservation Corps,
   (CCC), 7
Coast Guard, 30, 204
combat, 2, 5–6, 10, 15–17, 19, 24, 26, 32, 39, 40,
   44–46, 53, 57, 59, 78, 80–82, 88–89, 102, 104,
   107–108, 125–132, 139–141, 144–145, 148–150,
   153, 156, 158–159, 169, 171, 177, 185–187, 189,
   194–199, 203
combat fatigue, 2, 125–130 133, 137, 141. See also
   post-traumatic stress syndrome; shellshock
combatants, 2, 15–18, 57–58, 61, 80, 82, 141
command post (CP), 118, 123–124, 143, 153–154,
   164
conscription, 2, 9, 62
corpsman, 5, 59, 68, 70, 81, 83–85, 104, 106, 114,
   117–118, 151–152, 196
Corregidor, 192
Cotton, Lenley, 106
Courtney, Harry, 90, 94, 115, 121, 154–155, 206–207

D-Day, 1
Day, James L., 74, 144, 148, 151, 204
DeMeis, Paolo "Paulie," 29, 147, 176, 189, 200
Depression, 7
Dereschuck, Dan, 100, 112
draft, 22, 31, 50, 52–53, 59, 81, 126, 142, 212, 214
Drago, Joe, 73, 133
drill instructor, 23, 28, 32, 35, 198
DWUK, 48–49, 160–161, 206

Ehrenreich, Barbara, 140
Eniwetok, 3
Enola Gay, 173, 180

film, 8–9
First Army, 169
Fifth Fleet, 3, 167
Fifty-two/Twenty Club (52/20 club), 187,
　　190–192
Fitzgerald, John "Jack," 47, 83, 100, 103, 130,
　　144, 153, 204
flamethrower, 76, 97, 105
food, 58, 62–63, 85, 107, 111–112, 122, 126,
　　128–129, 149, 156–157, 175, 214
Formosa, 10, 12; Formosa Straits, 179
Fox, Edward "Buzzy," 85, 99, 147
foxholes, 53, 58, 73–74, 81, 87, 92, 94, 97, 104,
　　106–107, 109–110, 118, 127, 129, 137,
　　141–142, 147, 149, 156, 187, 196
Fussell, Paul, 22, 80, 173

Geiger, Roy, 2, 3, 208
German's surrender, 4
GI, 162
GI Bill, 186, 190, 192–193, 195, 215
Gillespie, Ray, 65
"good war," 215
Gray, J. Glenn, 58, 88,
Great Lakes, 59, 190, 192
"greatest generation," 16
Green Beach, 11, 44, 46
Guadalcanal, 24, 34, 43, 48, 54, 78, 81, 83, 107,
　　111, 144, 146, 160, 163, 192, 197
Guam, 5, 51, 55, 103, 113, 132, 136, 138, 148,
　　154, 157, 160–161, 167, 173–176, 179–180,
　　205, 207

Hagushi Beach, 11. See also Green Beach; Red
　　Beach
Half Moon Hill, 12, 96, 111
headquarters, 41, 114, 130, 145, 205, 208
Hedo Point, 53, 205
Higa, Tomiko, 108
Himeyuri, 62–63
Hiroshima, 4–5, 172–173, 177–178
Hoag, Jack, 152
Hollywood, 8, 9
Holmes, Richard, 125, 128
homecoming, 185, 187–188
Honis, Don, 40, 69, 77, 89, 112, 117, 141, 190,
　　198
Horseshoe Ridge, 12
hospital, 51, 59, 63, 66, 114, 115, 117, 119, 122,
　　126, 132–136, 146, 155, 178, 214, 216–217
Howell, Pete, 137
Hynes, Samuel, 15, 57, 78, 81, 112, 140

Ie Shima, 45
incendiary bombs, 4
Iwo Jima, 4, 10, 40, 43, 51, 58, 143, 168, 173,
　　190, 200

Jackson, Jack, 6
Jacksonville, NC, 36
Japan, 2–6, 9–10, 55, 62, 74, 77, 79–80, 87–88,
　　90, 113, 144, 168–170, 172–180, 185, 200,
　　206
Japanese Army, 6, 12, 62, 80; Thirty-second, 2,
　　6, 9, 10, 12–14
Japanese Naval Headquarters, 61
Japanese people and culture, 1–4, 6, 9–13, 21,
　　26, 43–44, 46, 51–52, 54, 58–59, 61, 63, 65,
　　67–70, 72, 75, 77–82, 84–87, 89, 93, 99,
　　101–103, 106–110, 115, 143, 145, 167, 169,
　　170–173, 177, 180, 182–183, 190, 198, 209,
　　211, 214–215
Japanese units on Okinawa, 10
jikyusen, 9
Jones, Tom, 46, 127, 130, 189, 199
Joralemon, DeWitt, 27, 49, 103, 129, 159, 187,
　　190, 217
Joyner, Tim, 157

Kadena Airfield, 12
Kamikaze, 11, 45, 54, 60, 156, 170, 175
Kemp, Henry, 24, 29, 143
Keramas, 11
Ket-su-go, 170
Korean comfort women, 171
Kraus, Steve, 76, 156
Krulack, Victor, 59, 167
Kyushu, 168–169

L-Day (Love Day), 3–4, 11, 43, 45–46, 52, 53,
　　196
landing, 3, 11, 14, 25, 27, 32, 36, 44–46, 48, 50,
　　53, 64, 75, 81, 93–94, 130, 133, 141, 168,
　　176, 181–182, 204
Larson, Henry, 144
leadership, 23, 89, 90, 139, 143–144
Linderman, Gerald, 7, 17, 59, 79, 125
Loftis, Garland, 142, 200
Long, Ken, 181
LST, 47– 49, 51, 115, 160–161, 179–180
Luckey, Robert 163

MacArthur, Douglas, 3, 10, 100, 168–170, 175,
　　181
maggots, 58, 60, 107–108, 111–112, 121,
　　123–124
Manchester, William, 89, 100
Manchuria, 10, 83, 170
Manell, Alan, 27

Marine, 2, 6, 8, 14, 22–23, 26, 28, 31, 37, 89, 95, 99, 111, 120–121, 132–133, 143–144, 146, 150, 155–158, 170, 181, 196–197

Marine Corps, 5–8, 12–13, 22, 26–29, 31–32, 36, 40, 46, 50, 84, 88, 97–98, 127, 143–146, 148, 150, 156, 159, 170, 175, 185–186, 188, 191, 199, 216; Marine Raiders, 9; Merchant Marines, 27, 50

Marine Corps hymn, 27, 215

Marine Divisions: First, 6, 45, 78, 105, 148, 204; Second, 6, 11; Sixth, 4–6, 24, 43, 45, 83, 128, 142, 151, 158, 167, 175, 192, 214– 216

Marine Regiments: Fifteenth Marines, 24; Fourth Marines, 6, 173–174; Twenty-ninth Marines, 6, 41, 52, 53, 133, 151; Twenty-second Marines, 6, 11

Marshall, George C., 172

Marshall, S. L. A., 16

Marshall Islands, 148

Mazado Ridge, 212

McConville, Joe, 51, 179

McGaugh, James, 19

McKinney, Thomas, 54, 67, 70, 86, 105, 109, 151, 152, 177, 181, 209

McKnight, Harry, 141, 154, 155,179, 180, 192

McTureous, Victor, 141, 154–155, 168

Medal of Honor (MOH), 27, 74, 82, 115, 148, 153–156

memory, 15–20, 38, 40, 127, 209

Miller, Charles, 28, 73, 88, 104, 142, 164

million-dollar wound, 58, 113

Mitscher, Marc, 3

Mog-Mog, 43

Moore, Glenn, 52, 108, 132, 192, 207

Motobu Peninsula, 11, 45, 46, 132, 155

Mount Yae-Dake, 12, 45, 146, 172, 180

movies, 8–9, 22, 31–32, 50, 60, 112, 166, 178–179, 185, 209

Nagasaki, 4, 172, 173, 178

Nago, 11, 53

Naha, 6, 12–13, 60, 70, 87, 114, 132, 151, 207–209

Naha Airfield, 14, 151

Naha Harbor, 179

nambu (machine gun), 96, 118, 153

Nanking, 78, 83, 173

National Origins Act (1924), 7

Navy, 2–3, 11, 21–22, 26, 30, 40, 45, 49, 61, 63, 99–100, 103, 131, 135, 156, 162–163, 169, 181–182, 204, 211

Navy Cross, 34, 151, 154

Niland, George, 27, 52, 65, 85, 96, 102, 107, 130, 153, 178, 188, 200

Nimitz, Chester, 3, 10, 45

non-combat casualties, 125, 128

non-combatant. See civilians

Normandy, 1, 4, 40, 47, 173, 190

officer candidate school (OCS), 29, 188

Okinawa, 1–14, 24–26, 32–34, 36, 43, 45–47, 57–58, 61, 63, 72, 75, 79, 81– 82, 85, 87, 95, 99, 101–102, 108, 110–112, 126–127, 130, 133, 142–144, 148–149, 151, 153, 156–157, 163–164, 168–173, 175, 177–178, 190–192, 196, 199, 201, 204–205, 215

Okinawan people and culture, 1, 8–9, 11, 61–67, 70–71, 77, 99, 104, 107, 178, 215

Okoru Peninsula, 14, 61, 209

operations: Coronet, 168–169; Downfall, 168–169, 171–172; Iceberg, 3, 10, 27, 34, 167; Olympic, 168–169

Ota, Masahide, 61

Ota, Minoru, 14, 61–63, 211–213

Pacific, 1–5, 7–10, 17, 24, 27, 31, 77–82, 90, 101, 107, 125, 133, 152, 168–169, 173–174, 185–186, 191, 195, 207–208

Parris Island, 7, 26, 28–29, 32–34, 36, 197

Patton, George, 126

Pearl Harbor, 7, 21–22, 25–27, 43, 77, 80, 90, 101, 139, 146, 152, 180

Pesley, Edward, 90–91, 155

pests, 106–107; fleas, 106, 110; flies, 58, 105, 107–108, 111–112, 128

Pfuhl, Richard "Heavy," 47, 127, 154, 204

Pierce, William, 75, 131, 175, 184, 187, 195–196

post-traumatic stress syndrome, 126, 187, 216. See also combat fatigue; shellshock

Potsdam, 168

prayer, 16, 51, 97, 113, 117, 178, 181, 196, 205

prisoner, 2, 4, 80–81, 84, 87, 102–103, 171, 178, 182

prisoner of war, 171, 173, 180

propaganda, 9, 58, 62, 64, 82–83, 170–171

Public Law 30, 170

public relations, 8, 22

Purple Heart, 112, 151, 190

Pyle, Ernie, 4, 7–8, 45, 64, 79, 81, 139, 204

Quantico, 22–23, 28–29, 38, 163, 216

racism, 172

rain, 6, 12, 58, 62, 96, 99, 107, 109–110, 128–130, 143, 180, 206

rations, 108, 110–112, 120, 124, 147, 149, 154

Rawlings, Bernard, 3

Red Beach, 11

replacements, 56, 85, 89, 96–97, 104–105, 125, 141–143, 146–147, 155, 192, 217

Rittenbury, Charlie, 24, 25, 87, 177, 197

Roosevelt, Franklin D., death of, 4, 45

Royal British Navy, 52
Russia, 83, 85
Russo-Japanese War, 80
Ryukyus, 9–11

Sams, William, 36, 45, 47, 60, 106, 108, 125,
    157, 160, 174, 178, 188, 208
San Diego, 7, 22, 24, 138
Schlinder, Raymond, 39, 97, 115–117, 154
sea bags, 168, 175, 177
sea stories, 203
seppuku, 61
Service Adjustment Act, 1944, 186–187
Shapley, Alan, 29, 45, 46, 146, 147
shellshock, 126, 134. *See also* combat fatigue;
    post-traumatic stress syndrome
Shepherd, Lemuel, 11, 46, 83, 88, 115, 136, 146,
    161
Sherer, Robert, 145, 208
ships: USS *Arizona*, 145; USS *Augusta*, 172;
    USS *Franklin*, 43; USS *Missouri*, 4,
    174–175; USS *Relief*, 115; USS *Sea Bass*, 24
Shuri Castle, 12
Shuri-Yonaburu Line, 12–13, 63
Sixth Marine Division Companies: Easy, 67,
    214; Fox, 67, 142, 145–146, 204, 214; Golf,
    100, 101, 113, 118, 142
Sixth Marine Division Monument, Quantico,
    216
Sledge, E. B., 78–79, 108
Soviet Union, 4
Soviets, 171–172
Spruance, Raymond A., 3
Stephens, Harold, 191
Stephenson, Jack, 192, 204
Stillwell, Joseph, 2
suicide, 2, 61–62, 83, 172, 176
Sukawatey, Edward, 84
Sugar Loaf Hill, 12–13, 16–17, 57, 60, 66, 73,
    90–92, 95, 100, 110, 115, 118–121, 128, 155,
    168, 172
surrender, 2, 4, 62, 70–71, 98–99, 102, 104,
    168–169, 172, 174–176, 178, 181, 200, 215

tanks, 5, 45, 105, 107, 109–110
Tarawa, 29, 33, 115, 198
Task Force Fifty-eight, 3
Task Force Fifty-one, 3
Taylor, George, 28, 101, 200, 207
Terauchi, Hisachi, 171
Terry, Howard, 98
Third Amphibious Corps, 3

Tibbets, Paul, 180
Tojo Line, 9
Tokyo, 4, 9–10, 63, 82, 170, 172
Tokyo Bay, 4, 174, 178, 181–182, 184
Tokyo Rose, 45
tracers, 54, 60
train, 22–23, 31–32, 39, 190, 194
training, 2, 4–5, 11, 21, 23–24, 28, 32, 52–53, 59,
    62, 81, 83, 97–98, 111, 116, 132, 141, 143,
    146–147, 170, 181, 185, 197, 199, 208
Tremblay, George, 32–33, 98
Truman, Harry S, 4, 168, 172, 177–178, 181,
    215
Tsingtao, 179, 208
Turner, Richmond Kelly, 3
typhoon, 174, 179
"typhoon of steel," 6, 11

Udo, Takehika, 45
Ulithe Atoll, 12, 43, 47, 51. *See also* Mog-Mog
Underwater Demolition Team (UDT), 34, 44
United Service Organization (USO), 24, 40
Ushijima, Mitsuru, 2, 6, 9–11, 14, 71, 86, 107

V-12, 142
Vandergrift, Alexander, 12
Vietnam, 126, 128, 185–187, 197, 214, 217

Wanamaker, Warren "Ike," 29, 54, 178, 185
Whaling, William J., 151
Whitaker, Richard, 25, 31, 33, 51, 57, 59, 72,
    99, 110, 128–129, 142, 145, 153, 158–159,
    177, 191, 199, 208
White, James, 33, 59, 95, 100, 107, 109–111,
    113, 115, 142, 145, 148, 167, 173, 176, 187
White, William, 50, 133, 145, 148, 167
Wilkins, Annie, 181
Wilkins, Claud, 53, 133, 150
Women's Reserve, 5–6
Woodhouse, Horatio, 90
World War I, 5, 8, 28, 126, 144, 151
World War II, 1–2, 4–5, 15–18, 20, 22, 62, 79,
    80, 86, 112, 126–129, 173, 181, 185–187,
    191, 200, 203, 215–216
wounded, 91, 94–97, 105, 112–114, 118,
    127–128, 132–133, 142, 145–147, 149–151,
    154–155, 168, 170, 174, 180, 185

Yahara, Hiramichi, 74
Yemassee, SC, 22, 31
Yokosuka Naval Shipyard, 182
Yontan Airfield, 11, 46, 53, 55, 151

ABOUT THE AUTHOR

Laura Lacey, whose father and mother served in the Foreign Service, was born in Ankara, Turkey. She grew up in a variety of countries, almost all in Asia, before settling in Virginia. Laura earned her Bachelor of Liberal Studies from Mary Washington College in 1991. Her interest in the Pacific Theater of World War II came from having been stationed on Okinawa with her husband, a Marine aviator. She received her Masters Degree in History from the University of Texas at Arlington. After a variety of duty stations, she has recently returned to Virginia with her husband and three children. She is the Sixth Marine Division's Historian and is also the Battle of Okinawa Museum's U.S. Representative.